The Lonely Path

A Novel

Dido G. Kotile

Copyright © 2020 Dido G. Kotile

The Lonely Path is a work of fiction. All characters, names,
and places depicted in the novel are either the product of the
author's imagination or are used fictitiously, and any
resemblance to actual persons living or dead, events, or
location is entirely coincidental.

To the generations of first immigrants in their journeys for a better life

Acknowledgements

To my family for their support and patience. In particular, Guyo for reading the draft a couple of times, and Lokho, for painstakingly going through the formatting process.

To my reviewers: Takuma Shimoyama, Tamer Abdelhamid, Zahra Williams, and Professor Abdulrasheed Na'allah. My cover designer, Aleksandar Milosavljevic, and editor, Jefferson (First Editing). The Lonely Path is better because of your feedback.

Chapter 1

Sami glanced at the letters on the small table, which was cluttered with old newspapers and junk mail. He stretched his hand to reach for them but then hesitated. After a moment, he picked up the letters and, flailing aimlessly, stumbled across the room with his face downcast. His wife put down the newspaper she was reading and watched him from the corner of her eye as he checked the envelopes one by one and dropped them on the table near the TV stand. Two letters had come from Kenya, his native country in Africa, one was from his brother, and the other one was from his friend. The other two letters had come from the companies where he'd applied for jobs.

"Why don't you open them? Are the letters not from home?" his wife, Sarah, prodded.

"I know," Sami growled.

"You did not open them! How do you know?" she blurted out, trying to hide the accumulated anger in her belly.

"Their responses," Sami mumbled. "Nothing new. The usual regrets and rejections. How long will this continue? I have stopped counting the number of times I've applied for jobs."

"Open and find out?" she exclaimed; her tone slightly agitated.

Sami turned around. "They call if they want you. They only mail these annoying regrets, repeatedly copied with the same one-size-fits-all response. All of them work the same way." He paused. "I graduated from one of the best universities, and I have a master's degree. Why do I still receive these regrets?" He paced the room.

"They probably have valid reasons, like experience, a field of study, legal documents. Remember, you're competing with new graduates."

Sami looked at his wife. "Are you blind? What reasons could they possibly have? I have a work permit until our visa expires. Most jobs only require that, except for federal job vacancies, where one has to be a citizen or a green cardholder. I intend to get that damn card." Sami twisted his lips and repeated, "I must have it." He puckered his lips with anguish. "I must get a permanent residency card."

"Good luck with that wishful thinking." Sarah chuckled and waved her hand. She tossed the letters towards him and shifted to an upright position; her wrist bangles snapped with an irritating sound. "Can you check the letters from home?"

"I know who sent them and what they want. The usual demands and requests for assistance with their constant, endless problems." He uttered, his words barely audible.

"You didn't even open the letters." Sarah stood up.

"Here!" He threw the envelopes at her with a glazed look on his face. One letter landed near the TV stand. It caught the attention of Adam, their youngest toddler. Adam grasped the envelope, but before he could transfer it to his waiting mouth, Sarah grabbed his hand.

"Give it to me, little rascal!" She glanced at her husband and noticed how he held his face in anticipation of jeering remarks.

Sami said, "All those letters that I've received from that

part of the world have contained one plea. They needed my help. Name a single letter with good news. None! So, what makes these any different? Problems, drought, poverty, and hunger bred in a den of misery." He shrugged off his words and turned away.

There was no point arguing with him over this, his wife decided.

She picked up the letters and looked at the envelopes while checking the address and the writing on them. Only the local ones had the addresses of the senders. The ones from overseas did not show who sent them, but she recognized the handwriting. Sami probably had, too. She noticed the peculiar way with words, joined at the base, and then tipped over to a slanting angle towards the left. Sarah tore open the glued envelope with difficulty. She straightened the letter, stretching it a little to remove crevices before reading its contents.

Sami watched as Sarah flipped pages. She read it slowly, with a pace that hastened his anxiety. From the corner of his eye, he tracked her movements. As she read the second letter, she stopped. She sobbed, a gush of tears engulfing her face.

"What is it?" Sami jumped up.

Sarah wailed unabated, making the atmosphere tense. Only her tears trickled down.

Sami fidgeted. He paced the room, no longer pretending not to know what the letter said. Sarah sneezed and wiped her tears. Sami balked at his intense feelings. There was no way he could avoid this persistent problem bedeviling him.

"It's her, right? Tell me how it happened?" For sure, the news in the letter was not pleasant. "What is it?" he asked again, his tone just below the level of urgency.

She did not reply. The atmosphere tightened with an eerie silence.

Sami twisted his face with the eminent panic of a man

faced with a multitude of unknown ambiguities. He started wondering what she could tell him. The daunting silence pierced the chamber of his heart. It tightened with each breath and quickened to the point of desperation. His mind, already clogged with the mounting pressure of unresolved issues, remained steadfast. The agony of waiting for her answer stiffened him. *Why did she weep when she read the letter from home? There can only be one dreadful answer, and I do not want to hear it.*

"It is her. Tell me it isn't. She had a premonition that she would die before we saw each other. Before she saw her grandchildren." Sami slumped in the chair with a sigh. "For heaven's sake, say something." He catapulted from the edge of the chair to a standing position again. It was apparent that he had to get the letter to read it. He paused, hesitating, not sure how her next move would turn.

After what appeared to be a tumultuous passage of time, his wife said, "It's your sister." A long silence pervaded the atmosphere. In the previous letters he'd received, they'd told him that she was sick. He didn't need to know what had happened. He stood motionless, looking at a blank space on the ceiling.

"Your mother, too, has been bedridden. Your brother wanted to take her to a private hospital in Nairobi. She needed surgery." Sarah lifted the second letter and read halfway through, holding back her tears. She paused and then announced, "Your uncle needed money for food. He lost a child. They did not get rain for the last two years, and some people have died of hunger, including some of your relatives."

Sami looked off into the distance, beyond the empty wall. He kept quiet, with a vacant mind. It was the most enduring silence he could ever imagine.

In the beginning, Sami had received news from home

every month from his nephew, who turned out to be the right conduit through which all the information from home reached him.

Then, gradually, Sami had failed to reply. He would argue that they asked the same kinds of questions, and he was too busy. The letters from home then came every two months, then three, four, and finally, once or twice in six months. In all, the messages they sent him always covered day-to-day activities and life in the village. They kept him informed of the deaths and the number of births in the family. There were more children born in the family than the number of deaths, although the figures seemed to fluctuate. Sami had stopped recording the number of people in the family, and yet every time they sent him a letter, they would update him. They would occasionally tell him who had gotten married and added another wife or had a child. His elder brother, with three wives, had three children, one after another, as if in a race to join the world, which would receive them with uncertainty. As expected, the cyclic nature of birth and death, like the night following the day, took a toll on the unsuspecting innocent lives. It would have been okay when the conditions were stable. The devastating drought had depleted and annihilated all their livestock, which they depended on for their survival. Sami knew all the problems and wished he could erase the misery from his memory. He shook his head slightly.

Having crossed the oceans into a strange world, he'd thought his problems would be over. He'd been wrong. The difficulties had multiplied and intensified in a way that only he alone could understand.

After a long silence, Sarah thought of giving him quiet time on his own. She felt sad that she'd nagged him with harsh words of condemnation just before he'd gotten the bad news.

"Adam is asleep. I will take the rest of the children to the mall," she announced.

The kids rushed to the door, ready to dash out, competing to see who would be the first to get out of their tiny, congested two-bedroom university house.

Chapter 2

Sami entered the bathroom with the letters in his hand. He straightened the pages with the palm of his hand as he sat on the toilet seat. He started reading. Tears rolled down his cheeks. He'd forgotten the last time he'd cried and wondered how he would be able to control these strange tears that seemed to appear from nowhere. He has seen his wife cry several times, even at the slightest sight of his kids getting a cold or a fever, but it had never occurred to him that he would break down in tears.

His family at home would never understand him, and he wouldn't tell them how much financial misery he had endured in this country. They would never understand or believe him. How could he tell his illiterate mother and brothers that he lived from paycheck to paycheck after all the education he'd acquired in the USA? A country they admired, a powerful nation with global scope, endowed with ebullient wealth and everything beyond what their minds could ever imagine? Sami could boast that he was the first from his village to have landed in America. The country they had heard so much about, and it would be incomprehensible for anybody in his family to think that he could not even spare a penny to save his mother.

Sami had been in a deep emotional state before. It

intensified whenever his problems piled up. Lately, he got consumed with how he could ease his ever-growing challenges. He had nowhere to turn to and did not see any way out of his current financial misery. On the outside, he appeared like everybody else, going about his student life. As an international student on a scholarship, he had a limited duration of study left to complete his education and go back home and rebuild his native country. That would remain an illusion and an unfulfilled dream.

Sami tried to lock the bathroom door. He then remembered they had disabled the lock on the door when his son had locked himself in the bathroom. How badly he wanted the door closed. He pushed the doorknob back and held the string hooked to the door panel.

Sami placed a chair in the bathroom. He took off his belt, made a loop, and hooked it to a nail attached to the wooden frame on the low ceiling. He pulled it down, satisfied that it could hold his 160-pound weight.

Sami stood on the chair and lowered the belt around his head. He kicked the chair out of the way. The noose he'd made with the strap yielded and became loose. It caught him by the chin, but the nail that was attached to the wall came out. Sami fell off the chair with an up thrust jolt towards the door, knocking it with a loud bang. The loose door frame caved in, and the whole door fell with him on top.

"Dada." Sami looked at his one-year-old son. Words failed to come out. "Dada," his son repeated.

"Yes, Adam. You talked!" Sami supported himself in a standing position after he regained balance. Adam left the bathroom and wobbled across the tiny room to play with his favorite singing Barney toy, pushing the button to make the song "I Love You" play.

Sami squatted on the toilet seat and broke down in tears. *Oh, my God. Adam spoke for the first time and called me Dada.* His mind flipped from thinking about the attempted commotion to the realization of what had happened. He repeated to himself, *what was I doing? Why?* He had no answer for why such a wicked thought had entered his mind.

Sami remained in the bathroom. He cupped his head between his sweaty palms, and his breathing accelerated. *Why? Why did it happen this way? Why?* When he felt the impulse, he wanted to act but never assessed what kind of outcome he could create. The thought of what would happen to his children came to his mind. A new dawn of reality emerged in his head. The tears began to pour again. He remembered his mother's voice: "Son, teach them good manners. I may not live to see them." Those were the last words she'd uttered when he'd talked with her four months ago.

Sami shivered and stayed slouched. He must have been like that for a long time because Adam's sharp cry brought him back to the present. He washed his face and looked at the mirror on the bathroom wall, keeping his gaze on the image that he could barely recognize. Closing his eyes, he was frightened by the ghastly replica of his embittered face.

He opened his eyes and looked at himself through a series of panoramic episodes from the time of his childhood. He vividly remembered these events, including the death of his father during the civil war, when the army seized and ambushed the whole village. His family members were ostracized from camp and later his journey from the rural village to the boarding school. At that young age, Sami had promised his mother that he would never disappoint her and the family.

Sami stood there, perplexed, and soaked in the zombie-like persona, awakening to reality. A surge of positive energy engulfed him, but he was still bitter. Several conflicting thoughts crowded his mind as he tried to figure out how he would deal with his new inspiration. A voice in his head rebuked him for this cowardly act of desperation: *You have gone this far. Don't let it happen again. Get up and fight for what you want.*

Just then, he heard the door open. His family was back, and soon the whole house would be upside down and filled with loud voices.

***

"Daddy!" Hawa, the oldest daughter, abruptly stopped and stared at him. "You look awful. What happened?" She hesitated.

"Nothing, sweetheart. Tripped and fell. Only tired," Sami replied, trying to deflect her attention.

His wife gave him a worrisome glance. His daughter rushed to the bathroom and stopped. "What happened here? It's like a war zone."

Hawa, the nine-year-old, seemed to read his mind. All his children, by now, knew when not to disturb daddy, although, in recent times, such times had become frequent. Their daddy needed to be alone.

"Ssh!" Hawa passed on the silent message to other kids without uttering a word.

The kids had conjured gestures of their own to interpret the situations. It was the way their father looked. The demeanor on his face was evident, and that scared everybody. The kids followed each other silently and stopped behind Hawa; Chaaltu, the seven-year-old girl; followed by Musa, a four-year-old boy. They all ended their haste to get ahead, but Musa tried to fight his way to come closer.

"I saw this cool toy; I have to have it, Daddy. Mommy told me to wait until next month. I can't wait to have it."

Hawa pushed Musa back, but he ignored her and continued with his fantasy story of the toy world. Hawa stepped aside as Chaaltu also juggled her way to the attention arena. She wouldn't let Musa steal the show. Hawa had already resigned herself to the back seat, as so often happened when the younger ones clamored for attention. This time, she stood her ground and used only facial signals to divert their attention. Her looks told it all: *Since when do we get new toys?* The message she delivered through her facial expressions did not get through.

Sami paced the room, wondering how he could tell his kids the desperate situation he faced. The kids received messages in various ways. As they watched TV, they could see their favorite toys advertised, and it was painful for Sami to watch. He hated those breaks and commercial gimmicks that drove wedges between him and his children. Every time the TV was on, they had to see numerous advertised products. It was apparent to him the commercials were targeting kids. You would think that the kids would not be interested in the news, but the moment those commercials came on, their eyes would turn towards the TV with glowing excitement.

Each one would have his or her favorite toys. "Buy me that, Daddy, Mommy. My friends have those toys, video games, and trading cards," the kids would say at the same time. By now, they knew what to expect when they requested toys and could read the answers from their parents' facial expressions.

Every time Sami received job rejection letters, the kids noticed how he reacted: tense, moody, and absentminded. Sami tried to hide it and took everything lightly, but it had become difficult to bear the burden. He muttered to himself in a self-loathing mood that he could not provide them with the simple things they wanted. They wanted to be like the other kids. They watched the new toys advertised and saw them in the stores. In their little minds, they believed that they had to get them, but as kids, they did not understand their father's situation. They didn't know that their dad couldn't afford health insurance or dental care for that matter. There were other things to think about, like the staggering amount of unpaid debt. And now, with the hospitalization of his mother, Sami had to consider taking on more obligations, withdrawing cash advances, and sending money to pay for her hospital bills. Yet, his children's only concern was new toys.

Sami got toys for his kids from the cheap thrift stores, and he could tell from the looks on their faces that they disapproved of them. Some of the toys were older than ten years and did not appeal to their insatiable appetite for what they saw in the commercials.

When he was growing up in Kenya, Sami and other children would make and play with anything they could find: scrap metal, papers, tires, cans, whatever was available to them.

"What is it you wanted to tell me, Hawa?"

"It's nothing, Daddy."

Sami glanced at his daughter and admired her maturity. She understood the situation. She'd observed the family conditions and acquired the intuition of a person who had lived long enough to have witnessed life events and developed barometers with which to sense the mood and act accordingly. She was ready to transmit the message to the rest of the children.

How would he explain to her that he deserved a better-paying job so that he could afford to buy her the twenty-dollar toy she wanted? The sad news about the death of their aunt, whom they had never met, might not mean much to them, but Sami could not explain to her that her grandmother in Africa was dying in the hospital and needed money for hospital bills, and he could not afford to visit. His children wouldn't know that his extended family in Africa was as dependent on him for their basic survival as his immediate family here on American soil, which they now called home. How could he tell her that his brothers expected him to help with the education of their children? In the part of the world where Sami had grown up, the whole tribe awaited the glory of his success, ready to rejoice with him. They considered him to be their son. He was their hero, and they regarded him as a pillar and pride of the whole community. The tribe expected him to support them in their entire well-being. Sami did not tell her any of those things, and even if he tried, he would not know where to begin.

"Here. Adam was playing with them." His daughter gave him the letters that were on the floor. Sami sat for a long time to look at the letters again. Mere words on paper, they had triggered a chain of reactions. Feelings of anger, sorrow, helplessness, and failure loomed in his mind and kept coming back after each disappointment. Sami clenched his fist, remembering the truth of the statement: "If you can't help yourself, how can you help anybody else?" His wife kept reminding him of that, but Sami did not want to admit the bitter truth. "It hurts when you know it, and the pain intensifies when somebody else reminds you of it," Sami recalled the traditional adage and questioned his fate and failures. He then wondered whether it was a mistake for him to come to this country.

It wasn't a curse of some sort. Nor was it fate, lousy luck, or the evil eye, as some African traditions believe! He brushed off these silly thoughts of a nostalgic past, but the fear kept flowing through his mind. He mused over the circumstance, came to terms with the reality of the job situation, and decided to take whatever was available. *I can't afford to be out of status at this moment,* he said to himself. Sami had mapped out what to do before the expiration of his visa.

Chapter 3

Sami's mood began to change, though murky thoughts continued to hang over his head. Even amid turmoil, there must be a speck of hope to rekindle the desolate spirit. After piles of problems, there will always be a little glimmer of aspiration that will help to regain lost confidence.

Sami answered the phone.

"Sekou quit without notice, and we need a dishwasher for the morning shift. Will you be available?"

"Yes," Sami answered without hesitation.

***

Sami picked up the dirty dishes and took them to the dishwasher. Then he cleaned the kitchen and the floors. He also collected the garbage and swept outside the front door of the restaurant.

"Hey, dishwasher! Catch!" a voice echoed. The plates, spoons, and utensils soon began to accumulate. "Quick, we are busy today," Ryan, the manager shouted as he glanced at the revolving door leading to the kitchen.

"We want clean plates," the cook demanded.

"Get those dirty plates and make them ready."

Sami jerked his head towards the voice. The irritable manager yelled across the counter again, "Dishwasher?"

"I'm not deaf. I can hear you." Sami left the plates in the

washer to respond to the call. The rattling, clicking, and clunking sound of the dishwasher echoed in the background. Nobody called him by his real name around here. Everybody called him "Dishwasher," as if that were his name. At first, Sami did not object; however, when the cook introduced him as a dishwasher, he protested, but to no avail.

Sami placed the plates on the table, picked up some more dishes, and continued working. When he returned, there were some more plates. Sami looked around and then understood where they were coming from. Matt, the senior cook, peeped through the revolving door, his eyes darting back and forth. Sami looked back, cursing silently.

"We need those plates now!" the cook insisted.

Sami did not speak. Matt had something ready for him to do even though there were enough plates in the kitchen. The manager, instead, instructed him to clean the floors. He wanted Sami to do something all the time, no matter whether it was a busy day or not. At first, Sami thought dishwashers were supposed to be on their feet all the time, but then Kumar mentioned taking a break and commented, "The other dishwashers did not clean the floors, so you can take a break as everybody does."

"Nobody told me. I assumed that was the nature of work here."

"Now, you know." Kumar nodded.

Sami tried to remain incognito if possible, not wanting to bring attention to his visa work status. With a minimum wage and a few hours of work, he neither expected much nor complained. The work environment, aside from the mean cook and strict manager, appeared friendly. The laughter, jokes, and noisy atmosphere sometimes gave him the serenity he needed during this chaotic moment.

The world of odd jobs was in total contrast to what he knew about casual jobs in his native country of Kenya. As time went by, he grew a thick skin, turned deaf ears to the constant demands from his home, and no longer whined his litany of complaints.

"It's a lunch break," said Kumar Mehta. He was originally from India and had worked there for the last two years. As a student, he found the working hours at the restaurant flexible.

"Kumar, how come your name is spelled differently in the roster, as Kummer. I thought Kumar is a typical Indian name."

Kumar came close to Sami and looked around to make sure nobody was listening. "Sami, the way you pronounce my name, with a strong r sound at the end, is not correct. Make it soft, easy on the letter r. Why do you make it so thick? Koom-uhr, that's how you can say it." He spoke softly, close to whispering. "You remain typical. Do you know the saying, 'When in Rome, do as the Romans do?' You need to blend in."

He paused for a moment and then added, "One more thing, Sami." He propelled his head forward. "Here, people don't talk about where they came from, but my colleagues know that I came from Great Britain and speak the Queen's English."

"Do they care where you're from?" Sami asked with a sneer. "With your accent and skin color, Africa is on their mind when they see you."

"I am working on the accent. Keep things down." Kumar nodded.

"Tell me about the other places you've worked at," said Sami. "I need to pick up some more hours elsewhere."

"Oh, I know one place you'll get a job for sure if you want. A meatpacking factory." Kumar smiled.

"Where?" Sami turned to face Kumar.

"You won't enjoy working there." The sudden look from

Sami made Kumar quiver. "Well, let me put it this way, Sami. There, you will have a job on the spot if you are interested in doing heavy manual labor in freezing conditions with an irritating cleaning detergent. A chemical that eats into your skin and gives you a cough that doesn't go away." He looked up and leaned towards Sami. "The place is full of illegal immigrants, and you will never see a shortage of workers. People who've just gotten out of prison, drug addicts, and new immigrants who barely speak English, you will find them all there."

Kumar adjusted the tone of his voice. "You'll see a person working there one day, disappearing the next, and returning in another week or so. People come and go." He lowered his voice even more as if dispersing total secrecy. "If you don't have legal work documents, it's okay. People who've lived under the cover of the night have found in that place a suitable environment to work. They were real jailbirds, those who were in halfway houses, and maybe even deadbeat dads. The strangest-looking group of people you'll ever see. You can try it out if you can tolerate the environment." He paused. "The pay was a little better than here, a dollar and a half difference. Terrible pay for the work conditions, but still better than what they pay here," Kumar finished with a sinister look on his face.

"Why did you leave?" asked Sami. "I am just curious."

"After two years of working under those conditions, I could not cope with the cleaning chemical. It made me sick, and I developed a chronic cough. I also made the mistake of arguing with one worker, a degenerate crackhead who threatened to kill me.

"Tell me more about the work, then."

"Try it on your own first and see. They used to have two shifts, morning, and evening. At that time, I worked on the morning shift."

"If I go there today, do you mean I can start the same day?"

"Yes, they will always need somebody to do the cleaning. You can show up and get the job the same day on the spot. Easy to get in and out. The evening manager was a guy from Africa." Kumar smiled, his facial expression depicting a cynical look that was difficult to decipher.

Sami sat for a while without saying anything. "Can I ask you something else?" He was not sure how to approach the issue on his mind. Finally, he asked, "How can I get a green card?"

Kumar turned around when a fellow worker popped his head through the door.

"You need a good document, and I know how to get one," Kumar whispered.

Sami raised his head in surprise, his face wrinkling up. He kept his mind in a reflective mood, expecting to hear more. "Do you mean a legal document?"

Kumar gave him a know-it-all kind of look and smiled.

"How can I get it?" The way Kumar had spoken indicated to Sami that the green card document might be illegal. "You know bribery is out of the question here in this country. You know that, right?"

"I heard anything is possible if you have the money."

"Yes, technically. With the right amount of money, you can have almost everything, like everywhere else. However, in America, things are quite different. There are all sorts of activities, and if things go wrong, they call it bad business or judgment of error." Sami agreed that in the part of the world where he came from, anything was also possible with the right amount of money, including even getting a new passport, birth certificate, or what have you.

Kumar understood what Sami had in mind and quickly corrected himself. "Don't get me wrong. The kind of deal I am talking about is different. No money exchanges hands in the manner done in developing countries. It's a smarter way of doing things. You'll get frustrated here if you expect the same thing."

Sami kept silent. Deep down in his heart, he would like to do the right thing. He turned to Kumar. "I hate corruption, and I don't like what happens in my country." He smiled. "At least there, you get the things you want if you provide the right amount."

Kumar laughed. "Do you mean bribe?"

Sami continued with his line of thought.

"Well, whatever you call it, it is still bribery, Sami. They have all kinds of words to describe it, like 'greed,' and bribery is considered a felony, and you can go to jail for it."

"Okay, that's scary. Let's get back to the issue. How do I get a green card?" Sami gestured for Kumar to continue.

"You will need enough money. Once you have saved enough, about five thousand dollars, let me know. I will tell you how to get it. I know a lady who can help." Sami's forehead muscle twitched. "What? You appeared perplexed," Kumar teased.

"That's a lot of money." Sami waited as if expecting more. Then he asked, "Who's the lady? Can I meet her? I don't have to wait until I save. I will take a loan to finance it."

"Sure, I can arrange a meeting. Let me know if you needed anything else."

"You will hear from me."

"Bye, for now, Sami."

Sami knew that the road ahead, whichever one he must tread upon, would be paved with uncertainty. His past numerous job rejections had shown him what to expect.

"I will get a job, a real job when I get a proper document," he whispered to himself.

Chapter 4

Sami punched in his card before the morning shift team streamed out, forming a congested line at the entrance. There was barely enough time for him to return the card to the slot pocket of a folder. It took him a while due to competing hands criss crossing over a hundred cards sticking out of the folder pockets. Towards the bottom of the column of names in alphabetical order stood the unfortunate letter S for Sami's name. The card read, "Sami, Jama." Whoever had organized his card had made a mistake and put Jama as his first name.

"Take your time. New to this work? It gets crazy around here during this time." The person next in line noticed how Sami was struggling to find his name. Another person down the line complained that the evening shift crew should wait before they punched in. Some of the people Sami worked with during the evening shift had checked in before the actual time of 3:00 p.m., although the work wouldn't begin until the end of the morning shift. Sami put on overalls, rubber gloves, rubber boots, and got ready to start.

"One more thing, Sami," Sami turned around to face Moses. "Try to avoid punching in when the morning crews are lining up to punch out their cards. You can do it a little before their time or wait until they punch out." Sami nodded.

With his second job and extra money, he hoped to regain

his sanity and help his relatives back home. A convivial spirit overcame him as he looked back. He didn't have to drive far to work, either; it took him about twenty minutes to get there.

"You will be working in this area for one week and will clean all these machines and the floor." Moses waved his hands back and forth, making sure that Sami understood the extent of the area he was expected to clean. "This will be your primary section, as I mentioned to you last week during orientation. Make sure you have carefully tucked in the gloves, and if you need any help in lifting heavy machines or any equipment, ask for help either from Nick here or me." He pointed at another worker standing close to the spot where Sami was assigned to work. "We work very closely together, and you will get the help you need anytime."

Sami connected the hose to the hot water tap, dismantled the machines, picked each piece apart, and placed the pieces on the floor. He hosed the blood with warm water first and then scraped each piece with a thick, heavy-duty scrub sponge dipped in chemical detergent. Within the first few minutes of working, the glove ruptured, and some chemicals got through to his fingers. He got burned and had to wear a bandage. Moses instructed him to wear two rubber gloves. It was uncomfortable, but it helped him to keep away from chemical exposure.

Moses stopped by frequently to check how Sami was doing. He walked around to each section and inspected each piece of equipment, making sure that Sami had cleaned them all. He sometimes joined the evening crew and helped them, mainly when workers were late. Moses assigned team members to different sections of the machines on a rotating basis.

That day, all eight evening crew team members were present. Everyone occupied their positions and got ready to work. Sami was a bit slow, but he repeated the steps in his mind. "Take the removable parts of the machine apart first, presoak, wash with steamy hot water. Apply foaming agent, scrub each part with a heavy-duty sponge using the chemical, rinse, dry it quickly using the paper towel, and spray oil on all parts of the metal." The critical step was to oil parts before the metal began to rust and then spread out on the dry paper on the small table in the assigned area. Moses's words rang in his head as he meticulously followed the directions.

Before he started the second machine, Sami went to Nick's section and saw with satisfaction that he followed the steps correctly. After that, it was a smooth transition to the next machine. Nick, the worker on his left, yelled across to him as he sprayed the top parts of the equipment, warning Sami about the water coming from his direction. The hot stream of water shooting from all over the sections could land anywhere in the work area, spreading splashes of water across the entire unit. The workers did not like this intrusion.

"You have to be on the lookout. Make sure you contain the spray from your side and do not cross over to the next section. Otherwise, tensions could arise," Moses warned Sami. From the way Moses looked at Nick, it was easy to see why the best idea would have been to watch out and carefully work your way across.

Moses passed by several times. "Still at one machine? Keep working," he would encourage. Sami cleaned areas close to the border, separating his section from Nick's several times. From the corner of his eye, he noticed Nick hosing the drainage towards his part; and affirmed that the water had not oozed from the concrete floor, as he'd earlier thought.

Sami stopped spraying and readjusted his gloves when he noticed the inner one was soaked and about to come off. He then had to take off the whole overcoat before he could put on gloves again. The intense, penetrating odor engulfed him. Every time he dipped the rough scratchpad, soaked with the chemicals, the smell multiplied and permeated the whole atmosphere. It was as if the air he breathed choked him out and left him to depend on this chemical-laced air for survival. Sami didn't see anybody wearing any form of a protective mask, so it never occurred to him that he needed anything different. However, he mentioned his concern to Moses that the chemical odor was overpowering.

"You will soon get used to it, my friend," Moses replied. Sami couldn't imagine he'd be able to make it until he got used to this toxic atmosphere. He sneezed, desperately in need of fresh air, wondering what kind of chemical they used here that nobody seemed to know about or care. "You will get used to this chemical," Moses said. "You will be fine for a few days. Except for a persistent cough," he added casually.

"Break time!" Nick howled across to Sami.

Thank God, Sami silently said. He desperately needed a break to pay attention to his itching body and find breathable air somewhere.

He burst into the luncheon room, filled with a cloud of smoke from cigarettes, cigars, and who knows what else. He sensed a sudden silence as he stepped into the room, humming with anticipation akin to relief. He gasped, stifled a cough, and tried to disperse the smoky cloud floating around his face with his hand. Then he dropped his overcoat and gloves on the table and hurried for the exit door. Before stepping out, he remembered his food for dinner.

He warmed his rice mixed with beef stew, a Kenya dish, *pilau*, in the microwave, wondering where he would sit to eat. The aroma from the smell of his rice meal, prepared by his lovely wife, turned heads towards the beep and ding sound coming from the microwave. He knew there would be some questions about his food. He would have to agree that his wife was the best cook, and she knew what he wanted.

Sami rushed to open the windows. "Close the windows!

It's cold!" Pablo shouted. His hoarse voice cracking streams of vulgar curses.

It's okay, Pablo. A little fresh air will do," Moses said, trying to calm the situation.

"No, I am cold." Pablo got up and closed the windows.

"Welcome! Feel free," Moses said, and ushered Sami with his hand, implying that he could sit next to the table where they were playing cards and smoking. Moses transferred the cigar from the right to the left side of his mouth, back and forth, freeing both hands to shuffle the cards.

"Today is my day; I will regain the ten dollars I lost," Moses fumed. With the cigar still in his mouth, he threw down a card. "For twenty dollars!" he shouted.

"Common, Moses, I had bad luck, and I will prove it to you today. Take this." Nick threw a matching card in return.

At the next table, Emilio and Sancho were also playing a game that Sami had not figured out yet. He later learned it was "conquian" a rummy game, and they used a Spanish-style deck. Everybody was busy doing something while enjoying the chit-chat or games. In another corner, four more crew members talked in Spanish, loud enough for everybody to hear. Sami thought they were talking or arguing about something. The group also had cards on the table. From their gestures and body language, one would think that they were talking about some pressing matter. The one called Jose appeared vocal, while Petros emphasized his points with his fingers. Rafael spoke with a raised voice, though at times, he lowered it, ostensibly only for his friend's ears. Pablo, on the opposite side of the table, occasionally joined the argument, but for the most part, he kept to himself. Nobody challenged him when he shut the windows. After a few minutes, Jose and Petros stepped outside. The exit door faced an open space with a parking lot for the night crew, and behind the parking lot, some trees with thick undergrowth marked the edge of the factory premises, beyond which was an open field.

Sami gulped his food down without a word. He could not wait to get outside for fresh air. A chilly breeze hit his face as he walked out. He buttoned his winter coat and stepped away from the door. Nick followed him to ask for cigarettes.

"I don't smoke." Sami could barely say a word as he tried to get away from the tense, smoky environment, and he wondered why Nick did not realize that he did not smoke. Everybody was talking, so Sami was not sure whether Nick heard him or not. Pablo came out last. He went straight to his car, parked around the corner. He opened the driver's seat, left the door open, and sat on the hood, smoking.

Sami stood and watched the vast space stretching before him. The security light dimly illuminated the parking lot, and close to the edge of the trees, he could only see vague images of people. The three-night crew members, with their distinctive yellow plastic aprons still visible, joined the elusive nightly visitors. From that distance, Sami could not figure out who they were. He cast his eyes to the open space and saw cars coming into the parking lot and then leaving as soon as they arrived. Sami counted two vehicles. *What kind of a friendly visit is this*? He wondered, still submerged under the unbearable labyrinthine situation.

Sami stretched and let his mind wander. He yawned, a sign of looming physical exhaustion. With his hand still aching from the chemical burn, Sami could not explain how he felt. He had stoically conditioned himself for any possible adversities, yet his mind refused to accept that he had a full-time job. He recalled the numerous applications that he'd sent out without success, and here he was, hired on the spot and working within a short distance from his apartment. He had hardly filled out a paper to indicate his qualifications. The only requirement for the job was availability.

A slight, nippy breeze blew over his face and chilled him. Sami glanced once more towards the parking lot area and saw the flicker of lights from cigarettes glowing in the dark. The dim environment blossomed like a twinkle of fireflies in the distance. He did not want to indulge in other peoples' affairs, but it appeared to him as if something was out of place. When he returned, the card-playing groups were playing dominos. Moses and Nick were drinking coffee and smoking. They talked loudly, and one could hardly hear what anybody was saying.

A sudden silence descended on the room when the three members who went outside earlier entered. They ignored the silence and melted into the evening routine pattern.

Sami's curiosity bugged him with an impulse of glances. He saw hands exchanging things swiftly with the usual interlocking technique. Jose shook a hand with his friend Rafael, a quick tapping of the palm and then closing it. Then he turned around and dipped it into his pocket as if it were a carefully planned activity. Whatever it was that had transpired with the exchanged hands remained buried, and the other team members did not even notice.

Sami quickly turned his eyes the other way. It was too late. Jose had seen him and returned a look accompanied by a frown. Sami wondered what the expression meant. He then heard Jose and his friend talking in Spanish, which he did not understand. Jose took his friend aside and whispered something to him, and then his friend looked over at Sami. It occurred to Sami that something he'd done might have triggered the mean looks from them, but he had no clue what had caused the appalling reaction. He pretended not to notice it, but a feeling of goosebumps trickled over his body.

Chapter 5

In a few hours, they would all go home. "How much more left to do? Is this the last one?" Moses had to ask two times before Sami heard him.

"Yes!" Sami shouted amidst the hissing sound of spouting water spray.

"By 10:00 p.m., you should plan to get done with a major part of the work and slowly work until the end of your shift," Moses reminded him again. Earlier on, he told him about what other crew members did and how they managed their time. "I do not mind people working quickly to get done and go home if they wanted to, but you know most of them wanted more hours."

Sami had to learn later that some crew members left light work towards the end and extended their work beyond the time prescribed for the night shift. In some sections, they could do the job in three hours, but they had to stick around to get their full eight hours. The group seemed to have formed a close-knit bond and covered for each other. If one of them wanted to leave early, he could complete his work by 9:30 p.m., and leave the premises. A colleague would clock him out later as if he had been present the whole time.

Moses was aware of this practice, and in fact, he allowed it as a favor that he accorded to some of his close friends, with no regard for a punctilious code of ethics. This wrong approach to handling things was his way of diffusing grievances and the grumbling of his unpredictable workers. Moses also helped them with their work as often as he could. With poor work habits, some of them were very unreliable and never showed up for work on time. Moses would exploit this predicament and used it as leverage. It was the only thing that he could rely on to get the job done. If one is gone, he will get another one soon.

Sami got the job when a worker failed to show up for two days. He later learned the worker was locked up in prison for domestic violence, and Moses was desperate to get a replacement. Sami, like most of the workers, found this job ideal. The only document that Moses asked him to produce was a driver's license.

Sami checked the parts he'd washed again and waited for Moses to inspect them.

"Look at this part! "Moses turned part of the machine around for closer scrutiny. "This spot here and another one there, a hidden area about to rust. The rest of the parts look perfect." Moses moved to the next section. Nick was not in his assigned area, but Moses went ahead and inspected. He moved to the next, making sure to complete all the designated areas. He would later check them when everybody punched out for the night.

Sami waited for Moses to return. He had completed the task satisfactorily. The rest of the crew members were back in the breakroom. Sami joined them.

"Are you done with the parts?" Moses lifted his head from the newspaper he was reading.

"Yes."

"I will check them later."

"Did you say that you were originally from Malawi?" Sami asked. Moses paused his reading. "Yes."

"How was the job situation for foreigners?"

"The job situation did not change. It was worse for those who did not have proper legal documents." Moses folded the paper. "Unfortunately, there were extra obstacles for foreigners, even for those who had green cards. Some foreign-born students did not get the job they deserved."

Sami recalled a brief discussion they'd had the day before about filling out the forms and how Moses instructed him not to fill in all the spaces, like where it required the level of education.

"What did you do with your degree?" Sami asked.

"Nothing. There was nothing I could do unless I got an opportunity to work in the area. I applied several times and got rejections."

"That's sad."

"You might be surprised. I had two master's degrees, one in health education and the other one in sociology and yet I could not get a job."

He nodded and continued. "With my degree in health education, I only needed a student teaching field experience, but I taught at a community college for two semesters."

"Why didn't you continue with teaching?"

"They didn't offer me any course to teach. Students complained about my accent. I am not sure whether that was part of the reason."

"I am just curious," Sami continued. "How long did you stay without getting a job in your area of expertise?"

Moses paused as if trying to remember.

"About nine years, and I have been working here for the last seven years. I was almost kicked out of the country when I graduated. My visa was about to expire, and I avoided deportation by taking classes that I did not need. Then luck struck me in the form of a green card lottery. Even with a green card, I kept working at odd jobs for two years. And I'm still doing the same kind of job as a night shift manager." Moses sighed. "This is my job. After all these years, I no longer consider my degree relevant. I could have gone back to school to do something else, but when you're out of school for many years, you lack motivation. Besides, I am in high debt." Moses had a solemn look on his face.

Sami felt a sense of déjà vu. "Should it be the same all over again for all these people who came all this way to get the best education that they will never utilize?"

"The circumstances we faced forced us to accept any job. After years of working in this kind of situation, your academic status and qualifications have no substantive value."

"Really!" Sami exclaimed.

"We keep sending resumes with a gap in years of experience, and when they see that it makes them wonder whether you are qualified. They think that you have no ambition." He bit his lips. "And yet they don't know what we go through. We work two to three jobs, educate ourselves, and help the family back home." Moses was ready to spill out the venom. "I feel bitter when people who don't know about your situation judge you. Some of them think that we are lazy and came here for handouts. Just look at the statistics, some of us who came to this country as students have made a mark. I just happen to be one of those who failed a little short of catching up with the dream." He consoled himself, adding, "With two master's degrees under my belt, I have no regrets. My only bitterness is that the system failed me." Moses paused and continued. "Even with that, I should have done something differently or adjusted my career quickly. I stayed long, waiting, and took so many years without changing my attitude."

Sami remained attentive.

"Anyway, for the last ten years, I have not done any work

related to my area of expertise. To be exact, after five years, I stopped applying for jobs and decided to hold on to any manual job that I could get. I was competing with fresh young students from college, and when they looked at my resume, they saw a big gap and probably thought that I was no longer relevant."

As Moses continued, Sami could see in his eyes a beaten spirit. "I started this job as a floor cleaner and worked in all sections. I worked hard and never hesitated that the job was beneath me. I put every effort into it and learned how to do it better every day. I even pretended to love the job and looked forward to doing it. I remembered the first two years; I did all kinds of odd jobs on the farm. I even went to Alaska during the summer to work in the fishing industry to load tons of fish. After five years of cleaning floors and bloody machines, they promoted me to the night shift manager. If I knew then what I know now, things would have been different. I missed opportunities. Anyway, the future is unknown, and we ended up talking about events after the fact." He took a deep breath. "Believe it or not, I still have a desire to go back to school and complete an MBA degree. I have enough knowledge about the meat industry. When I return to Africa one day, I can build a meat-processing factory."

More wishful thinking, Sami thought.

After everyone was gone, Moses waited for a night delivery worker to deliver some hog carcasses.

Sami put his overcoat, gloves, boots, and other things he needed at work in the locker. He sneezed. The stench from the chemicals they used for cleaning followed him. He might be the only one sensing all the smells of this unbearable, corrosive chlorinated chemical.

"Bless you, amigo! That was a long sneeze. You will get used to the chemical we used for cleaning." Jose looked over. "How was your first week, amigo?"

"Oh, it was okay. I will look for a mask next time." Sami sneezed again and again.

"You know, amigo, once you get this chemical into your body, it will give you a persistent cough that won't go away, and you can't forget about the smell." He shook his head. "You will have it in your head for days and nights."

Sami continued with his final packing without saying a word. Jose came closer and whispered to him, "Amigo." Sami stopped.

Jose paused. He scratched his square-shaped head. It was the kind of scratch that was not triggered by itch but perpetuated by a desire to deflect attention by sweeping his fingers over his head and follow it with a sly smile. "You look innocent and pure, and I can see that you're not used to this kind of work. Here is my friendly advice to you." He looked around as if he did not want anybody else to hear what he was going to say. "Anything you see here should remain here. Find alliances if you can and keep out of other people's business. Don't trust what you see and hear. Most of the people around here have criminal records. They can disappear without a trace, and nobody will notice or miss them. Some of them don't have any support system, and they don't care about anyone. No families, no noting."

Sami understood that Jose meant nothing. "You may be surprised that even the names we use here are untraceable and fake. The people who work here..." Jose glanced around. "They are here today, and tomorrow they will be in Illinois or other states doing similar jobs under different names and with proper identification. If you need to know anything else around here, let me know. I have worked here for the last five years and have a good reputation."

Sami could only give a friendly nod to this frightening cautionary advice.

Moses was punching out some cards when Sami

approached. "Are you punching out," he asked when Sami came closer. "Go ahead, and I can talk with you later."

Sami noticed that Moses punched out cards for some people who'd left earlier. Jose was right behind him, and Sami remembered his advice: "Whatever happens here, stays here." Sami wondered what would happen if the owner of the factory showed up.

The night crew had already devised a way of fooling any intruder. When they completed the main work, the team would take a break and pretend to clean the lunchroom. The crew had a secret signal to alert each other too, yelling across to each other using of terms they commonly used while cleaning. If caught in the break room at the wrong time, they could say they were taking their break at that time, and one person was always on the lookout. In any case, one had to pass through another room where the light was often turned off. The moment the lights came on, the workers knew that somebody from outside was entering. They would then have enough time to regroup for action.

Moses cleaned the lunch table and beckoned Sami to sit. "I am sure Jose advised you on certain things. He means good for everybody. I know you are noticing the dynamics of the group, and in general, you can work with them if you keep to yourself. Don't get involved in anybody's affairs. You may see something that you don't like, and it's okay to look the other way. I don't allow them to do any drugs in the building, but any of them can go out in the parking lot and do their stuff, and I don't bother them. I pretend not to see it, although I am clear with them that they do it at their own risk." Moses pulled out chewing tobacco." I was trying to quit cigarettes and found it challenging. It was harder to quit smoking. I have attempted sugarless chewing gum to minimize cravings."

He continued. "Smoking weed for some of them seems to

be the main issue here: Petros, Emilio, and Pablo even served jail terms, and they may carry on with their habits. The crime of indulging in this is considered an aggravated misdemeanor, and you should know that Iowa is stricter than other states. On the other hand, they don't want this place raided. It would be the end of their job, and they don't want to jeopardize it. They will not get any other job elsewhere."

Sami nodded. "That won't bother me. I have never done any drugs."

"Stay out of it. Don't associate with anybody. I didn't mean to scare you. These workers are generally good people, easy to work with, and with good hearts once they accept you. The discussions during the break can sometimes appear frightening and hostile. Don't think much about it. You will feel totally out of place, and that's okay as long as you don't interfere. In a nutshell, don't cross anybody's path." Moses smiled. "Of all the people who work the evening shift, I think Pablo is the most difficult to deal with, and you should be careful; he has anger issues. You saw how he reacted to the window that you opened, but he is a hard worker, and most of the time, he is friendly if you don't bother him."

Sami was not sure how to interpret these messages. "You can go home now. We can talk later," Moses said, and then he left the room to check the office and bathrooms.

Chapter 6

"Hello, is Kumar working today?"

"Hold on." A lady's voice on the other side of the phone kept him waiting. In the background, soft music played. After what seemed like two or three minutes, Kumar came on the line.

"Yes, what do you know? What's up, man!"

"It's me," Sami tried to answer, but it looked like Kumar knew who he was. Sami laughed, amazed that Kumar could adapt so quickly in his manner of speaking, except for his typical Indian accent, which showed no matter how much Kumar tried to suppress it. Kumar had adopted all the mannerisms of American speaking, and he practiced the new things he learned. Sami wondered why he would use a term like "What do you know?" when something like "How are you doing?" would suffice. At first, Sami did not know what to say, but then Kumar told him that was another form of greeting.

"Sami, call me only during break time. The restaurant's coffee shop serves customers throughout the day, and it can be jam-packed."

Sami quickly got to the point. "Okay, Kumar, I understand. It's urgent. When can we talk about the document?"

"Anytime if you're ready."

"See you in twenty minutes. I am ready."

Kumar hesitated. "I would rather not talk further over the phone, but I could spare you a few minutes."

"Let me get directly to the point," Kumar said when they finally met. "Have you made up your mind?"

"Yes." Sami nodded.

"You've probably heard a lot of stories about getting a green card through marriage." Kumar waited for Sami to affirm that he had.

"Kind of," Sami said.

"Some people risk their lives to come to this country. How far are you willing to go?" Are you ready for a significant risk?"

"What do you mean?"

"Okay, my friend. Let me remind you." Kumar elevated his voice. "A marriage visa is where you marry a US citizen and get a green card through the marriage. Some people will do anything to get what they want."

"My best option for a visa is through work, and with all my disappointments with the job situation, it did not work for me." Sami sighed. "As for marriage option, I am skeptical."

"Let me explain, Sami. Getting a visa through marriage is the best route for an unmarried person. However, a married man could divorce his wife and marry a citizen, and you can stay low until everything goes through with the documents. One to two years in a marriage if you want to avoid any suspicion. After that, you can get back to your wife."

"I didn't know that a phony marriage could take that long," Sami wondered.

"Let me take that back. It depends. Some people have abused the system and made it a money-making scheme." Sami squinted his eyes in a manner that showed disapproval or doubt in his mind.

"Really?"

"Yes, Sami, without question, you will get a green card," Kumar emphasized.

Sami sat speechless for a moment and wondered whether he was ready for such a drastic shift in his life. Though doubt crept into his mind, this approach was too hard to resist. "Do you think I would have any chance with this arrangement?" he asked as if he wanted to hear the same answer he had in mind.

"As I said, it all depends on you and your willingness to take a risk, and nothing is guaranteed." Kumar held his head up for attention. "Let me tell you what I heard. There was a woman who signed onto multiple marriage deals. She demanded payments in advance and then vanished."

"How could this happen?"

"Who would ever accuse her of fraud? They were all in the game, each one afraid to report the matter. In such a situation," Kumar lowered his voice, "it would be difficult to trace the culprit. She could be anywhere in one of the big cities, doing a similar thing." Kumar was painting a picture that didn't look pleasant. "There were many reported incidents, and I heard one ended in brutal death."

Sami looked up with an expression of disquiet on his face. Kumar noticed the discomfort and smiled. "I am telling you the extreme scenario. The reality may be different." He paused. "There was a network where some men were involved. They hired women for fake marriages, and the strategy worked for both." Sami remained silent, confused, and lost in thought. Kumar moved on. "With Jasmine, something like that would never happen."

Sami glowed with a sparkle in his eyes. "Are you sure about this?"

Kumar nodded. "There is another simple solution to these hassles." He smiled as if harboring a secret. "Older women who are available will do the deal for real unless they've encountered bogus marriages and gotten frightened."

"I don't know how this can help a married man," Sami murmured.

Kumar looked around as if dispersing a secret message, and he lowered his head. "Divorce your real wife and marry for the document," he suggested.

"Are you serious? This is not a joke?" Sami tilted his head and faced Kumar directly.

"Yes." Kumar laughed and added., "You know polygamy is illegal here, and with your situation, it's the only way."

Both Sami and Kumar looked at each other at the same time.

"Real divorce without any justifiable cause is unlikely. I love my wife and would never imagine committing such an act," Sami declared. The words coming out of his mouth were barely audible as if talking to himself, and then, as an afterthought, he asked, "What if my wife does not agree to the divorce.?

"Sami, this is not like a real, real divorce. You may have to make a deal with your wife if you want to do this." Kumar winked.

"A divorce is a divorce no matter what," Sami added.

"There are no specific grounds for divorce in Iowa. The state is what they call a 'no-fault' divorce state. In other words, no reason or justification needed. One party can cite the reason as irreconcilable differences that led to the breakdown of the marriage."

"This can't be as simple as you put it," Sami said. "I guess my wife and I will be needed at the court to witness, right?" Sami asked.

"Actually, no. Once the document is signed, it's enough for one person to present it to the court."

"What if one person does not want to sign?"

Kumar turned, and Sami waited, wondering what was behind the strange look. "I thought you wanted the card."

"Yes, I do."

"Then, you will find ways. Don't get bogged down with little, insignificant things. Your wife does not need to appear in court. Okay, I have to go now. If you are ready to take this on, let me know." Kumar waved goodbye.

Sami spun the bizarre notion in his head. He pictured the image of Jasmine, a name that sounded like Yasmine, a familiar name from the region where he came.

Chapter 7

At the initial introductions, Jasmine began with her brief biography. She was born in Brooklyn, New York, and lived in three other states: Louisiana, Texas, and Iowa. Sami listened attentively, not sure what to make of all those places she'd lived.

"Can I call you Yasmin?"

Jasmine smiled. "Call me, Jasmine. I heard it originated from Persia and meant flowering plant."

Jasmine glanced at Sami from the corner of her eye as they ate lunch. Sami also stole a few glances, pretending that both were there strictly for business. He brushed off the weird thoughts seeping through his head. An image of marrying this strange lady on paper emerged, allowing for a twisted fantasy to brew. He had no idea what kind of a marriage this would be, and with curiosity shaping up in his mind, he berated his softening attitude. Jasmine looked pretty, at least, on the first impression. She was a little chubby, and that was acceptable within his parameters of preference. A figure he could approve. Besides, she had a pleasant face and exotic, glowing charm akin to Mona Lisa's smile, which intrigued him.

Realizing the need for professional etiquette, Sami turned his eyes quickly to the balsamic glazed salmon skillet lunch and devoured it. *It won't hurt to pretend to be like a husband, too,* he thought.

"Kumar told me that you came from Africa," Jasmine said, breaking the silence. She looked at Kumar, who kept munching his food and was almost oblivious to his surroundings.

"Yes, East Africa." Sami waited to see whether she could ask for a specific country.

"I would love to visit Africa one day." She sipped her water and resumed eating.

"Which country in Africa?" Sami inquired.

"Maybe Ghana, that part of Africa. They tell me that I look like the people from that region. What do you think?"

Sami was not ready for this question, although he had to appear knowledgeable about the continent. "Your physical features are quite similar, and I am sure you can pass as one of them."

They talked briefly about their lives and hobbies, and then, after lunch, they went to a nearby park. Sami searched for an appropriate opening line, but the proper words evaded him. Lucky for him, she initiated the conversation by thanking him for lunch, and she wanted to know when he would leave for work. "Somebody I knew worked there some years back and told me that it was a great place to hide," she slyly commented.

"I was wondering…" Sami began, but then she interrupted him, patting him softly on the shoulder and smiling.

"Relax. You look tense. Take it easy. I can see you are a bit nervous."

Sami faked a smile. She was right, and he was sweating and looked miserable. He then suddenly felt like going to the bathroom.

"I am fine. "Let's talk about the amount," he said softly, raising his head until their eyes met.

"Kumar told me that you had all the information." She glanced at him and gave him a seductive wink.

"Yes, but I have a different amount in mind, not more than two thousand," Sami stated.

Jasmine waited for a few minutes. Another smile accompanied her gesture towards him. He felt a little intimidated; a feeling of surrender overcame him.

"You look nice and good-natured, and frankly when I saw you, I liked you. I think Kumar might have told you that I would not accept less than five thousand dollars. You can pay half of the amount this month and the rest in the future. If you do that on time, I will take off $250. Remember, this offer was only for you."

Sami stared at her vacantly. It took a moment to realize that his gesture had resulted in a stalemate. In a split second, many things went through his mind. They all came to rest on the issue of money.

"I will pay half of the amount you said and the rest when we process the document," he said with a grimace. He had grown up in an environment where people bargained vigorously for a good deal.

He made eye contact with a lingering gaze. She stared back with a smile, a sign that he interpreted as a soft spot. He needed a couple of days to work on her. She had the leverage in the form of the document. She switched the topic from money one moment and then brought it back again, a reminder that he had to produce something, and, without money, he would not get the document.

As if caught in the mischievous act, Jasmine leaned towards him. "I repeat, I am willing to bend my own rules for the first time, and you seem to be one lucky fellow." She paused with a deep breath and continued. "Okay, I can reduce it to $4,500. You can pay $2,500 now and the remaining amount towards the end."

She noticed a worried look on Sami's face. She paused for a while before continuing. "I can understand if you think negatively about me and this deal. You may be right to think that way. Sadly, it is the American way. People here think of themselves first and ask what is in it for them. Nobody does anything for free. The end game is what matters about the deal. We have to keep our end of the bargain intact."

Sami sat and watched as she unfolded her tantalizing enigma. She went on and on. "I hope you won't judge me by this act and the monetary value tied to this sacred gift of marriage. I can feel it in your eyes." She smiled. "I mean..." She paused. "You're married with children, a family man with your burden. I understand that."

Sami sat with the same somber mood and listened. She spoke the truth. It was a bitter truth that he hated to admit.

"You now know about me in detail. Maybe you can share with me more about yourself later," she concluded.

"I believe our deal is private, and I want it that way," Sami interjected.

"Oh, yes, this is only between you and me, and of course, Kumar knows." She smiled.

"The matchmaker."

"I would not involve Marvin in a matter like this. With his rage, he can be destructive, and I will not allow him to stay with me. He's gone back to New York," Jasmine noted.

Sami puckered his lips in anticipation of more questions. "No need for me to worry about any of your former husbands or boyfriends, right?"

Jasmine did not expect that kind of question. She paused. "Oh, you don't have to be concerned. The only other person who might show up is Antonio, my former husband. We were separated. He was in prison until recently. In any case, you have nothing to worry about. I am on my own."

After a moment, she added, "Just so you know, I have a

few credits left before I graduate, and I will soon take some courses to complete my degree. We may bump into each other on campus."

"I would prefer not to meet with Marvin, Antonio, or any other of your associates," Sami declared.

"Oh, no, I was just giving you a head start. As I told you, I cut off my relationship with Marvin, and he knows it. I had to let him go. We no longer live together anymore."

"What about Antonio?"

"He's a drifter and got out of prison recently. He has some issues with anger management. I had a short-married life with him." Jasmine shook her head. "You don't have to worry about them."

Jasmine checked her watch and apologized for taking too long. She did something else that softened his feelings towards her. She planted a soft kiss on his cheek, held his hand, and delivered a smooth, tinkling squeeze. The tender and pleasant scent of her perfume wafted across his face. He paused and returned the accommodating affection, telling himself that it was okay, and she might not have anything else in mind other than the transactions of the business. He brushed off the wicked thoughts percolating in his mind.

Sami turned around to leave and looked back twice. As his eyes met hers, she sent smiles and waved. He shrugged off that gesture as a routine courtesy in the business world.

Sami drove back to work, wondering and replaying the events in his mind. Whatever little information Kumar had shared about Jasmine was enough to gain his trust. In the brief discussions that he'd had with her, Sami realized that she did not want to talk much about her previous history. The only passing statement she shared was about her children and grandmother, and a little about her current boyfriend and former husband.

On the other hand, if one disapproved of her present

actions, one could easily blame the past for influencing her errors of judgment. From her first appearance, Jasmine had looked great, probably a reasonable person in a spoiled, rotten environment that numbed, submerged, and dragged her down. Sami thought she needed a helping hand in the form of encouragement and recognition.

Sami had nothing else to say about the sealed deal. He had listened to her well-planned side of her brief life story and remained skeptical. There appeared to be some gaps and deletions. She told her story either to convince or to scare, and the impact left Sami in a dilemma, especially when she'd warned him jokingly that her boyfriend could cause trouble. She'd hinted at how her boyfriend had boasted about his adventure in the Caribbean, where he'd made people disappear. Sami shuddered and reflected on each word she'd uttered, wondering why she'd bothered telling him all that.

Jasmine's motives were clear, and even Sami's charming look would not give him an extra edge. He'd gotten a good deal, according to Kumar, who told him about the nature of this business, where they stated their price and stuck with it. It was a plan contrived, carefully crafted, experimented upon several times with masterful precision, and then apparently kept alive by a person like him. If there were any shimmering light of hope of getting a green card, Sami vowed to try his best to do anything to go forward. In his current dire situation, he had no other option left. Without his wife's collaboration, he would have to trust Kumar's tactics to work.

Sami recalled the scenes from his past experiences and wondered what Kumar wanted in return for the favor. He remembered Kumar's statement: "It is straightforward. Get the application from the library, fill out the necessary parts, and I can help if needed, and let me know when you want to go to the court. You can surprise her later with the green card."

Sami was not sure what to make of all these competing items. The desperate need for this document blinded him. He weighed his options and went along with the plan, and he reached the point of arranging to get a loan to finance the deal. In a day or two, he would meet with Jasmine and pay the amount agreed.

***

The following day before he went to work, Sami received a call from Kumar.

"I am fine, thanks," Sami acknowledged.

"Let me know if you need anything. Jasmine seemed to like the idea and is pleased to work with you. She was impressed with your demeanor, and I think she likes you. She found you to be funny and original."

"Come on, Kumar, this is a business deal, and you know it."

"Yeah, but there seems to be a chemistry between you and her, and that's a good sign," Kumar observed.

"Kumar, I had to do a lot of homework on my side. My wife probably won't buy into this, and I don't know how it would work."

"As I told you, work on the divorce papers first. We can work things out."

"Okay, Kumar, I have to go." Sami's voice trailed in the distance.

Chapter 8

As he drove home from work, Sami pondered the endless drama of his life. Although his financial situation had improved a little, his salary was far below what a person with his academic qualifications could earn.

Sami had to support his large family at home in Kenya. He'd promised his mother and brothers that he would uplift them from the jaws of poverty and deprivation. Sami had grown up thinking that one had to go to school to learn, get a job, build a family and community, and then live until death came upon him in old age. He was not even sure whether he now believed in anything like fairness, equality, and justice. Those beautiful words enshrined in the true meaning of life worth living, and yet the reality he'd encountered had proven otherwise.

Sami had promised himself not to think about anything else after work. This was a problematic pledge to keep for a man who lived through contradictions. His mind was always alert and consumed with regrets. He knew it would take a long time for him to fall asleep.

The past few nights, Sami had found another outlet to numb his sleepless nights. As he drove through downtown one night, he diverted his attention to the neon lights that advertised entertainments and adult movies, a bizarre way to assuage the nightly concerns. The colorful lights calmly beckoned to his eyes, awakening in him overwhelming hedonistic feelings. He tried to avoid the temptations, but it required a five-minute stop before he developed a crack in his fickle mind. Sami thought he could stop by the store to satisfy his curiosity. He needed only five minutes to browse through some pictures in the magazines and the items displayed. This later extended to 30 minutes, then an hour, and later, some nights, he would stay until past midnight. It came to the point where he had to pass by this peculiar place at least twice a week. There was also a room that one could rent for a movie. Like a person deprived of all worldly goods, Sami plunged into this secret world with the impervious force of willpower to enjoy the newfound time-wasting indulgences.

Sami reminded himself that it was no big deal, and yet every time he passed through downtown, he had to glance towards the direction of the store. The next thing he knew, he had to look for a parking space in the next lot. Just like the mysterious power of Calypso, the daughter of Atlas, who enchanted and detained Odysseus on her island, his mind and heart remained captive to the late-night movie encounters. He was trapped and knew how to keep the frequent exposure secret even as he parked his car at the far end of the parking lot in a busy town. Sami would then wait for a few minutes in the car, making sure that nobody he knew spotted him going to the store. With the guilt of shame, he would lower his head and put on a hat in disguise. He did not like being seen going into that store.

"What are you afraid of," he would scold himself when these contradictory thoughts came into his mind, even though he believed he was not doing anything wrong or illegal. He watched the materials available in the public domain. It was his moral upbringing that could not accept his actions. Sami could not explain the degrading, shameful text written in those magazines, and he had a choice not to see or read them. A proud father of four children, a husband, and a man of learning and profound cultural upbringing if he added the whole list of his acquired trophy of wisdom. Besides, there was whatever remained of his vague religious awareness. Confused, Sami was trying to downplay his actions. He believed that some of the TV channels his colleagues talked about showed more graphic adult materials than what he read, so he brushed it off as usual.

Sami arrived home a little past midnight. He parked his car and walked across to his apartment. He yawned and sneezed as he clutched at his house key. The muscles in his hand ached from exhaustion, and it took him a while to open the door. He showered immediately to remove the odor of the chemical that seemed to linger on in his head. He then tiptoed to the kids' room to check on them. They were all asleep. The university family apartment was as quiet as ever during the night, exemplifying the serenity of this peaceful community life.

As usual, by the time he came home, his wife was asleep. Sami put all his working clothes in a plastic bag and kept them in the corner of a bedroom. He put some of the papers he'd brought from work in the top bedroom drawer and returned the envelope with his certificates and resume to the bottom drawer. These were the documents he'd carried with him earlier out of instinct, thinking that his employers would need to see his qualifications for the meatpacking job. Sami admired his certificates, saddened that he could present a master's degree to an employer who just needed a high school level of education for a job. He twitched the corner of his mouth, dreading the inevitable reality, and Sami had no qualms about accepting this job. Without the proper legal document, like many people with a similar fate, he would likely get jobs well below his educational level. The lowest-paying, unpredictable, risky, and unsanitary jobs.

Sami jerked his head when he heard his kids' laughter. He checked and confirmed that it was a dream. He then tucked in their blankets and glanced at the ticking clock on the wall. It was past midnight. He sat on the bed and wondered if his wife felt his presence. Some days, she would stick her head out to ask or tell him something, family communication reduced to where and why. The answers, in most cases, eluded him.

Sami did not expect anything to be different that night. Guided by the bedside light, he looked at the layout of the terrain. His side of the bed was crinkled and had no sign of ever being made. He straightened the loose end of the bedsheet and swept the surface with his palm. As if there were something on top of the bed. He had the reverent attitude he'd acquired from his childhood days when he used to share a bed with his brothers. His younger brother had had a habit of playing tricks by leaving unwanted objects on his side of the bed, pieces of broken sticks, animal bones, metallic objects, and everything that appeared to obstruct. Breaking old habits was hard. Sami had to wipe the bed or shake the bedsheet before he could lay down to sleep. He then slowly found his way under the blanket. Some days, he would be tempted not to take a bath, but if he didn't, his wife would surely pick up the scent. He would then receive an unspoken reaction. She would face the opposite side of the bed suddenly, with a violent turn that would tilt the whole blanket and the bedsheets over towards her, leaving him to hang onto the loose end of the bedsheet.

Sami lay on his back and turned on his left side and then on the right side. As he waited for sleep to come into his head, his mind became cluttered with all sorts of things competing for attention. He had developed a habit of checking the time, and after some time, he raised his head to get a clear view of the clock on the little table near his bedside. It was about one o'clock, but still, sleep did not come into his head. This trend had become part of his nightly routine.

Sami wondered how much sleep his wife would get with his constant and continuous turning. The matter was getting worse because of his cough and sneeze. This endless misery in the form of respite took a toll on his sleeping partner. Tonight, though, his wife didn't turn as she had in the past. She stayed calm, with what looked like a perfect state of tranquility spreading over her face. Sami looked at her as she slept on her back. He felt the presence of her whole beautiful being, and from the way she was breathing, he knew she was not entirely asleep.

Sami admired the contour of her immaculate figure. The bedding materials emphasized her distinct configuration from head to toe, creating an appearance of a rolling plain with jutting hills and valley. Sami felt his side of the bed; it was slightly cold, just as it always was since his wife rarely ventured into his territory. The only place where they ever had any form of contact remained aloof and could not even alleviate the daily problems he faced. His bed was supposed to be where he could bury his worries and fatigue or renew his energy for tomorrow's battle. As time moved on, it turned out to be a place where all the demons in him were released to torment him with concerns and fears of failure.

No wonder Sami woke up every morning tired and grumpy, and not looking forward to a new day with a hopeful and optimistic outlook. A bitter feeling slowly numbed his mind into thinking the gloomy side of life again. Every time he consciously decided to shorten his misery, the scenic views of his children and his whole life drama appeared to him in the form of a picture. He shuddered. *How the papers would print one more unfortunate event in the life of an international student, and then what life awaits his children*, he thought. He then consoled himself in his mind and turned slowly to one side, facing the wall, in anticipation of the desperately needed sleep. It would be another short night.

He sneezed. It came without warning as he tried to hold it in, and it shook the whole bed.

"Can't you do it in the living room? You have ruined my sleep," his wife snapped. After another sneeze, Sami realized that he had to step out and sleep in the living room.

Some days, he would get a note from his wife, stuck on the TV screen or the door. He would do the same in case he needed to tell her something. Their little exchange of information was limited to the needs of children, a hapless circumstance of life. Sami and his wife still used old-fashioned ways to communicate; they couldn't afford the cellular phone. He picked up a notebook, tore off a sheet of paper, and wrote a message for his wife. His explanatory note read: "Sorry, dear, we used this chemical at work, and it made me sneeze over and over." He looked at the hand-scribbled message with scrutiny. "We are in this together, I promise. I will get a decent job, but until then, be patient."

He knew she had done her part with glowing success. Her social work degree and certification in nutrition health and wellness might land her a permanent full-time job. Sami noticed how confident she was about getting a job in her field. She'd interviewed for nutrition, health, and wellness position at a clinic, and with her certification, she was sure to get the job. His wife kept telling him that the demand and job outlook appeared promising, and she might even get a visa through employment. The disappointment with Sami's job situation had made him lose hope in his field of study.

***

When Sami woke up, his wife, as usual, had packed everything the kids needed while at the babysitter. She would never entrust him with that kind of detail because he would do it in his clumsy way, leaving some essential things out, or wrong items would find their way into the package. She would never forget the day when he'd almost driven over the baby. He'd thought the baby was in the car. Sami would rather do the delivery than the packing.

He noticed a note his wife had left on the table about the concern the babysitter had about Musa not listening. Sami and his wife knew Isabella, the babysitter, was overwhelmed, and their kids did not enjoy the crowded environment. Their faces would twist in anguish and uncertainty wherever he left them. Besides, they regularly came home with a cough and running nose and spread it among themselves. It was this issue of health that became the point of family discussions.

The children had gone through five babysitters, one after another. They'd been the mothers of international students here for short visits.

Sarah kept the babysitters' contact, and the most recent was Isabella, a Peruvian lady. She was a short, joyful woman with a broad, friendly face and squinty eyes. An active kid would have trouble getting her attention.

Isabella was at the door when Sami arrived. She handed him a note, which said, "Your payment of $10 is due now."

"Okay, I see." Sami had another appointment, which he would not delay, with the Department of Human Services. He was required to meet with them after he reported the changes in income. He tried to explain. "Let me drop the kids off first and get the money from the bank. I don't have the cash with me right now."

Isabella kept pointing to the note. Sami tried all the gestures he could manage to convey the message. Isabella could only repeat, "No English." He understood the condition of daily payment of five dollars for the five hours his two kids stayed with the babysitter, and he had not paid yesterday.

As he was leaving, she kept pointing to Musa. "Nino destructivo." She had many kids from the neighborhood. You would find several students from Latin America lining up to drop off their kids. The two-bedroom apartment was packed. There was little space for kids to play, and one would wonder how she managed them all. She charged little and provided cheap service. Parents would pack food for their children and pay on time. At a dollar per hour, most of the students with limited time and money could afford to leave their kids two to three hours while attending classes or doing some work. Sami's two younger children would stay with a babysitter for five hours before his wife would pick them. By that time, the two older ones had returned from school. The bus would drop them off by the apartment. It was the convenience and affordability that dictated the choice they made, with quality sacrificed in situations like this, where you struggle with life to make ends meet.

Sami withdrew the money needed. He had one more hour left before his appointment and then another hour before his morning shift at the restaurant, which started at 10:00 a.m.,

"Let's see what you've got." The social worker browsed through the documents and copied both paystubs from Sami's two jobs. As a Medicaid recipient, he would receive a monthly Medical Identification Card, and he was obliged to notify the County Human Services Office. Sami had heard all kinds of stories about how they could deny benefits or reduce them if his income reached a certain level. He knew this would put him back to where he'd started.

"Will this impact our situation?" he asked.

"I will run a quick calculation and let you know." The lady punched some numbers in the calculator and checked a sliding scale, to determine the final figure. "With a family of six, you still qualify for the benefits. What both of you made was not enough to reduce welfare assistance." She handed him some documents to read and a list of other agencies to contact if he needed them. Sami got back into his car, thinking that even with two manual jobs, there was not enough money for his immediate family needs.

Chapter 9

Sami checked off the job positions to which he'd applied and transferred the rejection letters into a big envelope and tossed them under the desk . He read through the stack of advertisements.

"This one requires just a minimum qualification, and yet they didn't invite me for an interview." He cocked his forehead and pursed his lips, creating the appearance of an angry man ready to explode. "They are outright biased. I won't get anything in this terrible environment," he murmured to himself.

"Maybe you were not the right candidate for them."

Sami shot a glance at his wife with a sudden twitch of facial expression. He thought he had been talking to himself out of her hearing range.

"You don't have to apologize for them. Why do you kowtow to their rules and expectations all the time?" he said with a raised voice.

She swung. "You're in the wrong frame of mind all the time. Pack up and go home if the system doesn't welcome your type."

The anger and frustration Sami had suppressed threatened to come out into the open in the form of an outburst. Tempted to take things into his own hands, he clenched his fist and made a scary grimace.

"The wrong frame of mind? Not at all." He tilted his head, projecting his voice. "I am in the wrong place?" He shook his head.

His wife shot a look back in his direction, recalling one of the few moments that they'd had a heated argument. "You have to mend your negative and crooked views regarding the job situation. With this kind of attitude, you are unlikely to get any job. Therefore, you keep getting rejections."

Sami returned the look. It irked and hurt him to hear his wife defending them.

He did not like what she'd said.

"We are not wanted here; don't you get it?" He shrugged off her sharp criticisms. "You assessed me wrong. I felt bitter and blamed myself every time for not getting a job. I think I tried everything possible within my power. I did my best. Don't ever think for a moment that I am a quitter!" he snapped with a burst of anger. His chocolate-colored facial muscles turned darker, and veins bulged in his forehead. It was the look that Sarah never liked to see: chilly, forceful, sad, dejected, and murderous. She knew not to reply with another word.

Sami paused to regain his composure. "I got your cruel point of view, but I intend to fight this struggle in the way I can. As for my children, I will make sure that they understand all their rights and what the Constitution guarantees them here." He took a deep breath as if waiting for a flash of wits to pour into his head. Like an injured animal, he fumed, ready to vent his steam of anger with harsh words.

His wife looked in the opposite direction. She did that whenever he brought up cultural issues.

"I have heard your lecture before; it's a long way from here." Sarah was determined to extend the argument. "You are here now. Where do you go back to? That wretched place won't offer you anything better." She lowered her eyes in the usual manner of her defiant portrayal against all that she believed to be ancient and irrelevant.

"No. Wake up! You are a self-hater and in denial. Don't you see after all these years?" He flounced forward with a tilt of his head, and his whole body followed the rhythm. "You missed my point, my dear." He shook his head in a gesture of dissatisfaction attuned to the mockery of her words. "I wonder where you belong. How naïve and easily brainwashed you can be. What's wrong with beating our own drums? When we go back, we will still belong to the culture of our tribe unless we give up our God-given rights and responsibilities. We must protect them. What do you expect to get from here? Nothing." He gestured with his hand. "At least I have dignity and respect at home, no matter how backward it may look to you." He expected her to comment. If there was one thing that made her furious, it was his persistent reminder that the life they had left behind might still hold some valuable things to offer.

"You're kidding. Who would respect a jobless man? A penniless, pathetic man. After all these miserable years in America, you have nothing to show for it. You don't have a house, land, or anything that they would consider of value. They would regard you as a crazy man. They would laugh at you and ask you why you spent so many years scraping floors and cleaning people ..."

He looked up. Sarah realized how he felt offended whenever she brought up the idea of cleaning. Sami had worked in all kinds of odd jobs, including cleaning rooms at the hotels and nursing homes where he worked, and somehow, he even got a nursing aide certificate to earn a living. She'd used the word in jest to drive her point home as if by saying it, he would be compelled to secure a job immediately. He understood her line of thought, and usually, as soon as she started it, he would even complete her sentences for her: ...*cleaning houses and washing dishes when you have all those degrees.*

Didn't you hear what your friend said the other day?" she continued, even though Sami raised his hand in a familiar gesture. He did not want to listen to this anymore. He knew what else she would say: the barrage of words describing his conditions, terms she had perfected over the years. How could he forget what his friend had said? *A refugee who came to America recently built a retail shop in Nairobi.* It was the yardstick by which they always judged each other. *Who has what? So and so has developed land and built a rental house after a few years of work. You see, he spent less than a year as a refugee in America, and now he has dozens of trucks conducting business all over Kenya, from the northern tip to the southern part of the country.* They compared each other and wondered why Sami didn't help himself or his relatives.

"I have heard enough of that already. I don't care what anybody says. Nobody knows my problems better than me." Sami stood up to turn on the TV, murmuring how the emotions and feelings of those people who were not even with him could affect his life and his way of thinking. He waited. "You have heard how those refugees got rich, right? Yes, I do agree, maybe they were hardworking people who worked two to three jobs and saved, but what we heard about some of those refugees was different."

After a long pause, he continued. "Some of those people you keep mentioning performed illegal schemes. You heard the story where four people who claimed to have families exploited the situation. They received housing assistance for their families and got four apartments with two to three rooms, with rental fees and food paid by the government, and yet they lived in one room and rented the rest. Of course, they never reported their earnings from the rental deals. Within a year, the amount of money they accumulated was enough to build a village in Africa and even feed the whole village. You heard other strange stories as well. People who were not even related came together as brothers and sisters or fathers and mothers, and when they reached here, they melted away, and money changed hands. The people up there don't know how they acquired this wealth, and I don't want to get rich through these kinds of routes. I want an honest living. They can say anything they want about me and my conditions. I care less about their glorification of wealth and prestige. I do not want to hear it." Sami flipped the channel and sat down.

"There will come a time when you will say enough is enough. If I'm not able to get any decent job here, there is a home I can go back to." He turned towards the sound coming from a couch where his wife sat. It was a familiar squeaky sound from the old sofa, which he'd collected from the dumpster across the street where students kept piles of recycled items, furniture, and all sorts of beddings. His wife had cursed the couch numerous times, an act he thought she did to provoke and torment him further. A constant reminder of their pathetic living situation. Sami remembered when he'd brought the furniture into the house. He'd asked his friend to help him carry it. With difficulty, they'd managed to place it in the room. It had taken a while, with a twist and several turns, before they finally forced it into the doorway and the tiny living room. The room was already cluttered with old stuff, junk from the outside world. Students moving out of the students' apartment would drop off items at the dumpster, and soon the things would find their way back into one of the rooms. Sami had become accustomed to the squeaky sound of the aging sofa. He never bothered greasing it to stop the irritating noise.

To make matters worse, he brought the couch into the

room at a time when his wife was not at home. Like adding fuel to the tense, fiery situation, Sarah kept fanning sharp embers of blame and criticism wherever the squawky sound reached her ears. The bulging couch had displaced some things in the overcrowded tiny room, and Sami knew for sure that he would continue receiving multitudes of curses for trampling on this vital space. How dare he violate the only area she considered sacred? Sarah had guided the furnishing of the living room carefully, and nothing that she did not approve of should claim any space. As a woman of the house, she believed that there was still some dignity left in her, and she made sure that things were in order and arranged the way she wanted. She used vast decorations to hide some torn parts of their possessions. Sami should never put anything in the room without telling her or without her consent. Otherwise, she would rebuke him.

Sami knew that in his culture, the woman of the house had the final say in household matters. He apologized for the mistake and violation of her rights, but that was not enough for her. She considered it disrespectful, and he would receive rebukes and criticisms every time anything broke in the house.

If a child tripped and fell in the house and items got misplaced, it was his fault. The new furniture, with its clumsy shapes, provided a perfect venue for all kinds of play. The kids found a convenient landing pad, where two kids could jump from it to the ground with a loud, exciting sound that thrilled them all. They would create characters from the movies they'd watched, like Woody from *Toy Story* or Batman, and staged their acts on the couch. All the characters had a spot for swift landing. They used this to extend their play and activities into the house even after being outside. Sami had given up telling them to stop playing on the couch. After a few minutes, they would start again. He threw up his hands and allowed them to have their fun. His wife, on the other hand, had a different approach. She would not tolerate any play on the couch, bed, or even on the floor. Kids should play outside in the park, and she would not accept filthy rooms and messy stuff around.

Chapter 10

Sami had more on his mind than worrying about the tattered , squawky couch, or awkward arrangement of the room. He looked past this daily nuisance. The more prominent issues remained unresolved. The statements of the bills threatening to cut services he desperately needed and the letters from home he feared opening for what he might read lingered in his psyche. He kept ignoring these demands of daily necessities, which did not go away. It became a recurring reminder that the world was full of misery that could plunge him to the ground.

Sarah lifted her head just a little, and then she raised it further up until she was reclining on the sofa with her face directly in line with Sami's. Like an antelope that picked up the scent of a predator, she stared. Her eyebrows formed a distinct shape, tightening up to create columns of lines stretching towards her cheeks.

"I will not go back there!" She shook her head.

"Where?" Sami asked, his train of thoughts lost in the distance. He straightened his shoulders with the anticipation of a person expected to solve an immediate problem. As usual, she would pick up statements from issues that he had forgotten, as if the whole world depended on them. It had occurred to him several times that his wife would start one topic and drift away to another before he could have a chance to think about them. "Do you mean home?" He knew what she meant, but he asked it anyway. "Yes, you're not going. You said that many times. I got it," he scoffed, staring at her.

"I have made up my mind, and my future is here. Also, I don't want to live in this house anymore."

A telephone interrupted them. Sami picked up the receiver and listened. Finally, he said, "I will send it," and hung up.

"As usual, they are charging late fees again." It had become a ritual. Whenever creditors called, his mood would turn gloomy. He picked up a statement of bills from the pending file. A junk letter addressed to him caught his attention. It declared that he had won a million dollars and he should claim it. He twitched his lips. *Rubbish! A million dollars to give away.* He still remembered the first time he'd received a letter like this. He got excited, wondering how they knew his name and called them. They told him to go to another location to claim his prize.

Later, Sami learned that he had to buy some items, subscribe to some magazines, and spend the night at a hotel. All these paid out of his pocket. He ended up spending money he could not afford and got in debt. *Those suckers*, he cursed with closed lips.

Sami pulled out an envelope from one of the piles of papers. They were offering him another credit card with a low payment rate until April of next year. *Sure, and hike it to 29% again?* He had gone through these numerous times, using the opportunity of the low rate and transferring some of the balances from the card with the high amount, but the obligations kept mounting, and doing this did not help him. Sami squinted his eyes to read the tiny font. With bare minimum payments, there was no way that he could pay it off. The debt got stuck, and every month, the amount remained the same. He realized the mistakes and the tricks of the credit card system too late.

Sami thought of all the events that had shaped his life, and he wondered why this had happened. Could his wife be right? That he could be part of the problem?

Sami stepped out of the house and sauntered to the small park near the preschool and daycare. There was no sign of activity in the park. The office hours had ended for the day. The short, therapeutic walk consoled him. He visualized a notion that he had a mission to accomplish. Challenging moments could come in different forms, leaping from within his body with a burst of anger that culminated in a strong desire to move forward.

A silent voice encouraged him. *You must never give up. It is time for you never to give up. It's time for you to gather the little courage you can garner and fight back with all the energy available to you.*

I don't care what other people say. He added as he recalled his wife's famous statement: "What would your friends say." Sami looked about himself, invincible. *You know what? This is my war, and I have to earn my worth. What they think of me is irrelevant. I must make my living and do decent work, but they were always rejecting me.*

Sami turned the thoughts in his mind. He cast out his feelings and quickly refocused his attention on the current matter at hand. The job search would continue. In the meantime, he needed to teach his kids about his native Oromo language and culture.

***

"That's an excellent drawing, Dad. What's it for?" Chaaltu asked.

"You will learn parts of this in our tribal language. Get the rest of the kids here." He cleared the table to make space. Chaaltu ran off to tell the rest of the kids about daddy's drawing.

"For the next thirty minutes, I will not speak to you in English," Sami warned. "Hawa, Chaaltu, Musa, and Adam, let's go through the whole thing again, and we will practice until you get it right."

"What for, Dad? I don't need it. Mommy said it, too, daddy!" Chaaltu protested, and it became a routine process for her. This was something his wife said, and now his daughter had borrowed the term. Sami ignored her plea and continued with the lesson.

"Daddy, it's boring," they all called out when he started the lesson in his native language. The look on his face said it all. Sami had an uphill battle to tackle, and he had to fight it alone.

"Mom?" The children would seek the alliance of an unwilling partner.

Sarah looked at the scene from the corner of her eye. "Keep me out of it." She went to the next room. It was a futile moment. As the children spoke to him in English, Sami wondered what would happen when, one day, they met his mother, who did not understand a word of English. Sami twitched his lips. Another failure he did not want to confront.

His mother had once told him, "Make sure they learn our language." Her words were fresh in his mind. It was the way she said it and the urgency with which she stressed.

He could only nod in agreement from a distance over the phone with a promise. "Yes, Mom, I will teach them," he'd repeatedly affirmed.

Sami lost the stamina to be consistent and persist due to the frustration of not getting what he wanted. He was not even sure whether he was mentally ready to hassle with his kids over the tribal language but giving up was not an option for him. Thirty minutes went by fast. "Wait, clean up first, Sami instructed before the kids dispersed. Chaaltu was already on the way to announce the ordeal to her mom. She ignored or maybe did not understand the look on her dad's face when she told him that she was going to share with her mom what they'd learned.

"Wait, Chaaltu, not now," It was too late. She was already in the next room.

Sami knew his wife was the main reason for his kids' failure to learn his tribal language. She'd grown up in the city and spoke Kiswahili, though not fluently. She expressed herself better in English. Sarah didn't want to look back. She would retort at the slightest mention of the language. "The tribal language is irrelevant. There's no need for my children to learn." She'd made it clear that she would not bother herself teaching them. "I don't want them to have an accent when they speak in English." Sami had laughed at that. "What are you laughing at?" Didn't you complain about an accent as one of the reasons why you could not get a job?"

"They won't have an accent because they were born here, don't you know?" Sami replied.

"Yes, even a trace of it. Period. They must speak with an American accent. They were born here," she'd proudly added.

Earlier on, Sami had thought it made sense for his children to learn English to catch up with other children at school. If they spoke English at home, it would help them learn faster. He regretted not speaking his native tongue at home with his children. At times, he wondered whether his daughter was right. Who needed his tribal language anymore except people like his mother, who did not speak English? After some years, he had noticed how his own ability to speak his mother's language had diminished. It was his mother who would have been happier than anyone else if his children learned her Oromo language.

Sami knew one thing for sure: he had joined the statistics of those immigrants who failed to pass on the torch, and yet he was not ready to bemoan this fact.

Sami watched his wife from a distance, his face distorted. This was another obstacle he had to overcome, a clear sign that his children would never learn the language of his mother. "I will give them the values of both worlds," he said. "The world I came from may not be modern or cool in their eyes because they don't understand. You know very well that we have solid, ageless, admirable, beautiful cultural values." He took a quick breath. "There!" He thrust his whole body forward as if saying the word itself epitomized his mere existence.

His wife looked on. She allowed him to rant on and on and only shot a word or two when he least expected. She could bring up the topic the next day.

Chapter 11

"Hey, Sami! A call for you!"

Sami jerked his head, surprised that anybody would call him at work.

"It's for you, amigo!" Jose said, repeating Sami's name twice. Everyone in the break room looked at Sami. None of the workers ever received a call at work.

"Yes," Sami said once he was on the phone softly. He didn't want his colleagues to overhear anything he said. A sparkle of surprise came over his face, and his tone of voice changed. "Oh, Jasmine, I didn't expect your call. Nice to hear from you. How did you get my number at work?" Sami got curious. He then realized that the company address, and telephone numbers were in the local directory.

"Antonio used to work there."

"Who?" Sami asked.

"My former husband I told you about," Jasmine replied. She asked him if he could meet her at a Hickory Park on South Duff Avenue for dinner later that evening.

Sami looked at his watch. "Yes, I can make it." He had one hour left to work. He heard a giggle at the other end of the line but kept silent.

"Are you sure?" Jasmine asked.

"No problem. I will be done by then and will plan on being

there. It's just…" Sami did not complete the sentence; his mind went blank.

She said something in Kiswahili, a language spoken in the Eastern part of Africa and one he'd never expected her to speak. He was looking for the right words to go along with what she had said: "Kwaheri kwa sasa," bye for now. It was impressive, and she sounded joyful with a melodic and mesmerizing voice. Suddenly a deadly fear gripped him. What if she was a spy, and this was a trap?

What-if questions raced through his mind. After he hung up, the phone rang again, and he turned to it with a feeling of apprehension, thinking that it might be another call from her. He picked it up.

"Hello, hello," he repeated several times. On the other end of the line, he could hear a male, raucous voice repeatedly demanding to talk to an English speaker.

"What?" Sami asked.

"Get me somebody who can speak and understand English, dumb-ass!"

"I speak English; how can I help you," Sami repeated.

"You don't. Damn it, get me somebody who understands and speaks English!"

The caller insisted on his demand.

"Okay." Sami put the phone down, went to the break room, and called Nick to the phone.

"Two calls for you. Amigo!" Jose teased him when Sami sat down. "The wife, girlfriend, or whoever called, has made you a bit worried."

Sami shot him a glance of bewilderment. It was Jose's way of making the evening go by quickly. It was also true that Sami had come back from his call with an elevated change of mood. He didn't know why, but he had calm and convivial feelings of satisfaction, followed by worrisome feelings about the second caller.

The call had filled him with mixed emotions. For the first time, he thought that his deal with Jasmine might go wrong. He trusted Kumar that everything would be fine; however, when Jasmine had spoken in Swahili, Sami had felt something sinister might be stirring up. He'd read stories about secret spies and people who worked undercover. His limbs convulsed with a chilling effect.

"What was the call about, amigo?" Jose asked.

"The first one was personal. Ask Nick about the second caller, a redneck son of a…" He held back the final word.

"Ask him what?"

"Ask Nick. He will tell you what the caller wanted."

Nick heard Jose as he entered the break room.

"The caller asked for somebody who could speak English. He had a hard time hearing Sami. A hog farmer. He wanted to know when to deliver the carcass."

"Amigo, you speak English very well. I have heard that comment many times. At one time, somebody told me to go back to the country from where I came. I then asked the caller which country I should go back to, and to my surprise, he said Mexico."

"How did he know that you were from Mexico?" Sami asked.

"I guess it was my accent or, like most people, he assumed. As if all Spanish-speaking people came from Mexico. Amigo, every fool knows Mexico."

"That's okay, Jose. I have had my share as well. Somebody told me once that the English language will die out like the Latin language did if everybody spoke English the way I do."

***

The call from Jasmine and her invitation to dinner had taken Sami by surprise. He promised himself that doing those little things would not keep him away from his family. After all, he would be home before midnight. He tried to dispel his hidden fear that mistrust and discomfort would result from meeting with her alone.

Jasmine's call kept popping up in his mind. He brushed off this goofy idea that anything could develop between them. He deliberated, admitting that he was curious but also afraid that this association could bring peril.

The idea of being invited by a lady bedazzled him. Where he came from, it was always men who initiated this request. However, Sami knew very well that in this country, the situation could be different. How could he ever forget the first invitation he'd received during the second week of his arrival in the USA. It was on a Friday after classes were over. His adviser, Professor Mueller, had ushered him into his office with a broad smile. "Sami, join us for social time."

There was a small café adjacent to the pub and grill across the campus, where students frequently gathered and had fun. Out of respect for his advisor, Sami could not decline the invitation. In his culture, collective community issues took precedence over the needs of the individuals. Later, as he told his friends about his cultural shock and experience, Sami would narrate how he had to pay for his food and drinks after being invited. It became clear to him only when one student decided to leave and paid for his bills and left without saying goodbye. Sami looked at other American students he'd come with, who were scattered all over the café. Some were playing pool and darts. Sami 's adviser was moving around, checking on his students, stopping at tables, chatting with some of his colleagues, and filling his glass as he continued to socialize. All this time, Sami sat at the same table, sipping his soda and appearing lost. Everyone had fun doing their things, and no one had told him what to expect. Even his professor, who'd invited him, did not stay long at his table. He stopped by and asked Sami if everything was okay, and then he moved on to the next. Sami observed what people did from the time he entered the café. It was contrary to the practice in his native country. The general trend there was for the person who'd offered the invitation to pay the bill.

The lesson he learned taught him that he was on his own and would walk a lonely path. He could leave anytime he wanted, and he didn't have to tell anybody. *It's okay to decline the offer even if it's made by a person one respects, and if invited, be prepared to pay your bills.*

The vivid memories of all those things that had happened in the past came back.

Chapter 12

Sami smiled at the idea of buying Jasmine dinner even though she had invited him. He withdrew some cash from the ATM and planned to treat the lady in an authentic African style.

He arrived at the restaurant early and passed by the flower shop adjacent to it. Several ideas ran through his mind. *Should I buy flowers for her?* He remembered some of the movies he'd watched where flowers were offered to women, probably as a gesture of goodwill and not necessarily as a token of affection. He thought it was the right thing to do in this culture. He perused the flowers arranged in different colors, finally picking up a bouquet of roses. Then he stopped. "How can I help you?" he heard a sound of a voice from behind the stall.

"No, thank you. I was just looking." He stepped back.

The lady encouraged him further. "They're fresh flowers, just arrived. She will like them."

At first, Sami was not sure what the lady had said, but after hearing her the second time, he became emboldened. A sense of guilt and shame came over him. He had never bought flowers for his wife, and he had been resisting the urge because it was not part of his culture, yet he was about to buy a bouquet of roses for a stranger to satisfy her cultural norms.

Sami returned to the flower shop and bought roses for his wife. He asked the lady to wrap them in plastic, and then he headed to his car to leave the flowers in it. It did not take long to notice Jasmine's car neatly parked beside his vehicle.

As he turned to the parking lot, he froze and waited. Jasmine was walking directly towards him. He was not sure about the protocol, whether to hug her or kiss on the cheek or hand. As Jasmine came closer to greet him, with her calculated gait, poise, and immaculate posture, a picture emerged in his mind. He held himself back, thinking that she was still a stranger to him, and he should behave. The flowers were in his right hand, and before he could transfer them to the other hand, Jasmine stepped right in front of him. She extended her right hand to receive them, and the rest was history. From then on, Sami played his role to perfection. He was surprised that he did what he did.

"Thanks. They're adorable." She admired the flowers. "How did you know my favorite color?"

Sami wanted to tell her that the flowers were not for her. Instead, he offered what appeared logical to him under the circumstance. "You looked great and liked wearing pink. A rose color would be a fine matching addition to embellish the glamorous color of your outfit."

A feeling of pride seeped through her mind. She had confidence in her ability to attract and command the eyes and the affection of men. She looked herself over, a little flattered, but she knew she had put on her best dress and makeup. She gave him her signature sideways smile and thanked him.

"How is y'all doing?"

"Hey." Sami strained his neck to get out the word.

"Oh boy, I slipped into my Southern accent. How are you and your children?"

They were seated, and the waiter came around. "Let me know when you're ready," he said before moving to the next table.

Sami flipped the pages of the menu.

"Let me," Jasmine recommended chicken parmigiana and Italian chopped salad. "I always get this to get a bit of everything."

Sami nodded and said, "I was hoping to see you earlier. The first part of the payment we talked about." He pushed the envelope towards her. Jasmine covered it with her purse and then slipped it in.

The waiter brought some salad dishes to set the mood for their appetites. Sami followed Jasmine's example and plunged right into eating and sipping his soft drink. It was clear he was excited with all the splendor and arrangements. He noticed that the table was even decorated with a bouquet, and set apart from the rest.

"Do you mind if I smoke?" asked Jasmine. "It's allowed in this section of the restaurant." She dipped her hand into her bag and fished out a glittering box. At first, Sami thought it was perfume or air freshener, but when their eyes met, he knew what it was. He was not surprised that she smoked. She'd told him earlier that she occasionally did when nervous. As they waited for their food, he wondered what was making her nervous. Jasmine rolled the cigarette between her fingers, back and forth, as if performing a ritual. She took a glittering lighter from her small bag and placed it on the table.

In those old Western movies he watched in Kenya, Sami had seen men lighting cigarettes for women. He picked up the lighter and tried, but it was a big embarrassment. He couldn't make it work. He flipped it over, desperately searching for a button to push. He tried many times and was not sure how to turn it on until Jasmine came to his rescue.

"Here." She pressed a small dent at the side, and a huge tongue of flame popped up. Sami pulled back his hands. "I understand. You wouldn't know if you aren't a smoker. Thanks." She smiled.

Sami sensed Jasmine had something on her mind. She glanced at him as if demanding a sort of reassurance before she said any word. He waited while suffocating on the smoke. Another person near their table started smoking. Sami looked at him and quickly returned his attention to Jasmine. She released a smoke of cloud that went up in a swirling pattern. She appeared agitated and seemed to take pride in her act. She apologized when Sami followed the trails of curled smoke with his eyes until it disappeared.

"It's Antonio," she announced. "I told you that he was out of jail."

Sami thrust his head forward. He had forgotten why the name Antonio meant anything. It only clicked when she mentioned his name in a fearful tone of voice. He stared at her. In a situation like this, it was safer not to interfere and make any comment. However, when he saw the bruises on her neck, he sat straight up and wrinkled his face. He tilted his head back and shook it side to side while looking at her intensively.

"He did that to you?" he inquired.

A moment of silence passed. "I have decided not to accept this anymore," she finally said.

Sami kept quiet. He didn't like what he'd heard. Jasmine harbored hidden scars, and he was not sure where this would lead. He didn't say anything offensive about Antonio, but his facial expression showed it. He said, "Sorry, my anger is not towards you." The news piqued his curiosity, and he was overwhelmed by vexation on hearing the name of Antonio.

"You had a similar issue with Marvin as well," he reminded her. With lips curled up in disgust, he wondered how she could stay with a person who'd abused her and mistreated her in the first place. After a little pause, he asked,

"What was the deal with these men in your life, if you don't mind me asking?"

"With Marvin, we had a deal and agreed to terms. Otherwise, he would remain behind bars for over half a century."

Sami raised his eyebrows. "What kind of crime could put one in jail for that long? What did he do? Do you trust him with baggage like that? What if he turned against you? You will never have time to tell your story if anything happens." Sami waited.

Jasmine did not answer him. Sami understood this could be one of those sensitive areas to avoid, and it was none of his business to indulge. Part of his mind, overtaken by curiosity, wanted to find out, but he kept silent because he had his burden.

Jasmine finally said. "He's gone right now and won't be back. If you needed to know, I would let you know. You can feel comfortable, and nothing will go wrong. I will keep my end of the bargain and remain true to our agreement. By the way, you can rest assured that he's not part of the deal, and I did not share anything with him. It's Antonio that I am more concerned. He showed up at my place." She twisted a strand of her hair. "He was supposed to serve two or more years. He spent only about two years for a felony conviction of marijuana possession."

The picture of Marvin, Antonio, and Kumar emerged in Sami's mind. "What was Kumar's part in the deal?"

Jasmine puffed out a cloud of smoke and put her cigarette out. She stood up. "I would not include Kumar in this category. He's a decent man, and other than the connection, he did not know the details of my plans, either. I made my own decisions in this matter." She then went to the bathroom.

Sami pondered all the things he'd heard. A situation like this could turn out ugly if he committed any error. Jasmine's emotions could get in the way. A need to protect, shield, and provide her with some buffer seized him. Sami had noticed her glances and friendly, cuddling nature. While this by itself might not lead to anything serious, with his wife's relationship at its lowest ebb, he was afraid that he could easily slip away. Some weird parts of his mind fantasized about growing closer to Jasmine. An idea popped up to fill the vacuum left in her life.

Jasmine came back from the bathroom just as the appetizer was being served. "I'm hungry. Let's eat!" She nudged Sami with her elbow to start. It was evident that she had applied makeup and changed the aroma in the air. They ate the three-course meal quietly. Sami entertained her questions about him and his school life. He appeared relaxed, although the news about Antonio bothered him.

"About this, Antonio, he doesn't live with you, right?"

"No, but he can be a pain to deal with. He's demanding. I fought with him and warned him not to come to my house again." Jasmine still showed some concern in her lingering voice and did not want to share more.

"If you were separated, why did you invite him over?"

Jasmine stared at Sami with the kind of look of a person pleading for help. "Sami, you don't understand. I would never invite him. Yes, I was married to him before. He claimed that he didn't have anybody around and wanted to remain a friend." She reached out to his hand and tapped it. "I will take care of this. No need to worry." She winked.

After dinner, Sami escorted Jasmine to her car, and before he said goodnight, she turned around. "I live close by here. You can stop by for a coffee if you're not in a hurry. Unless…" She looked at her watch. "If it is too late, I understand."

Sami checked his watch. "I still have time, until 11:30 pm, when I usually leave work."

"Good, you can follow me, then." She glanced at him,

leaving a mild perfume odor lingering in the air.

It's normal to have an uneasiness in the stomach when visiting anybody for the first time, Sami thought, trying to convince himself, and then he gleefully surrendered to pleasant feelings. He was confident that he would not fall for anything unusual.

Chapter 13

The room was neat and immaculately arranged. Sami looked around, trying to adjust to the environment. A framed photo attracted his attention. "These are my three children, and this is my grandmother in Louisiana . She adopted my siblings and me."

"You are lucky that your grandmother still keeps in touch with your children."

"Oh, yes, I needed a break, and she was always there for me." She held that last sentence as if she needed to think about something to add. "My mother. I don't call her Grandma. I barely knew my mother." She sighed.

The more he thought about her childhood story, the more he felt like doing something about her current condition. Jasmine had gone through a painful childhood, with her mother being given a life sentence in jail when Jasmine was a toddler.

Sami's earlier perception of Jasmine slowly disappeared. In the beginning, before he'd even had a chance to see her, Kumar had painted a picture of a beautiful person who could be trusted. Sami thought he might be right, but it was too early to conclude.

"Make yourself at home," she said with a friendly smile. "Coffee?"

He nodded, and Jasmine went to the kitchen and started making some. The sweet aroma filled the living room and merged with the colorful illumination of the background and the humming of the refrigerator. Sami sat oblivious to the alien atmosphere as his eyes slowly adjusted to the dim lights.

"Sami." She opened the fridge and turned. "Which one do you prefer?" She held up two bottles.

Sami looked from one to another and asked for coffee instead.

She poured herself a glass of sparkling, colorful grape juice. She tipped the glass as she poured, filling it to the brim. Small bubbles rose to the surface, and Sami could see the spectacular sparkling color trapped within the glass. In the background, the blue fluorescent light-infused a feeling of harmony in him. He allowed his mind to transcend this scene of tranquility and kept watching Jasmine, making sure about the source of his soft drink. Sami did not doubt in his mind about the aura of this charming setting. He let his mind roam in the fantasy world of his imagination. It was one of those moments when the whole episode begins to unfold, and he did not notice when Jasmine sat down near him. He wondered whether to remain seated or make an excuse to leave.

Suddenly, he picked up his cup of coffee and took a large gulp. "I have to go."

"Oh, did I make you uncomfortable?" Jasmine asked.

"No," he quickly responded. He was not sure whether whatever she'd drunk had gone to her head. What if she'd planned this meeting with something else in mind? What if this was her customary way to treat a guest? What would happen to his situation if he didn't go along with her? Sami even wondered what he was supposed to do under these circumstances, but his natural intuition was jovial to the surrounding. Such proximity to a woman who was not his wife was an unacceptable norm and inappropriate, yet he sat back down and kept drinking coffee.

Suddenly, a phone rang. He swerved his head and felt uncertainty building up in his throat. Jasmine hesitated. Then she stood up and came close to the phone, but she did not pick it up. She let the phone ring until it stopped.

Sami's mind kept tossing around different moods and uneasiness. Swallowed by the ecstasy of the moment and engulfed in the presence of a stranger, Sami continued drinking coffee, and he poured himself another cup. He was not even sure about his state of mind until it became clear that the distance between him and her had narrowed. He gulped down the last drop of coffee, looked at his watch, and announced that he had to leave. He didn't notice that Jasmine had changed the setting of the room and had lowered the curtain. Sami heard a melody playing, but he didn't know where it was coming from.

To his great relief, Jasmine asked him some questions. "Tell me more about your area of origin. I heard that my great-grandfather had his roots in the East African part of the World, and I could claim some relatives there. It's possible, although most slaves shipped to the Americas were from West Africa."

Sami entertained her illusionary discussions for a while and then switched the topic. "Is Marvin still around?"

The question came from out of nowhere, and Jasmine took her time before she answered him. She replied in a funny way that made Sami laugh.

"He's history, honey! I am all yours now!" She glanced at him.

Sami was rather engrossed in a state of dilemma and was not sure whether he understood her correctly. He smiled and nodded because he was not sure what to do. In any case, he thought Jasmine must be kidding, and this was one of the language nuances he had to learn. *I am all yours.* He stared at her in bewilderment.

"Relax. I can sense the stiffness in your muscles. Let me." She told him to recline.

"No, I think I have to go. It's getting late."

Jasmine patted him on the back. "Don't worry. It will help you relax," She brought out some cream and rubbed the back of his neck, working it with her smooth hands. She spread the palm of her hands across the length of his shoulders.

Sami quickly gathered courage as if awakened out of the trance. "I have to go, Jasmine. Thank you very much." He stood up to leave, much to the chagrin of Jasmine's hospitality. He felt embarrassed and guilty. He took a step forward, but he slipped when his feet got caught up in the carpet corner.

Jasmine laughed, realizing how nervous Sami was. "I didn't mean to cause this reaction, and I had no ill intent."

The phone rang again. Jasmine hesitated and then picked it up. She gestured for Sami to wait while she answered it. "Yes." She remained mute, and after a long silence, she said, "I would rather have you back in jail again, you son of a…" She did not complete the word. She must have forgotten that Sami was still in the room.

"I don't care from where you're calling. Don't ever call me again." Jasmine slammed the phone.

Jasmine held on to the edge of the table. She picked up the empty glass and poured herself a drink from a small bottle. Then, with a shaky hand, she took a quick gulp and sat down.

"What's wrong?"

"Antonio. I forgot to change my phone number." She stared blankly at the phone and let out a sigh of distress. "Why did they let him out early?"

"Jasmine, are you afraid of him?"

"Not really." She avoided eye contact. "He was jailed for repeated possession of marijuana. A felony charge that carried up to two years of imprisonment and some fines, and now they have released him. I don't know how long ago he was released."

"Let me know what I can do to help."

"I will be fine and will take extra care." She paused before continuing. "Antonio can do foolish things, and I am glad he's out of my life."

Sami looked at her with mixed feelings.

***

The short drive home gave Sami time to reflect on the transient duration of the evening. He'd heard strange stories about men lacing drinks with sedatives to make unsuspecting girls unconscious. However, he remembered very well that he'd drunk coffee with a regular, sugary taste. Whatever was in it, and probably the dose of caffeine had unwittingly altered his mood. This encounter in an unknown territory had exposed how vulnerable he could be, and regardless of the situation, he should not have condoned it. He brushed off his questioning thoughts; he did not want to get too deep into this one encounter. With unanswered questions in his mind, he concluded that there was nothing abnormal about the events. He then recalled her reaction to Antonio's phone call. Undoubtedly, it had scared her.

After a quick shower, Sami tiptoed into bed without any slight disturbance to the sleeping body. As if nothing had happened, he raised the blanket and slipped under the sheet. He had just enough to cover part of his body. His wife had tucked in all the corners of the blanket under the mattress. She laid on her side with her knees pulled up to her chest, basking in her favorite fetal sleeping position. One hand hugged the bedsheet materials, while the other hand extended over into his domain, creating an intimate encounter in a territory each of them tried to claim as their own. The sweet aroma from her nightly perfume perfused the air and maintained a pulsating pace.

He hesitated to pull parts of the blanket tucked under her. If he did, she would wake up, and he would not do that today. She clung to the sheet as if that was all she had for nightly comfort. Just then, he realized a faint perfume scent had come with him or was it his imagination? Sami was sure there was no trace of it on his shirt and neck. The cream Jasmine used had a distinct, attractive smell, but he'd gotten rid of it when he'd taken a shower.

Convinced that this was just his imagination, and still shaken from his evening encounter, Sami got under the silent blanket and joined the sleeping body. As always, it would be a while before sleep came.

Chapter 14

Jasmine was tossing around an idea in her mind when the phone rang again. She hesitated before slowly picking it up. " Yes." She wanted to hang up, but she kept listening.

On the other end of the line, Antonio said animatedly, "I wanted to apologize for what I did, and I would like you to forgive me."

Jasmine shook her head. "Antonio, we went through this process already, and I don't want to go back. Keep away from me and don't come to my house, or I will call the police."

"Hey, baby, you don't want to do that. I have nobody else." Antonio started his usual tactics. Jasmine knew what he was up to, and she blamed herself for being soft.

"Antonio, it's over. Get over it. We are not together. Don't you get it?" She became agitated by his constant demands. She knew his next move. He would shower her with gifts, plead incessantly, and apologize, and then he would go back to his old habits again. How could she forget? Antonio had introduced her to marijuana, and she knew she might fall back into the practice of smoking it if he came close.

"Are you still there?" Antonio asked. "I know you're listening. Please say something. I want to hear your therapeutic voice."

"Antonio, I am seeing a very respectable person, and I

don't want you to ruin my life. I am done with you and will never take you back if that's what you are thinking."

"No, no, I am fine with that, Jasmine. I won't bother you."

"Can you give me your word? Are you still in the habit?"

Antonio kept quiet. Then he said, "I stopped taking it. The jail term helped me get over it, and I am clean now." This was a lie.

"I hope so." Jasmine twisted her mouth into an expression of disappointment. She regretted the mistake she'd made earlier and taken full responsibility for her actions. She noticed her hand was trembling. Antonio reminded her of that dark part of her life, and she was not ready to fall back again. She hung up the phone with a mixture of fear and resentment.

***

"Hey, amigo, you are almost late today."

"Caught up. I am here now." Sami tucked in the corner of his shirt before he put on the apron to begin work. Jose walked with him to the workstation.

"We have a new worker, a mere teenager. Probably fresh from high school. I wonder whether he can survive and stick around. He's too emaciated to endure this hard work."

"He will make it, Jose. Don't underestimate his physical stature."

Just then, Moses approached them. He was taking the new worker around to different sections of the cleaning stations. "Sami meet our new employee, John. Sami has been here for about three or four months, right, Sami?"

Moses turned the corner as John tagged along, heading towards the cold storage area.

"He is starting with the cold turkey storage room, and I bet the kid won't come back tomorrow." Jose walked to his workstation.

"I think he will," said Sami. "Let's make a bet, a five-dollar bill?"

Jose laughed loudly. "Amigo, I did not expect this from you. Welcome to the club."

"What club?"

Jose laughed again. "You're now like one of us, almost ready for the elite club."

Sami was not sure what he meant, although it was clear as he got to know them that an atmosphere of comradery had evolved. Just like other workers, John would either hang around for a while and form part of the core team or disappear. Moses had tried hard to make sure that workers stayed. He facilitated transportation for those who did not have a ride, and he picked up Nick and Jack every day from the halfway house. Although the quality of work they did was not what he desired, their presence created the psychological satisfaction that he had all his workers in place.

After months of work, Sami could do his job with the efficiency required. Moses stopped by his station and complimented him. Sami coughed as if in response to his statement and then prolonged it with a long sneeze.

The other workers in their assigned stations echoed the work rhythm. Steaming-hot water splashed over the concrete floor and meat-slicer machines, creating a mist that floated up to the ceiling. "Break time!" Like a class bell ringer, Jose had taken it upon himself to remind everybody, though each worker knew when it was time to take a break.

The discussions during the break revolved around social problems, which they took pleasure in sharing. It was as if each of them had had a chapter of their lives exposed to scrutiny. Sami tried to keep to himself, but as he was quietly eating his dinner, Jose interrupted. "Amigo, remember, we did not complete the initiation ceremony for you. It will soon be your turn to tell a story."

Sami continued to eat his food quietly.

"Amigo, do you want to make money?"

Sami whirled and faced him.

"I won six hundred dollars at a casino over the weekend." Jose blurted out. Sami listened carefully as getting extra money seemed palatable. "It required only a few quarters to start with," Jose explained, but he didn't tell Sami that he'd lost all the money. He'd gotten drunk that night, and his friend who had given him a ride had ended up getting a speeding ticket. It was an unexpected extra headache because they'd had to share the cost. All these nasty habits came because Jose liked to look good and only told the part of the story he wanted people to hear.

"Amigo, you can try your luck. You'll never know until you take this step. Who knows, you might hit the jackpot." Jose needed only an attentive listener, and in Sami, he'd found a receptive one with genuine interest. "There are no entrance fees, amigo. You can start with as little as a dollar. The slot machines take quarters."

Sami did not want to look ignorant, and at the same time, he had no clue about what happened at a casino. Jose told him everything and invited him to come along with him during the coming weekend. He added, "You can even take a loan right there nearby; there's a bank that offers loans for those who need money on hand. They give loans to gamble, with no questions asked. Can you believe that?"

"No, thanks," Sami said. The only knowledge he had about casinos was from what he'd seen in the movies. The little demons in him reminded him about the debt he owed and all the financial burdens he faced, and yet his gut feeling told him that he should not fall for it. Gambling was the worst habit to develop. All religions condemned it as evil and wicked, and it could destroy finances and marriages, and Sami felt he would never engage in it.

That same Saturday, however, Moses invited all his colleagues to his birthday party at the casino. Many months passed, and Sami went back to the casino twice, a thirty-minute drive outside of town, both times at the invitation of his colleagues at work. It was a disaster and a lesson to remember. He tried to gamble and lost $150, and he resolved not to try it again. He swore never to accept an invitation to that dreadful place.

Life continued as usual, and Sami did not share his tale of adventure and loss.

At break time one day, they all took their usual spot at the game of cards.

Sami occasionally browsed through the advertisements in the paper for jobs closely related to his profession.

"Hey, amigo, "Do you want to learn about this game?"

With a brooding expression, Sami ignored the offer. He continued browsing through the *Des Moines Register* and checked the jobs section. Engrossed in the newspaper, Sami did not notice Sancho was also looking at the same page over his shoulder.

"Looking for a job?"

Sami did not expect this sudden intrusion. "What about it?" he asked.

"Nothing, simply curious. Are you ready to tell your story today? I heard it was your turn."

"Amigo, Sancho is right. It is the initiation ceremony. It is your turn to tell the story, and if you don't, be prepared to serve pizza, as the group agreed. We gave you several months to prepare, and it is time." After a moment, Jose continued. "No need to tell your whole life history. None of us like to talk about our lives in detail."

Sancho glanced at Jose when he stopped talking. "You are in college, right?"

"Yes, I am pursuing a second degree." As soon as he

uttered the word "degree," Sancho announced to the whole team about his discovery. "Tenemos un profesor aquí!" he shouted.

"Hey, amigo, el profesor!" Jose whistled. Soon everybody started calling Sami a professor. This discovery also brought mixed feelings. Some workers began shunning him, teasing him about why in the world he was rotting in this downtrodden, filthy, miserable den where drug addicts, crooks, the homeless, and all those at the end of the social rope abounded.

Pablo and Petros exchanged glances. "Maybe he was assigned, to uncover something," Pablo whispered to Petros.

Moses tried to calm this suspicious behavior. "Come on, guys, he's innocent and needs to work. He's struggling to get a job like most of you here."

Sami did not hear the side conversations and continued reading the paper. At least for now, he had a job and was ready to join this unlikely team even though he detested some of their deplorable character traits. Life would move on for Jose, Sancho, and all the other illegal immigrants. Daniel, a student with an expired visa, did not show up for work and was believed to have been deported. Emilio had escaped from a Honduran jail. Petros was a cunning trickster who got himself into problems by forging papers. Pablo had been jailed for forgery and marijuana possession and now blended in with the group but stayed aloof. They and all the other petty criminals and peddlers who could not get a better job elsewhere had a short respite here to earn quick bucks and disappear. These workers seemed to know their place on the social ladder.

It was bizarre how this little bit of information changed the group dynamics and everyone's perceptions. Suddenly, it became apparent to them that Sami was an outsider and in the wrong crowd. He did not blame them if they thought about him differently. With all his education, he felt out of place, and it was a contradiction that he could not reconcile. In any case, it did not matter anymore to him as long as he did decent work and earned his living. The physical exhaustion of the job naturally drained his energy, but regardless of the situation, he resolved to stay on and look for a better job.

The disclosure of his little secret, while it did not change his relationships with his coworkers that much, brought him a little discomfort. It's human nature to wonder, and for a strange reason that he could not understand, some of his co-workers felt that he was not supposed to be there. It's funny how groups come into existence and how individuals in those groups align their interests. Sami hated to see the happy relationships perturbed, and he wanted the little common bond that existed within the group to remain. He had to figure out what story to tell his colleagues now. He checked his watch and was satisfied that the evening was still young, and there was enough time to overcome his plight.

As he started rehearsing the story, Jose approached him. "Amigo don't feel bad about the teasing nature of our discussions. You should be proud of yourself for your academic achievements. It's unfortunate that you still work at this job. You deserve better than this. Sadly, life turns out strange. They say that when you work hard, you will achieve the American dream. For a foreigner like me and you, and especially those of us with no education, what can we dream?"

"Many people have made it, Jose."

"We are running from one state to another, and being hunted like a rat, and exploited. Do you call this the American dream?"

Jose had a way of expressing his point with a facial gesture that was difficult to understand. You didn't know whether he was expressing contempt or anger, with a corner of his top lip pulled up and back, creating an elliptical shape, and his eyes sometimes having a mischievous glint. "The kind of work we do is all the same everywhere: manual labor. The only difference is the larger amount of money one can get from the currency exchange when converting to Mexican pesos. Our life of hard work, from paycheck to paycheck, barely helps us pay the bills.

After a long pause, he added, "I don't ever see myself becoming rich. Even you, amigo." He turned to Sami. "They don't give you the job you qualify for, and you're doing the same manual job those of us without an education do. I feel for you. This kind of manual, backbreaking job was what I did all my life, and I am good at it. You have more options and are eligible for a better-paying job. I heard that some international students who do not return to their countries of origin end up doing all kinds of jobs, and some of them work as taxi drivers or earning their livelihood in different service industries. Did you know that Moses, the night shift manager, has two master's degrees and worked the same manual job I'm doing for five years?"

Sami listened with a confused facial expression at this vivid portrayal of his own life. The truth hit him hard.

Sancho joined the argument. "Only, those who do not have a proper document like a green card end up doing this kind of job."

"I don't think so. Moses had a green card for five years and had to do a manual job. He has been a naturalized citizen for the last three years. I think Pablo may have a green card, too." Jose looked at Pablo.

"What do you think?" Pablo answered.

"Probably a fake one." Sancho laughed.

"I heard that!" Pablo yelled and added, "Let the one without sin cast the first stone."

Sami was surprised by this consolatory and contradictory move from Jose and how they all exchanged words. Jose continued. "Amigo, you see, all of us here are either high school dropouts or have a high school level of education. All of us had brushed with the law, or incarcerated at some point in our lives. Pablo was out of jail recently." He came closer to Sami and whispered, "Be careful around Pablo and stay away from any of his activities. By the way..." Jose scanned with his eyes as if making sure that nobody else heard. "If you want something fixed, there are people who can do the service, and Pablo claims that he did it once."

"Did what, Jose?"

Jose laughed. "Amigo, you need to learn about our world, the elite club. He's a hitman. That kind of service and anything else needed for a fee. It is a simple task that many of us here can easily do." He stretched. "With the right amount, I can do it as well, but the amount must be big enough for me to leave the country."

After a pause, Jose said. "Moses also served for a minor crime. Did you know that?" Sami squinted his eyes as if caught by surprise. "No, problema, amigo. We often talk about the crimes we've committed. The more dangerous the crime, the higher the prestige, and the more popular the man is in the eyes of his colleagues. And the more favor he gets here in our midst." Jose nodded and smiled. "Yes, there is a code of secrecy in this place. As an initiation ceremony, a newcomer is required to recount his past deeds." He nodded to affirm his statement.

Sami knew Jose had told him several times that if a worker failed to narrate to his co-workers about his past adventure, he would have to treat the group to a pizza party.

Chapter 15

Sami had done the mental math. The cost of pizza would be equal to the amount he would earn for two good hours of work. As he struggled to decide what story to tell, Moses came to his rescue. "These people will believe anything from that part of the world. Invent something , and you will be amazed at how little they know about Africa. Somebody asked me how many hours it took me to drive here from Africa. You cannot believe that kind of ignorance. Or hear this ." He stooped slightly. "A person once asked me the color of my blood, and I told him it was black. He believed it. Where in the world was he from?"

Sami had no shortage of strange stories to tell. He wanted to come up with a good one, though.

"Amigo, you can start."

"I don't think you will like this story," Sami began. "It's about witchcraft and the strange things that happen to the people associated with this practice. Have you heard about cannibalism?"

"Yuck! You did that?" Emilio exclaimed.

"Wait." Sami waved his hand up and down, indicating to him to slow down. "The incident happened during one of those times when the tribes were desperately in need of rain after a long, dry, scorching season. One evening, a dark cloud gathered over the horizon. The village elders gathered to discuss what the dark cloud's omen portended and circulated rumors about the magician of the forest who could cleanse the evil spirit and appease the demons. Whispers kept bouncing that the spirit of the demon was angry with the villagers for the sins they'd committed. The local magician, who also played the role of a spiritual healer, was summoned to interpret the strange happenings. At work with concoctions, charms, amulets, and various paraphernalia, the magician chanted and sprinkled perfumed liquid, sipped a mouthful, and spat in a circular motion. He then proclaimed that in two days, they should sacrifice a ram to cleanse the spirit and demons. The pronouncement of the oracle revealed that a young man who'd recently arrived in the village should taste the first piece of flesh and blood of the sacrificed ram, mimicking human flesh. Unknown to the magician's plan, I'd arrived in the village for my vacation a day earlier."

"Are you a magician?"

"No, I was supposed to be the human-flesh taster."

Some of the workers started murmuring. "What!" Emilio shouted, raising his eyes from the deck of cards that he was lifting. "Did you eat human flesh?" he asked.

"Yes," Sami replied. Emilio's hand froze in midair as he was about to drop the card.

"No way," Petros exclaimed.

An instant commotion brought attention to the silent room. All eyes turned to Jack. "What a mess!" Nick shouted, dropping the card on the floor.

Jack was on his knees, holding the table with one hand, wincing amidst the protests and shouting, as he puked up the dinner he'd just eaten.

Moses rushed onto the scene. "What happened? Jack! Are you all right?"

Jack nodded as all the workers gathered around him. "I am

fine." He stood up and walked to the bathroom.

Sancho, Pablo, and Petros raised their eyebrows, "It may be an overdose." Sancho winked. Petros shook his head.

Pablo laughed loudly and added. "He's a pro; a little dose won't affect him. I think Sami's story shook and scared him."

The team silently resumed work. John trailed the group as they walked back, hurrying to catch up with the rest. He had a strange look on his face, and he furtively glanced in all directions.

Sami was the last one to leave the break room. Moses called him aside. "Hey, man, what have you done? They were terrified and traumatized. I think that story was not funny. You knew people had a strange notion about Africa already, and these workers believed what you said." He leaned towards Sami and murmured, "They might even think that you will chop a pound of flesh from their body and eat it. Besides, meat and blood are everywhere around us. Didn't you see the reaction on their faces? Poor Jack believed you." Sami laughed, and Moses added, "You and I can laugh about this, but it was not a laughing matter for them. Jose may be the only one who did not buy the story."

"What can we do, then?" Sami asked.

"We can reverse the trend of thoughts and deflect the scary thoughts," Moses suggested.

"I thought they enjoyed the story."

"Yes, but the idea was to tell a real story that happened to you, and if you admitted that you ate human flesh, what do you expect?" Moses shook his head in disagreement. "I think you have to retract this story and tell some other ones."

Later, before the crew punched out to leave, Moses conveyed a brief meeting. It took a while to convince the group that Sami's story was a little exaggerated, and Sami was ready to take back his created tale. Jose started laughing as if that was nothing to what he had experienced. "Amigo, I know anything is possible. They call it ritual cleansing. Curanderos or healers who do purification rites."

John, the young new employee, appeared shaken. Jose added a twist to the story on the sideline and made the new employee believe this bizarre story until Moses intervened. Sami's story ended there, but surprisingly, he gained respect and earned the title "the cannibal man." The crew now considered him to be one of them.

Jose was one of those people you don't forget quickly. "I tink you owe nobody noting. Outside of here, you don know me. I don know you. Leave everything here. Whatever you do is none of my business," he reminded Sami with that distinct accent. Sami understood him well: *tink*, *don*, and *noting* meant think, don't, and nothing. These were some of the words that Jose used too often, and anybody would probably have spelled them just the way Jose said them.

Sami learned a lot from this easygoing immigrant who took every day as it came with nothing to leave behind except his burden. With a family and relatives in Vera Cruz, Mexico, Jose had jokes and entertainment for his colleagues at work and made them feel at ease despite the physical exhaustion of daily tasks. In addition to the laughter that would rejuvenate and energize the spirit, Sami needed this relaxed attitude. He could feel comfortable conversing with Jose, who generously shared the sagacity of his working life. Sami had to admit that Jose put extra effort into educating him about the outside world. Up to that time, Sami had lived on its periphery. He'd never lived in it in the way he was supposed to. Outside the classroom and beyond his field of studies in animal science, Sami probably was as helpless as a fish would feel on a dry riverbed. He was never prepared to face the world of manual labor, which epitomized and encouraged the brute force of street attitude for survival.

As always, Jose took his time and punched out last. When

asked why he would say that every minute counted when added together to yield extra cash. He would then record his hours in a notebook that he carried around in his pocket.

Jose looked left and right, making sure that nobody was watching. "Amigo, it is gold, and in excellent working condition. Do you want to try?" he asked Sami one day, one eye on the hidden treasure that was still half in his pocket, and the other looking out to make sure that nobody noticed him. "It's Rolex, I tink," he said, stressing the word "Rolex."

"Where did you get it?" Sami asked.

Jose's glance did not require any explanation: Sami should not have asked.

"No more questions, it's safe, amigo. It came a long way. For you, half the price. You know, don't ask too many ting. You don know Jose. I don know you! Remember." The look in his eyes said it all.

"I got it," Sami said apologetically, wondering whether he understood this man. He judged Jose by the way he looked. A man of stout structure, probably in his late thirties, about five and a half feet in height, he stooped slightly with caved-in shoulder, giving him the appearance of a deformity. When you met him for the first time, you wanted to take a second look—only then would it become clear that it was the way he held his shoulders that gave him the appearance of the deformity. Jose was a man of few words, and you'd never know what was locked up in his mind. For now, Sami had to accept his word.

"You pay later, not now. We can arrange it," Jose said, interrupting Sami's thoughts.

Sami didn't need to ask how he would get his money back. The harsh, rugged nature of this man who, within a second, could portray a devious character was enough of a warning and a testimony to his capability. Sami had seen him annoyed and heard him say with conviction that nobody would double-cross him and live. If one could believe all the previous stories Jose had told, you would not want to cross his path. He said he had strangled a man with his bare hands during a robbery attempt, and an instant glance revealed sizable calloused hand for his dwarf-like body, hardened by years of manual labor. Jose portrayed himself as a professional crook, which, incidentally, seemed to be a heroic career for this group.

Sami brushed it off. "Thanks, amigo. I am not interested in a watch."

"Oh, come on, amigo! It is an excellent commodity to own. You can even sell and make more money on top," Jose insisted.

Sami did not cave into the demand.

The group cohesion and work dynamic continued unabated, irrefutable of the ideals they envisioned for themselves. The shift of alliance in the group quickly took shape, and the person with the most horror stories to tell got more attention and, for a while, was considered the leader of the pack. Sami curbed the temptation to follow the group blindly and spoke little about his past. He occasionally veered away from the questions asked about his personal life, but when he shared with them his academic achievement, it was a disaster.

He could see it in their eyes: education was a disgraced field for this group. None of them had ever finished high school, yet Sami was in the same position as they were, struggling to get minimum pay. What difference did his degrees make if they could not fetch him a decent job in the market? Yes, he would soon have two master's degrees. Moses had two, and with Jose and Emilio, their life-acquired degrees helped them survive on the street and got them respect from their peers. They used their harsh life experiences and hard-earned practical adventures efficiently.

Ready to plunge into work. Jose would proudly show his hardened hands as evidence. His experiences had shaped his destiny.

Sami thought to himself and got annoyed when they did not show interest in improving their lives through education, which was the only thing that he wanted to share with them. Regardless of the situation, Sami still believed that he was far better with education than without.

Chapter 16

The following day, Emilio and Jose were in the locker room, talking, when Sami joined them. "Hey, Sami, are you married?" Emilio asked.

Sami did not answer him immediately, but from the way he looked at Emilio, he expected him to know.

"Sure, with four kids. What about you?"

Emilio smiled and replied, "What do you think?" He held up his left hand to reveal the wedding ring.

The rest of the members of the group burst into prolonged laughter. Sami never got a chance to ask for clarification because, at that time, the break ended, and everybody rushed to work. The next time he could, Sami brought up the topic of marriage again.

"Jose, why did you laugh aloud yesterday when I asked whether Emilio was married or not?"

"Amigo, that was a fake marriage for the document, and it has become another trend. You should be careful. Marriage is for love." Jose then asked, "Do you want one?"

"You know I am married, Jose. Hey, are you a matchmaker? That's interesting to know."

"Amigo, you know, with enough money, one can get a wife."

Sami looked puzzled. "What do you mean?"

"That's right, amigo, you just need money."

"Interesting, Jose. Did you ever try?"

"No, but I know some marriage connections operate under known legal entities in the form of businesses. They use some other fancy names to attract people to the cross-cultural marriages, and that maybe the safer way for single people."

"Jose, how come you don't have any proper documents after all these years?"

Jose turned abruptly. He had forgotten that he'd told everybody about his status in the euphoria of excitement during one of those endless marathon storytelling exploits that had become the center of attraction and amusement for the group in the evenings. He looked at Sami as if the answer were written on his face. "What do you tink, amigo? Remember, our secrets should remain here with us, right? You don know Jose, and Jose don know Sami! You know only enough to have fun at work and ease work tension, okay!"

Sami turned to face him.

"Do you want to see my green card?" Jose flashed it from his wallet. Like a village elder dispatching age-old wisdom, he swiftly changed the topic of discussion, making up another joke about his friend in Mexico. Sami knew that was one of the ways Jose deliberately avoided answering questions. He wanted to keep this part of his life secret. According to Emilio, Jose had smuggled himself into the country after being deported, got a fake green card, and changed his name. Everything he said could be mistaken for a joke. Jose, the illegal immigrant, lived one day at a time. He'd lived in California, New Mexico, Nevada, and Texas under different names. Probably, Jose was a convenient name for now.

Sudden laughter from Emilio brought Sami's attention back. He was about to move on when Emilio erupted with laughter again and said, "Tell him about the train story."

"Nothing important to tell. My story is no different from the rest," Jose said with full confidence. There was something else that he didn't want Sami to know. The rest of the things Sami had heard were not significant or even personal. He wondered why they'd even shared them.

"Tell him about the train episode," Emilio insisted.

"I borrowed a ticket and discovered that the train was going in the wrong direction. When I arrived, the police caught me."

"Who would borrow a ticket for a ride?" Emilio asked mockingly. He laughed and added, "Jose put the guard out of action for a while and escaped. He then crossed the border and landed here in the states." More laughter. Every time someone told a story, someone else would add or subtract parts. Jose's version of his story did not change, but he insisted that he did not harm the guard. The incident with the ticket was right, and the escape was also correct.

"What about the informer who disappeared?" Emilio nudged his friend with a leering gesture.

Jose kept silent; he didn't want anyone to ask him about it. Finally, he said, "The guard did not die. He was temporarily disabled. As for the informer..." He shrugged. "No comment." With a side glance, Jose added, "One has to do what's needed. They can keep you there forever. Amigo, most of us here have heavy baggage to carry around. What about you? You didn't say much about yourself other than the flesh-eating cannibal stuff." he turned to Sami.

Just then, all eyes turned towards the entrance as Pablo walked in with a bandaged face.

Jose whistled. "What happened, man!"

Pablo approached Moses.

Jose and Emilio stopped talking and tried to listen.

"I wonder who messed up his face like that. A vicious attacker," Emilio speculated.

"It could have been his wife. I heard she sent him to jail."

"What happened?" Jose asked Pablo.

Pablo ignored him and felt the bandage, stroking it lightly with his left hand.

Emilio turned to Pablo. "What's the deal with your face? Wow! What a battle? Who did that to you?"

Pablo kept quiet, still stroking the bandage. "She will regret it. I swear," he murmured.

Chapter 17

As each evening went by, the team shared more about themselves, with tales mixed with truth and falsehood. At the same time, a real bond had developed between them. It was during one of those moments of laughter that Sami tried to share with them a little bit of his work experience in his home country.

He cleared his throat. "Okay, Jose, I can share my work experience in Kenya."

"It must be interesting," Jose replied.

"Okay, I will try. It's about how I got a scholarship to come to the USA and the nature of my previous job."

"What happened to your job?"

"At the time I was employed, there were people in bogus positions that never existed. We call it ghost workers. I approved farm loans for applicants who did not exist." Sami paused for a moment. "I regret what I did, Jose."

"Cool. How much did you get away with?"

"No, Jose, I did not take any money. I followed blindly against my natural inclinations and got entangled in the messy system."

Jose whistled. "Loans for ghosts, how?"

"The minister would send some names of the people to approve for loans without question. After a year of working in these conditions, you would either get fed up and move out or sink to the bottom and siphon as much as you could while, at the same time, covering your tracks. I can vividly remember the evening before I got the scholarship."

"What happened?" Jose was eager for Sami to extend the story.

"I accepted an invitation to a dinner with a government minister and a member of Parliament from my district in a private hotel room. We ate an expensive meal in the place reserved for three. For the first time in my life, I felt a spine-chilling moment. I was afraid and did not want to sign the loan form they brought with them. I did not even read through it. It was the standard loan application document, with tagged signature label pages to sign. I hesitated at first and only agreed after the member of Parliament told me about the scholarship."

Sami noticed how impatient Jose looked while listening. "The minister pulled out another folder from his briefcase and showed me the agreement that the government had with a faith-based organization that would sponsor me for a full scholarship, which included tuition and board for three and half years." Sami waited for Jose to take it in. "Six years later, I'm still revisiting the incident in my mind." He waited for the silence to settle. "That sums up my brief story of how I came to America."

"Wow, amigo, you were as guilty as those people. What happened after you left?"

Sami smiled. "It was the best thing that happened to me. There was a scandal about the loan scheme. They kept playing their games, and finally, the law caught up with them. After the election, the new regime tried to make things a little transparent. They tried to blame everything on me and were eager to see me return and face the court. My cousin told me that there was a plan to force me to return and face charges in the country. They debated and agreed to let time pass and move on until the end of the election. The two crooks were both voted out during the election, so nobody carried out their plans."

"Then?" Emilio asked.

"I wanted to correct my record."

"How?"

"I didn't get far. My file disappeared."

Jose laughed. "Is this more magic stuff."

"No, Jose, they couldn't find the whole loan transaction on my record."

There was a prolonged uproar, with Emilio asking how that could be possible.

Moses intervened. "Listen, guys; everything is possible in that part of the world. With a hundred dollars, you can erase the whole previous record and create another one or flavor it to your liking."

Sami smiled.

"Amigo, if I were you, I would seek political asylum," suggested Jose. "You won't go back. You are wanted for a crime in your own country."

"I think it is better if you don't attract attention to yourself," Petros interjected. "Your government has a case against you. They will use that to take action against you here and initiate the extradition process."

"What if your file resurfaces?" Emilio asked.

"Emilio, surely you know the file was intended to disappear," Moses replied.

"You're a criminal whether you like to believe it or not. That's how the system would look at it, especially if they pressured you from there. You don't have a country anymore."

"I have no idea." Sami agreed partially.

"Amigo, they won't grant you any asylum here, either. All

those filthy records you accumulated will come to the surface, and the gringos would love to hand you over. Welcome to our world."

"What are gringos?" Sami asked.

Emilio burst into laughter. "Amigo, it is another way of saying American, or even foreigner, a kind of slang word."

Sami twisted his lips in an anticipatory mood. He would not reminisce about this chapter of his life, and he did not share with them how another document at a loan department implicated his role. The two crooked politicians had turned the scholarship money into a loan for him to pay back.

After a long silence, Emilio chuckled. "I think you can file for asylum, an easier way to the dream card."

"Amigo, it is not easy," Jose added. "You will need a lot of documentation. You must prove that when you return, you will be a dead man. Your government will chop off your head." Jose demonstrated with his hand across the neck. "Wait! There is a term they use, but I forgot it."

"Political asylum," Emilio said.

"No, not that word."

"I got it! The prosecution!"

"No, they do that in court. It is not that word, amigo. The word sounds like prosecution, but I forgot."

"Do you mean persecution?" asked Sami.

"Yes, that's the word. One should file a document to avoid persecution." Jose felt a sense of satisfaction and continued. "Injustice and all forms of daily torture are not new to us, but here they will only consider massive executions, like what happened in the Bosnia incidents. In any case, they will reject it. However, if your case is active, you will get a work permit. They can deport you, too. They deported somebody I knew in California. They waited for him until he came to apply for a renewal of his work permit, and then they seized him. Some people whose visas or work permit expired moved on to different states and remained illegal for fear of deportation."

After the break, Emilio tried to push the giant garbage cart. It tipped over and spilled.

Emilio cursed in his native language and called out to Moses for help. In the real team spirit, Sami and Jose rushed to help. Jose started singing a joyous old song with a nostalgic melody, "Quanta la Mera." He had a happy smile on his face but hidden beneath the countenance lay a dark, sad, torturous life from which he was running.

The evening crew members appeared repulsive and indecent in their discussions, yet Sami had no qualms about engaging them in any debate. When some of his colleagues shared with him their troubles and ordeals, Sami became relieved, and he received some answers to his problems as well. They shared all the information they could get without any hesitation. He acquiesced halfheartedly to their silent comradery despite the drudgery of evening life. The crew did not abandon him despite his aloofness and reservations. They brought out of him the best he could ever be.

Sami learned to laugh and look at his own life from a different perspective. He learned to look at his world and accepted what he could not change. He learned to let go of some of those bitter feelings that he'd harbored for a long time, and he listened and allowed the fact that life was sometimes an illusion.

The famous words rang through his mind again: *We have received a large pool of highly qualified applicants, and you have an impressive resume, but you have not been selected for the interview.* Oh, how he hated those words. However, for now, he had to work on forgiving himself and accept life the way he found it. He believed he could change his life if only he had a green card in his hands.

With his mind bemused by all those unresolved issues, Sami let his thoughts stray to all other areas of his life.

Chapter 18

"You haven't mentioned your venture lately. You're fully on board, right?" Kumar asked, breaking the silence.

"Sort of," Sami replied.

"I can see the expressions on your face. Anything else?"

"Jasmine seemed shaken since Antonio was out of jail."

"That despicable scum is a pain in the rear. He belongs in jail. He's a parasite of a man, blackmailing her." Kumar spat air with a distasteful expression on his face.

Sami laughed.

"This is not a laughing matter, my friend. This thug deserves to rot in jail, and I am shocked that they let him out. He's abusive and very demanding, and he won't leave her alone. In any case, you don't have to worry. Your situation is different unless you got too close."

"What do you mean? How close do you expect me to be?" Sami asked. When Kumar did not say anything, Sami said, "You know my predicament, with a wife and children. A lot of questions popped up in my head. What if she is setting a trap or is an FBI informer? How well do you know this lady?"

"I understand your concerns. You don't have to worry about Jasmine. As I told you earlier, consider it safe." Kumar nodded. "It is perfectly normal to take precautions, as we talked about earlier because some ugly incidents happened in the past with this kind of work where fraud and deception occurred. However, I wouldn't be overly worried about Jasmine."

"What makes you certain about her?"

"Trust me; I have been around."

Kumar's confident and audacious approach won Sami over. With a glimpse of hope, Sami stepped outside his comfort zone and trusted him.

Kumar turned around. "By the way, once again, I will guarantee you that Jasmine is reliable. I know somebody she helped. Besides, she's going back to school to finish her degree here. You might end up in the same class. You never know."

Sami needed reassurance more than anything else. He had more on his mind than expected. The issue of how he could come up with the remaining amount to complete the deal lingered in his mind. "I have to find ways of making my final payment."

"You can still negotiate, you know. Jasmine might change her mind on the price range, and if you get to know her better, who knows?" Kumar shrugged in a manner suggesting that Sami could try once more.

"She wouldn't change. In any case, we had set the deal." Sami nodded. "The worst scenario would be if she disappeared. I took a loan to finance this deal."

He had to secure the precarious financial transaction that would blossom and deepen his debt hole out of control. As Sami looked back, he could not expunge the memory of the poverty with which he'd grown up. Money had always been a problem.

Back to the situation at hand, Sami diverted his mind to thinking about money, willy-nilly, a reliance only serendipity could provide. After so many setbacks in striving for a job, he had little hope left. What had kept him going so far was a belief that he had not exhausted all options. The mere fact that he was trying something gave him a twitch in his muscles.

***

"The kids have gone to bed, right?" Sarah turned to give a slight glance recognition of his presence. Sami didn't expect her to answer. A look in his direction could construe a sign of affirmative.

"Yes," she replied after a moment of hesitation. Sami had to set the tone for what he intended to share. They were two people who loved each other, were married, had four children, and yet, for no apparent reason, they had stopped talking to each other. They looked at each other with stone faces as if they had nothing in common and nothing to discuss. A long silence would engulf between them before any of them would say something. Sami attributed this to the nature of their life, working two jobs and with no time left for each other to lead a healthy life.

"It is about our search for legal documents," Sami began. Sarah raised her eyebrows, hoping to expect new information other than what they already knew. In the past, both exchanged information they received from friends without implementing anything. Like many international students, Sami had come to the USA on a student visa, and he had extended his time to fulfill his visa requirements by taking classes irrelevant to his selected field of study.

Sarah shifted in her seat, tilting forward. "We could try the green card lottery. You know, some people get a green card through it."

Sami had waited for this moment, an opportunity that he could take advantage of. He cleared his throat. "Yes, but there are other options as well. I've heard that people try everything possible to get this card. They will never bend the

118

rules, and as a matter of fact, they have tightened them and changed the regulations, although people always find some loopholes and leeway. The options available include green card through asylum and marriage if one marries a citizen."

She looked at him once and followed it with another glance, giving him the impression that this marriage option was a dead end. Then his youngest son cried, and she rushed to find out what was happening. With this interruption, Sami knew it would be a while before he got the courage to tell her what was on his mind.

"What about it?" she said after she sat down.

Sami tried to remember where he'd stopped. "As I said, we could try one of the options." He glanced at her from the corner of his eye. She did not react. He slowly tilted his head until his face came directly in line with hers. Still no reaction. "I think we should try something," he said, trying to attract her attention. "With money, anything is possible. Do you remember about the guy I told you who said that he knew a person who could arrange for the green card process?"

She burst into laughter. Unprepared for this sudden shift, Sami waited. The laughter continued and got a little louder. Finally, Sami joined her, only to realize that she'd stopped abruptly.

"Are you out of your mind?" She guffawed between hiccups. "What! For a married man? Which option? How does it work? Interesting." She finally calmed down.

Sami had trouble explaining this even to himself. It was one of those things that people do without thinking about the consequences. "Let me explain the way I understand it. Couples get divorced on paper while remaining married." He threw up his hands in a foolish gesture of desperation. How could he explain the obvious? After a little silence, he gained courage. "What this means is it's not a real divorce as such. You can call it a temporary divorce to allow the documentation process to go forward and legalize the new marriage."

She cut him short. "What do you mean? Like deceiving the authorities?"

Sami had waited for this moment to lay out his plan. He had learned one or two things from his wife, and this would be the time to use them. *Never give a direct answer to an ambiguous question.* "We talked about it already. I am sure you have heard how some people got their green cards. They file divorce proceedings on paper and remain together. In other words, it's meant for the eyes of the immigration world only, while the two still live together, sort of..." His voice faded away.

"Well," he continued after he realized she was expecting a further explanation, "then, when the divorce papers are finalized, the man could be free to marry the lady on paper. They will then process the legal papers to adjust the status for a green card. After that, the man can divorce the lady and get back to his former wife. Something like that."

Sami felt a chilling silence; he could hear his own heart throbbing with palpitating thrusts into the left side of his ribs. Like a physician closely examining his patient, he waited. He did not look his wife in the eyes. Deep down inside, he knew something was wrong. He had veered and trampled on a delicate, sacred spot that required a careful approach. Sami shot wary looks towards her. His mind drifted. What was wrong with the society in which he lived? He'd been asking himself that question for a while. What was wrong with him? He had asked himself about that, too. What was wrong with what he planned to do? He did not ask himself about that; well, maybe he did or perhaps not. Or he did not want to hear the answer he would get. What was right or wrong was no longer a question he needed to ask. He knew it was unfair that he had no job while he was qualified. It was unfair that children were dying of malnutrition and hunger in the world. It was wrong that oppression and injustice were being tolerated and accepted as a part of norms. *Yes, there are a lot of things morally wrong that people have made acceptable,* he said slowly in his head while his eyes and ears awaited an answer.

A society is devoid of decency when half of the population looks at the world in which they live with contempt. In the world where Sami had grown up, one could find a similar trend. The affluent would always move ahead and enjoy what this world could offer. However, there were some real differences. There were fewer opportunities for Sami in his country of origin, less freedom to do what he wanted, and he had to know somebody to be somewhere. In this world that he'd come to admire, the situation was very different, and yet it was similar in every aspect.

In some cases, prejudices and biases based not on an individual's potential but on how they looked could come into play. You might have all the opportunities without the means to enjoy them. Sami had come to accept the two worlds as the same. Whether he was worse off now than when he'd left his country of origin was a question that he had to consider someday. As for now, Sami had to convince his wife that they had to face reality. They lived in a world full of illusions, and the question was how comfortable he would be with the choice he made.

Sami saw his wife's face change: her facial muscles pulled together, showing whatever little defiance left in her. It took a while before she said anything. He hesitated to tell her the details of his green card plans. He mentioned bits and pieces and anticipated that she would shut down the idea as an impossible, unrealistic conundrum destined for failure. The waiting intensified. Sami glanced at her from the corner of his eye, dreading the outcome of her response. He'd known his wife for fifteen years. If she delayed her answer, you could expect one of two things: she would slash and burn the question or leave you dry with a conspicuous silence. Sami had to deal with whatever omen the quietude of the moment portended.

"You know it's wrong, immoral, illegal, a lie, and a fraud to pursue this opportunistic route to a green card. It is degrading and sinful, to say the least." She left her seat to go to the inner room. One look had convinced him that this topic was over for now.

Sami sat still. He had concluded the deal, and there was no way he could back out.

Chapter 19

The childcare center across from where Sami lived had an open space where kids from around the students' apartment buildings played . You would see couples pushing strollers along the sidewalk.

"Push harder! Faster! It's my turn now!" The kids all spoke at the same time, demanding attention. Some other kids were on the playground as well. Sami hurried to help each of his kids. With his mind still bogged down by the demands of parenting and social life, he'd learned to filter some things out. Some things needed his attention all the time, and no matter what, he had to find ways to fix them. He then sat and watched as kids played.

Sami revisited the scenario of obtaining a green card in his head and wrestled with how he should approach his wife again with this odd issue. Last night, he hadn't gotten far, and her previous words still lingered in his head. What if she refused to understand? What if the woman disappeared with his money? What if...? What about the kids, especially Hawa? What if she noticed and asked questions? How long could he keep it a secret from them? In the back of his mind, there were other things that he needed to address. The issue of money for the card preparation stood out and kept popping up for attention. He pushed the idea aside and picked up a newspaper left on the bench where he was sitting. The headline was about the detasseling season and how, each summer, students made money, and there was a need for hand laborers in all counties to help with it. Sami had already planned to participate in the detasseling season. Detasseling was the process of removing the pollen-producing flowers from corn. These activities, conducted by hired hand laborers, including high school students, served as a form of pollination control.

During the season of corn detasseling, which lasted for a period of three or four weeks, seed companies would conduct an intensive, rigorous manual labor. Thousands of acres of seed company corn farms extended across the vast land as far as the eye could see. The length of the planted cornrows, spaced thirty inches apart, could continue for miles and miles, depending on the size of the farm.

Like a swarm of hungry locusts devouring the last standing foliage, high school children, college students desperately in need of cash, and immigrant workers all converged and crisscrossed the narrow farm roads for corn detasseling tasks. The seed companies would initially use machinery (cutters) to cut off the top part of the corn plants and remove portions of the tassel. However, some would still be intact. Therefore, they required human labor to go down each row, check for tassels, and pull them out by hand.

That evening, a student who had signed a contract with one of the seed companies for detasseling came to Sami's house.

"Hey, brother Sami." Thoma beamed with the broad smile of a happy man about to give good news. "Thanks for taking the time to welcome me into your humble home. I will be brief." He sounded apologetic. Thoma, a foreign graduate student from Central Africa, had a contract to detassel eighty acres of corn. "Let me get to the point. We have enough acres available for work. The pay is from forty to seventy-five dollars per acre, and the more acres you clean, the more money you will receive. Fill out this form and sign it." He paused as if expecting a response from Sami. "It is as simple as that." Thoma waited for his words to sink in.

Sami's interest widened. He raised his eyebrows. Thoma asked, "Do you know how big an acre of land is? It's the first question they always ask."

"I don't know. We use the metric system in my country," Sami acknowledged.

"It is roughly about two hectares of land." Thoma held two fingers up. "If you want to make quick money, that's the way to go." He paused. "I have to warn you, though." He smiled. "It is arduous and tiring work. I will show you the field tomorrow, and next week, we will start the work. Now, can I see you outside for a minute?"

Sami stepped outside with him. "I have a tradition of welcoming my summer crew members, and this is a twenty-dollar bill. Take your family out for dinner." With that, Thoma departed.

Shortly after Thoma left, Sami and his wife discussed the proposal. Sarah was not excited about this prospect. She'd quietly listened as Thoma had explained things. True to her upbringing and cultural norm, she did not want to embarrass the visitor. She knew her secret veto weapon and when to use it. The superfluous proposal was too good to pass up without her second look.

Sami came into the room. His financial hopes raised with excitement. "I think the welcoming dinner was another way of making sure that we take the proposal. What do you think?" he asked his wife.

"A self-proclaimed contractor. What a charlatan."

Sami was surprised by her reaction. He turned towards her. "You don't even know him. How can you condemn him using such a strong term?"

"I don't need to know him. It was written all over his face. Easy to notice his fake plastic smile, the mark of a con man. It would be foolhardy to consider that this man would give you a fair share. The way he acted and twisted words and went over the number of acres, and how he hinted that the price could change, indicated to me that he was not to be trusted at all."

"We just got into this, and let's find out our availability and readiness first." Sami waited for her reaction.

Sarah reiterated, "I will take off from work to help, but I suspect that this is too good to be true." She sat back gleefully, with elevated pride.

"Everyone knows this is a detasseling season. It was in the papers, and they advertised the detasseling job, eight bucks an hour. A good amount of money considering that the minimum hourly rate in the state is still five dollars, and some people get paid lower than that. I think it is a good deal. There's no reason for me not to believe what he said. If we can get seventy-five dollars an acre for cleaning the field, my dear, that could boost and supplement our meager income."

"Do you know what the work entails?"

"No, I saw lush, green, tall corn plants when we drove to Des Moines from Ames. You remember. We even took several pictures of the corn plants and silos last summer."

"It is absurd that they have not adapted to the metric system. The measurement was in feet and acres. How do you know all the other hidden conditions?"

"I don't think it will be worse than what he was saying. I will find out," Sami replied.

"It's obvious he was making things appear simple. How can you get seventy-five dollars an acre just for walking through a field and pulling out some tassels missed by the tractor? He did not even say anything about the distance you have to walk or the preparation we need to get the work done. He only emphasized how easy it was to complete the work. That was what concerned me. Besides, the corn plant is very tall. How can we reach the top?"

"Come on, dear, think of two thousand dollars just within a week. Thoma confirmed they would cut the top so even a child can reach it. The risk is worthy. This amount of money could do miracles," he reassured her, and he even touted that he could afford to purchase the sapphire bracelets, her favorite blue color, she admired. However, in the back of his mind, Sami had a serious plan that would require a serious discussion with his wife again: the unfinished business of getting a green card and secure a document that would give them permanent residency in the United States. Sami even contemplated working for the federal government.

Chapter 20

Sami was engrossed in plans on how to convince his wife about the green card. At work, during break time, Jose picked the topic of family life again.

"There is no woman whom you cannot find a tiny bit of goodness in if you can only look and choose to focus on that character. Our problem is that we tend to put more emphasis on the qualities we do not want in our partners." The rest of the workers clustered over the playing cards. "Take the case of my friend's wife, "Jose continued. "She was a great cook, wonderful with kids, and kept her house and finances in order, and yet at the slightest drop of a spoon, she would go berserk and burst into terrifying anger. For her, every little thing was as if the world was about to end. You had to do everything her way, or there would be no peace. I would be terrified and can't imagine that a simple thing like that could make such a divine person act so devilish when angry. For me, it doesn't matter where the chair is facing, whether this way or that way." He swung his hands left and right, demonstrating how things could be scattered. "Or whether you arranged shoes in line or put clothes in the cabinet drawer or laid on the chair. If I have space somewhere to sit, it's enough for me." He sighed and paused for a long time. "I now know why some men want to drink themselves to death.

They are not equipped to deal with such simple and yet powerful emotions."

"Well, that's somebody else's wife you're talking about, Jose. What about your wife?" Emilio asked.

"You can only talk positively about your wife. Never should any negative things come outside the home. Don't you know the golden rule?" Jose replied.

"How did you deal with it," Emilio shot across to him with laughter. It was a kind of sinister laugh with hidden meaning that only the person who laughed could tell.

"This is one secret that no man would want to share." Jose paused. "Pablo, did you say that your wife sent you to jail?"

"No, but I think she was happy that I went to jail."

"Why?" Sami asked.

"First, she got a credit card in my name and put me into debt, and when I confronted her, she kicked me out. She ruined my credit record, and I will make her pay for it."

"Do you still live with her?"

"No, she filed for divorce, citing irreconcilable difference, and it ended. Nothing tied us together anymore."

"Are you married?" Sami asked.

"No, as free as one can get. Right now, I am in the mood for payback."

Moses jumped in and tried to change the direction of the discussion. "I will guarantee you that once you're married, you will find ways to get around your problems in the house. For some people, it may take years to figure out. Others will do it in a month or two. Some will give up, and that means parting with each other for good. Don't ever think that those who stay married have a heavenly life together. No, no, they just found a little niche where there are some spaces to maneuver things around when the going gets rough. They hang on to the thin string. If they let the string go, it will be the end. The string could be children, family ties, religion, a similar background, or even a little shade of love that flickers on and off. Whatever it is, there will always be something that can come with marriage." He looked at Emilio and Jose. "But you will only learn this if you are married. You better get a wife first."

"All of us here have some elements of fault and crookedness within," Emilio said. "Although incarcerated at some points in our lives, we value what is good in others."

"For some people, prison life is far better," said Pablo. Everyone looked at him.

"What?" Jose whistled.

"There are people who managed to do a million dollars' worth of transactions from behind bars. You hear that all the time. Others were ruined financially by their jail terms, with all their credits and debts unpaid. I prefer to make money by any means possible."

"Did you serve a jail term in your home country of Honduras?" Jose asked.

"Not yet, but what difference does it make? If you are in jail anywhere, you're a slave."

"Amigo, you're the only person with a clean record. Keep it that way," Jose said to Sami.

Pablo got interested. "Not even a misdemeanor?" he asked.

"He's clean. Don't taint him," Jose warned. "By the way, Pablo, you didn't tell us what you were in jail for the last time. You said the first time was for possession of marijuana. What did you do to spend two years in jail?"

Pablo smiled and shook his head. "It was a felony."

"For what crime?"

"No comment on this, Jose. I will keep this to myself."

"Sure, Pablo, just as we shared a lot of things, there were certain things that each of us kept to ourselves. You also did not share your other names. Pablo is not the only fake name you've carried, right?"

Pablo laughed. "I had to keep my other names top secret, too. I have three fake names fully documented just in case something happens to Pablo."

"Sami, this is our world. We all use these evasive tactics. If compelled to leave this state, you need a new name and identity, so we plan," Jose added.

"Do you want a document?"

"No, Jose. I am fine."

As Sami gathered wisdom, he wondered whether Jose was who he claimed to be, a de facto leader of the pack with philosophical wit and experiences that he shared freely. No wonder he hadn't wasted the six years spent in prison. Jose often boasted of the valuable knowledge he'd acquired reading history, philosophy, literature, and social studies while in prison.

Sami reflected on the discussions with excitement. He agreed with the group consensus that each home was unique and a treasure of an inviolable sanctuary.

Chapter 21

Sami stretched out his arm to press snooze on the alarm clock. He squinted his eyes, inched his hand over to bedside lamp , and turned it off. In the meantime , Sarah had showered, made breakfast, and prepared the kids. She packed the sandwiches for lunch and put the kids' lunch in a bag to give to the neighbor, who had agreed to babysit.

They left early for the field on the outskirt of Ames, Iowa, to avoid the traffic. The yellow buses transporting high school children to various farms, and trucks, minibuses, and passenger cars ferried people of all ages to detasseling sites. The farm road narrowed to where two cars could barely pass one another. Sami had to stop several times to avoid the oncoming trucks and buses. He silently cursed when the vehicles swarmed by, splashing a pool of muddy water on his windshield.

They arrived at the farm at around five in the morning. "I think this is a good time. They recommended starting before sunrise," Sami said. He slowed down and stopped his 1988 Chevrolet Corsica at the edge of the farm. "You will need gloves and goggles to keep the pollen from entering your eyes."

With a surprised look on her face, Sarah gazed at the vast forest of foliage. She stretched out her five-foot-six-inch frame, straining her neck to look up and down. She could not see the end of the farm due to the corn bustling all around her.

"This is the beginning of the cornrow that we need to pull tassels out. I will take one row, and you will take the other. We will follow them until the end of the row and then move to the next rows to begin again, following a serpentine pattern. You can take a break and keep going. I will be in the same row even if I get ahead of you."

Sarah looked at the rows of corn, which had majestic heights, and the towering waves of leaves swooshing and hovering from side to side. She stared again, transfixed, her mind engrossed in awe as if an unknown formidable force gripped her. The light breeze on her face added a peaceful, nostalgic feeling that only the outside natural vegetation could provide. She paused as if in communication with a telepathic message emitted through the breeze of the pleasant morning air. She was not sure how to describe the smell; it was like nothing she'd ever experienced before. The air smelled different and had distinct aroma laden with a pollen scent. As she stepped into the row, the atmosphere unhitched a stream of airflow that descended from above. Sarah raised her head and stretched her hand as far as she could. The corn was taller than she could reach.

Sami stopped, again and again, to make sure that his wife was within eyesight as they trod through the cornrows at a slow pace.

Sarah had never imagined that she would see a pool of water in the middle of a cornfield. "How did it get here?" she wondered aloud. "Do we have to go through the water?" The fear of the unknown engulfed her. She realized how much she didn't know what she was getting into. She was clear about her role and what to do with the corn tassels, but right there in the field, she had to struggle with other unknown obstacles that her physical structure could not support. Her inner anger swept over her mood. "How come you didn't tell me about all these hurdles? It's not even worth it, crippling yourself physically and allowing emotional drain. I doubt whether I can recover from this by the end of the day," she moaned.

Sami had to find a suitable word to assuage her anger towards him, which had gone beyond control and could trigger bad luck. He stopped and called out, "Keep moving; we have to finish what we started." He could only see the extra money that he needed; no fatigue could stop him. "You can take a break. I will wait for a little. This water is still below knee-height. Let me hold your hand and help you across." Sami stretched his hands towards her. She snatched her hand away.

"No, I can do it myself. I am not a baby to be held by the hand." She swung her hand to pull away from him, and in the process, she missed her step and tilted her body in an unbalanced motion. She fell forward and down into the pool of muddy water. She stood up quickly, but lost control again and fell on her face. With all her limbs in the murky water, she struggled to touch the soft ground for support. Both her hands sank up to the elbow in the pool of dirty water. The splash from it trickled down her shivering body, and with a panic-stricken face, she roared. She looked like a creature from the shady world of the underground.

The sight could instantly spark uncontrollable laughter, and Sami held himself back with difficulty. He couldn't dare laugh at her discomfort. The look on his face gave it away, another sign of looming incredulity. Sarah read his composure, twisted her mouth, and looked at him with a gloomy expression. He rushed to help, stretching his hand to hold her. She swung away from him violently, refusing to hold his hand, and again, she missed her balance and fell on her side. Sami froze for a moment and instantly reached out to hold her hand.

Sarah swung at him with a force of vengeance. "How can you laugh at me? You dragged me into this horrible mess!" she shouted between bursts of emotions. Her eyebrows squeezed together and tightened like a closed fist, spreading tensed creases all over her face. Sami could only imagine the heated venom about to spill over.

"I was trying to," he started to say, but she cut him off by flinging a ball of mud across his face. She hurled at him without cessation, and the abrupt incident caught Sami unexpectedly and left him baffled.

"Why would you do such a thing?" he shouted, but he quickly curbed the seething anger. He spat out the dirt and ducked another missile of muddy rain coming from her direction. He swerved through a shower of slung mud and tried to move out of her range. Despite his dodging, the third shower of mud caught him on the hand and stomach. Sami yelped while shielding himself with his hand, and he quickly stepped behind the cornrow. He writhed with anger that he had to curb, panting, and gasping for air. Then he waited with eyes fixed on her, just in case. The rows of corn shielded him from further barrages of vicious hostility.

There was a long silence for the remainder of the mud-slinging saga. They came out of the pool of water, close to the edge of their rows. Sarah sat down and waited. There was a road that divided the farms at the end of the row. "I am not going back there again!" she shouted.

"To get back to where we started, we must go the same way, back to the beginning. There is no way around it. We would end up in a different field if we tried to go around."

Sami did not know what to do next. He sat down until she made up her mind. He pulled up a blade of grass, wiped off some mud that was splattered all over his shirt, and quietly waited. Sami knew that one way or another, they had to walk back, and for the next four rows, they would cross this pool of water.

After what looked like an eternity, Sarah stood up and resumed her task with silence. She plodded on, tilting her head, and kept the pace by turning left and right. The energy in her legs already depleted. The picture of what detasseling was all about had emerged to her in two words: "blood money." In the meantime, Sami kept up the momentum. His mind flooded with wishful thinking, focusing on the amount of money in light of these new difficulties. A thousand dollars in a week was a colossal amount of money for him, and he was determined to get it despite the signs of physical exhaustion. Sami knew that by the end of the week, he might not have energy left in any part of his body to respond to this task. His own body was already showing signs, and now that his wife was threatening to quit, he might as well forget about the amount he'd fantasized.

The cornrows thinned out, leading to an open area with no corn. There were no tassels to pull out for a segment of that row. As Sami walked facing the east, a moment of reflection came upon him. He took a deep breath to look at the bright, magnificent rising sun. The head of the sun had just popped up. The light of its rays emerged from its disc and spread across the horizon. He remembered in his science class that the color of sunlight was white, composed of a mixture of seven colors, yet he was looking at a splendid red and yellow. Sami returned his attention to the rows of corn and resumed the task.

The long silence gave him time to ponder over his life in general. At the meatpacking factory, he understood what real-life work was, although he sometimes appeared aloof and lonely. Nevertheless, he felt comfortable in the company of his colleagues at work, especially Jose, the Mexican illegal immigrant who'd proven to be a valuable friend.

Sami remembered the hard times in the village during the drought season when everything was in short supply, and people barely survived. He shared a bowl of milk with his siblings during those tough times. You could only sip and pass it on to the next person and then take another sip when it came back around to you, circulating the meager amount until the last drop. The temptations to gulp down the whole quantity increased considerably after the first round, but even under these dire conditions, the family rule remained intact. The youngest sibling got the last sip, and as a middle child of seven, Sami's chance would usually dry up by the second round.

It was a path that he knew so well, and yet the complacent thought had crept into his mind that with higher education, he would get a good job, and things would get better. Time was passing by quickly, and his life had taken a different path, unknown to his upbringing.

Sami moved one step at a time, his hands-on the tassel, and his eyes focused ahead. He paused, making sure that he had not gone too far ahead. He moved on again when he heard the faint sound from his wife's row.

The final steps to the end of the rows appeared in sight. Sami could see the edge of the next farm. A glimmer of hope raised his spirit. He had four more rows to go. His body might not hold on long enough to let him finish the job. In any case, Sami had vowed to make sure that he got the money he needed. He hurried to complete his row first so that he could help his wife.

Chapter 22

"We are about halfway to the end of the rows. You can rest a bit and start again," Sami suggested.

Sarah snapped, "This will be my last row. I am not going back."

Sami pointed with his mouth to indicate the remaining rows. He knew she understood what to do, but she said nothing. Instead, she drank the water from her bottle, wiped some sweat from her face, took off her soaked gloves, and adjusted her boots. Sami also drank some water and waited. It would be a while before they talked again. He felt a little embarrassed and cheated that he had to put his wife through these difficulties. He knew it was his responsibility to make sure that everything was okay with her. He'd failed to provide; that was a fact, considering that he had enough education to earn a decent living. The quick money had tempted Sarah as well, and she'd been more than determined to help. It was a family decision to support and help each other, and a little extra money would always be needed.

Sami looked at his wife. Her usual radiant, lovely face appeared rough, crisscrossed with lines from corn leaves, and darkened beyond the causal effect of the summer sun. The leaves from the corn had cut into her soft skin and made some cracks. Sarah kept scratching herself, the pollen from the falling tassels had magnified the itch. Sami eventually had to ask her what had happened. She did not respond. She washed her face.

Sarah scratched and scratched. Sami looked on.

"In less than five minutes, we will be at the end of the row, and I can take you home." Afraid that she might bleed herself out in the middle of nowhere, Sami stepped closer to his wife, and not sure how she would react, he offered an apology. "I am sorry for getting you into all this trouble. I didn't know it myself, and the money promised was tempting."

He stretched his hand towards her and withdrew when the mudslinging picture appeared in his mind. Sarah's appearance showed the mark of melancholy, misery, and defeat. Sami saw the edge of the farm and wondered what to do with the two rows left to detassel. If he took her home, it would be difficult to come back again. On the other hand, she could wait while he continued with the task, but the distance from the beginning of one row to the end could be up to a mile long, and he could not leave her alone.

As he came closer to the end of his row, he saw Thoma.

"Don't tell me that you're still at the first acre? At this pace, you won't get done with this field today." Thoma smiled, but he stopped when he saw Sami's face wrinkle up. Sami ground his teeth and took a deep breath that seemed disconnected. The whole of his arm muscles, armpits, chest muscles, legs, fingers, and every joint in his body ached, drained of energy, and ready to collapse. He gulped in a stream of pollen-impregnated air and twisted his tightened lips in disgust.

"You promised a walk through the field," he fumed. "We harvested the whole acre by hand. The tassels were uncut, contrary to what you said." Sami forced out his words; his anger seemed to have taken over. "Are all of them like this one?"

"Frankly, I don't know," Thoma said quietly. "They told me that they cut the tassels in all the fields. The ones missed came out later, as I told you earlier."

"You didn't tell me the details," Sami repeated. "Where are the fields with fewer tassels to pull out." Thoma tried to speak, but Sami continued. "Not a single one of them was cut. We had to pull tassels from a forest of corn taller than me." Sami curled his upper lip. "The distance we covered was ridiculous, and what's more, there's a pool of standing water in the middle of the cornfield. You never disclosed all these obstructions that slowed us down." He shook his head.

Throughout the time he'd started contracting for detasseling, Thoma had played on the psyche of his student customers. He knew their financial conditions and enticed them with easy money. Once they got into it, they would do the job no matter what they said at the beginning.

"I told you it was not an easy task," he said, trying to console Sami. "Some students got help from their fellow countrymen. You could pay them a little money if they were willing to help." Thoma nodded. "Students who are not legally allowed to work would appreciate any little offer. I followed the company's terms and deadlines."

In a situation like this, Thoma usually raised the bar and added an extra ten or twenty dollars for each acre completed. He had calculated well in advance and knew how to manipulate the inexperienced students new to the country. They had no clue about what to expect and the tasks involved. Thoma would pretend to care and make things easy for them. In the past, he'd given them a ride to the field until they completed all the tasks. By isolating them during the detasseling period, he ensured their undivided focus. Thoma liked to remind students of this in a boastful manner.

Sami listened on, debating whether his wife was right about Thoma.

"Brother, I was the first international student from Mother Africa who got a contract. I helped a lot of students with their financial needs, gave them little loans. You know, we help each other."

Thoma had devised strategies to hook students immediately. On the first day of work, he brought them food and drinks while they were in the field. Some students wrongly misinterpreted this as a favor they had to return. Strange as it seemed, Sami had felt the same way before he'd begun the work. Thoma knew how students shared information, and he tried as much as he could to hide his past activities. He argued that students who tarnished his reputation were jealous and didn't want him to succeed. He'd warned Sami that the detasseling agreement should be kept confidential.

Sami could not hold himself back anymore. "Why do you provide vague information in pieces, as if you're hiding something. They did not cut the tassels." He threw up his hands in a mocking gesture. "Besides, the corn height was almost twice mine, so how do you expect me to reach the top part" Sami was furious.

"Calm down, brother. You don't have to complain about the height of corn. If you're short and can't reach it, how is that my problem?"

Sami got angrier. "I am taller than you. Don't you see?"

"Hey, wait a minute. It isn't about my height. You might be the tallest in your village, but here you would be considered short."

"What about you, midget!"

"Stop it. This kind of talk won't get us anywhere," Thoma warned. "Now, back to your question. I know the first time is not easy, and I do understand how you feel. You know..." He paused. "I go by what they tell me, and I believed it when they said they'd cut the tassels. It was to their advantage to do so. After a week, tassels will regrow, and if not removed during that operation, the uncut tassels will show up as fully grown again.

In some cases, they cut a second time. The next field will be fine. Now, take a few minutes to rest, eat, and drink a lot of liquid." He offered Sami a sandwich and a cold Coke. "Where is your wife?" he asked.

"Oh, she does not feel okay. I will take her home," Sami said nonchalantly.

Thoma turned his eyes toward the approaching sounds of Sarah's hands, sweeping through the rows of corn from left to right, rattling the corn leaves. He waited until she settled down.

"Hi, madam, how are you doing?"

Her voice barely audible, Sarah croaked, "Okay." After a long pause, she moved towards the car and opened the back door, where she kept some of her extra things, including first aid kits.

She emptied the bottle of water and sat down without touching the food. The two men looked at her, but she ignored their attention. She was fed up, and her only concern at that time was how to get her skin and energy back.

Thoma kept looking at Sarah. "Is madam alright?"

"What do you think? She was in a pool of water up to her knees, and you call that a field? Come on, give me a break. I was about to leave this field. I did not come here to wade through this muddy pool, and my wife is extremely disappointed."

"I understand," Thoma said, trying to calm Sami.

"You don't," Sami retorted. "I did not expect this."

Thoma looked on without saying a word.

Sarah was still within hearing range. She howled, "I need to go!" and she opened the passenger door and sat.

On the way home, Sami and his wife did not exchange a

single word. The old, beaten-up Chevrolet without air conditioning wound its way along the bumpy farm road. For the next thirty minutes, the only sound came from a cassette tape, Reggae music, and with all windows open, the dust poured in.

"You need to fix the air conditioner." Sarah wiped the dust off with her hand. Sami kept quiet. One of those pending to-do items that could wait.

"I have to get back and finish the remaining sections," Sami announced.

His wife did not speak. He dropped her off at home and returned to the farm.

Chapter 23

Sami identified the row where they'd stopped, and he resumed the ordeal of the tortuous final eight. The steam of energy that started early in the morning was long gone. He frequently nursed his hands to relieve the pain. With wet leaves, muddy soil, and uncomfortable outfits, each step Sami took became a reminder of what was to come. The first acre he'd done with his wife in the morning had dented his hopes, and it was unlikely that he could manage an acre within five or six hours. Sami brushed off the negative thoughts and ideas of failure flowing into his mind.

Just as Sami was finishing the last row, Thoma came out to the farm again. "Are you alone now? It will be dark around 9:00 p.m., and you don't have much time left. Was madam upset? I noticed intense anger on her face."

Sami wanted to tell him to get lost, but he kept it to himself. "We are not happy about the deal. It was very unfair. I would like to see the copy of the contract I signed with the acre price of one to two hundred dollars."

"Oh, my friend, that was just an estimate, and while I promised you seventy-five dollars per acre, in the end, after you completed the work, you might receive less or more." Thoma softened his voice. "My brother, you got a better deal than the rest, and I will add a bonus as well. Let's get the job done first." He started moving. "I will let you finish the evening work." Sami did not even turn around to look at him; he now believed what his wife had confirmed. Thoma was a cunning and mischievous crook. The glossy air of confidence he'd shown earlier no longer charmed.

Sami felt a repulsive feeling towards Thoma.

The long, rugged farm road stretched Sami's imagination as he drove back home after that day's pitiless ordeal. He recalled all the things he'd talked about with Thoma, Jose, and Kumar, and everything that they'd spoken about revolved around survival and how to live a better life in this country.

**

That night, Sami and his wife didn't talk much. Sarah held her hands to the light. Lines extended towards her elbow, and she scratched continuously, distorting her face in discomfort. "This was not what I expected!" She kept nursing her fingers with Vaseline.

Sami, on the other hand, inundated by his guilt and exhaustion, gritted his teeth, suppressing his anger. He feared that his plans would be thwarted, and he realized that Thoma should not be trusted. He twisted his lips, regretting that he'd ignored the signs and what other people had told him about Thoma. One of the students had warned Sami about Thoma and how he'd finagled recently arrived students out of the detasseling money. It was the student's final comment that made Sami even more bitter: "I hope you are not working for him. Everybody knows his greed." Sami was embarrassed to admit that he had become a victim of his own choice.

Thoma had grown up in a corrupt system, just like Sami. The detasseling contract opportunity had opened up a way for him to make more money at the expense of others. Sami had trusted him and believed in fairness, justice, and doing the right thing.

Sami sought with his glances whether to say anything to his wife or not. "I understand the Vaseline will soothe the pain," he offered.

"My fingers won't even close, and by the end of the week, I don't think I will have any fingers left."

"I know. I feel the same way. Keep folding and unfolding your fingers. The exercise will relax the stiffness. It's like readjusting to relearn the motion." He demonstrated to her what he meant. With difficulty, he managed to rub his hands together, but the whole of his back and body still ached. He offered to massage her back and feet, and that simple gesture seemed to unhinge the pressure building up to sever the thin thread of the relationship.

The next day, Sami left early in the morning. He did not bother to wake his wife up. The promise of money was too tempting to give up at this early stage. This time, the corn appeared shorter, and he plunged right into work, devouring the distance in the jungle of the cornfield.

Thoma would tell the company representative after each day of work, and they would return to the area and inspect the fields until the end of the week.

Thoma came again around midday and asked Sami the usual question. He checked what Sami had done and left without saying a word. Sami did four acres in two days.

Before Sami was about to leave for home, Thoma appeared again as usual to check the field. "Hey, brother, you are almost there. I like your determination. You stuck to the task." He reminded Sami to recheck the previous fields.

The next day, Sami went back to the previous fields to check. He stayed in the area until 9:00 p.m., taking advantage of the long summer day. The following week, he repeated the same pattern.

"What was it again?" Sami angrily remarked when Thoma told him to recheck the field. "Look here, it has been two weeks, and you are telling me to do the same thing over and over. You haven't seen how the first field looked. It was hell on earth, impossible to eliminate the so-called tassels from an acre," Sami grumbled. "It hurts to say this, but you can go ahead and shove it." He threw his hands up.

"Hold on, that was a very harsh language. You're on the final leg of work. You don't need to do any major work at all. Take a walk through the field and look for tassels that might have appeared and pull them out. The inspectors do not like to see more than three tassels in an acre. There's no reason to get angry with me. I don't want you to lose money because of one or two tassels."

"What inspectors? These kids have no clue about what they are doing. They will find the tassels if they come intending to do so."

"Listen, brother. There is no way of knowing their intentions. The inspectors will walk through the field in a random, zig-zag fashion and scout for the tassels, and if they find more than five percent in an acre, they will consider the field undone. Yes, they will consider it undone."

"Five tassels? You are freaking me out. And I lose the acre? Give me a break! Get real!" Sami shrieked.

"No, calm down, brother. Certainly, you won't lose the acre. Let me ask you, wouldn't you rather come to the field to pull out one tassel instead of losing an acre's worth of money?"

"What do you mean, lose?" Sami asked. "I pulled out so many tassels already."

"If the company representative sends their team, regardless of how much work you did in the field, they will claim the money for the team who showed up and did the work." Thoma looked at Sami. "I know how you feel about this, but that was part of the contract."

"I feel cheated and misused," Sami shot back. "I consider

this an unfair deal and a scam."

"Hold on. Just so you know, I will ask the company representative to check again, and if you were not going to do it, let me know right now."

"You're going to do it?" Sami snapped. "There's nothing to do in the field. I did all the work, and you're going to take the credit? You are all the same."

Sami had sworn not to step into those fields again, and yet, as he stood there, trying to figure out the available option, he realized how this adept con man had connived to defraud him.

"If I were you, I would not give up at the last minute when the fruits of your hard labor are so close. Watch your language. Insulting words won't help."

Sami did not even look at him.

***

Sami spent most of his time checking for tassels. As he approached the cornfield, he noticed the company representative coming out of the farmhouse. Sami waved his hand to signal him to stop. "How long do I have to come back to the same field?" he asked.

"This field is almost clear of any tassel, but we have to make sure. We can give it three days. If, after three days, you have not heard from us, then everything is set to go." With that, he entered his truck and drove away.

Sami looked after him with stern disapproval. "How many tassels did you see?" he yelled after him." The man had driven away and did not hear him.

Sami was already boiling with anger about the nature of the work. He noticed that all the field inspectors were very young, the age of first-year college students. Sami complained and vented his anger, but in the end, he grudgingly obliged. With no other alternative left, he cursed and vented on his way to the field for the next three days.

On the final day, Sami saw Thoma and the field inspector in the field and wondered whether they were targeting him. Thoma approached Sami. "You did the right thing, and if you didn't show up, the inspector would have declared this field incomplete, and somebody else would have taken it for free after you did all the work of removing the tassels."

Thoma, not wanting to look directly into Sami's eyes, waited for Sami to respond. A picture of Thoma, his greedy attitude, and his scheme to manipulate had emerged in Sami's mind. It was the moment for the truth to come out. With his lame excuses claiming that the field was not done well, or the company would not pay as much as they'd initially estimated. Thoma was known to slash the amount by half. Sami had all the rumors ready to confirm, and looking at Thoma, he could see a hidden agenda behind his statements.

"Are you saying that all the work I did in this field would amount to no work done because of one tassel?" Sami didn't need to wait for his answer. "Tell me exactly how much I will get for this deathly job."

There was silence. Thoma noticed the situation had turned delicate.

"I do understand how you feel about this repetitive work. The company has rules that do not make any sense. In any case, we have to abide by the conditions of the contract."

Sami knew he'd said the same thing the first week when he gave him the field to work, and there was nothing new. As for the second question about money, Thoma avoided it by saying that he wouldn't know how much he would get paid for each acre. The information he'd given earlier was an estimate that could be either a minimum or maximum possible.

"You can't be serious, Thoma. By now, you should know when we will get paid. I want to know now." Sami did not take his eyes off Thoma.

"I will know today for sure." Thoma appeared apologetic in his demeanor.

There was nothing Sami could expect from him anymore. "I need to know what I will get today, and you better have an answer when I call."

"Sure," Thoma said, and then he turned and left.

Sami walked through the field again. Most of the time, he had nothing to pick; he walked and walked and got only three tassels. He wondered how many miles he'd covered walking the length of an acre the whole day.

Chapter 24

As promised, Thoma called the next day with more surprising news for Sami.

"Yes, speak. I am listening."

Thoma spent half the time apologizing for how things had turned out.

Sami hung up. He called Thoma back later. "I cannot believe what you are saying. I wish I'd listened to what people told me," he fumed. "We have to meet face to face about this."

"Look here, Sami. You seem to be angry. It is not a good idea to meet with me when you are angry. Besides, there's nothing more that I can add to what I've already conveyed. I told you the truth, and you don't want to believe."

"What truth?" Sami glared into the phone, gripping it with murderous anguish. "What a scoundrel!" he yelled, and he hit the table with his fist, trying to prove his point. The glass on the edge of the table tipped over and fell on the floor with a smash. Sami hung up quickly to defuse the situation. His younger son was about to walk around the table, and broken glass was all over the place. A sharp, painful cry brought the rest of the kids to the little den.

"Keep away! There's broken glass!" Sami shouted. He

quickly got a bandage and contained the flow of blood. The glass had gone deep into his youngest son's little foot.

Later, at the emergency clinic, he had to face a barrage of questions from an unsympathetic nurse, who frowned when she saw four other kids all jammed around him. He'd had to bring his children with him, for his wife was at work. The nurse looked at the wound. "How did it happen?"

"As I told you, the kid stepped on broken glass."

She looked at his bandaged knuckle with a displeased facial expression. "What about your hand.?"

Sami returned the look with a frown. "What about it? I told you I cut myself. Let's take care of the kid first; I am fine."

"You should be more careful. Where is the mother of the children?"

"At work."

"Oh, your hands are full. Are all these children yours?" She looked at him with a condescending attitude. Sami held himself back. He hesitated, wondering whether to answer her or not. "Which children do you mean?" He looked at his children. "Why would I bring somebody else's kids with me to the clinic." The question did not amuse Sami, so he twisted her question to get back at her, not sure why she would ask it.

"It's routine procedure to ask when a child is in danger," she grumbled without even looking at him.

Sami left the clinic angrier than when he'd arrived. Anger breeds resentment. One little error could tip the massive problems he faced. He turned his anger towards the nurse; she seemed to be suggesting that he had been careless, and she had formed preconceived ideas about the incident. From the way she looked at his kids and the way she looked him up and down, from his tennis shoes to the Iowa Cyclones t-shirt he wore, it was apparent that the nurse did not approve of his rugged appearance. The accident happened so fast, and Sami didn't get enough time to think or change clothes. Still drenched with summer sweat, he was not in a pleasant state to be around.

He tried to control himself and patted his kids, who were mostly calm once they returned home.

Sami dialed Thoma's number one more time and boomed into the receiver. Thoma listened as Sami vented. "I was warned about your deceptive, crooked history of thieving and exploitation of innocent, gullible students. I wish I'd listened to my gut feelings and advice from other people."

Thoma remained at ease, most likely used to this kind of threat during the detasseling season. He had grown a thick skin over the years, and this was why he recruited inexperienced and new students who were vulnerable or those who lacked proper documentation.

"Listen, bro, this empty threat won't help you. Do you want your share of the money or not? Enough of this. I am telling you what the company offered. They used a formula to calculate the money you earned based on each row rather than the whole acre. Each row you worked was worth a dollar, and after a deduction, you will receive forty dollars per acre."

Sami boiled with rage. He needed better answers than what he was getting. He paced the room, not sure how to address the new development.

"Do you mean forty dollars? Four zero?" Sami shouted.

"That's right. Many people did not even get that much."

Sami checked his notebook. Ten acres. He'd circled the words and added a calculation and the amount he would receive per acre. He could not believe the pathetic pittance of four hundred dollars from Thoma. He had been expecting two hundred dollars per acre, and now he could not even get the amount he'd been promised (seventy-five dollars per acre).

With this news, Sami could not face his wife to tell her that the two weeks they'd suffered had come to nothing. He had not yet recovered from the fatigue and hand injury, and his wife's itch and skin rash continued to give her problems. It was a detasseling debacle, a big lie, and a rip-off. In the same two weeks, his kids had lacked proper attention, and the damage to his old car due to the rough, bumpy farm road had left him with massive expenses to the tune of six hundred dollars. He needed new tires and transmission. He did not put a cost on all other miserable experiences of the detasseling. What a pitiful sum of money!

Sami gnashed his teeth, suppressing his frustration. He turned his mind to the job situation again, condemning himself for not getting a better one. He clenched his fist. "I would not have had to struggle with this low, mean, filthy crook whose main purpose in life is to take advantage of others and thrive on them. Ptui." Sami spat his traditional way of disapproval; his face contorted in anger.

What made his situation worse was that the person who'd cheated him was an immigrant like him who should have known the problems they all faced. A man who came from a country torn apart by civil war. A country whose people had tried to wipe each other off the face of the earth. *How can a man faced with such enormous tragedies in life, subjected to a severe form of oppression, has room in his heart to do injustice to others? Or could it be that a person brought up in such an environment has nothing good left in his chest but can only continue down the same pattern of destruction? Blinded from the truth, with a heart clogged and cloaked by the coat of venom, ready to lash out and inflict perpetual misery on others?* Sami paused to reflect. *Something like this should not happen here. It should never happen anywhere in the world!* A moment of silence engulfed him. He took a deep breath.

As his anger turned to pity, Sami began to accept that the world was full of imperfections, but people lived throughout the ages knowing that things would improve one way or another. Regardless, he still retained little hope for future improvement.

Chapter 25

"Can we come in?" Two social workers showed up at the door. It was around 11:00 a.m., on a Saturday, and Sami was alone in the kitchen with his children.

He'd hesitated when he'd heard the knock. He wiped his wet hand on his pants and stood in the doorway with a wearisome look on his face.

"We wanted to stop by if you don't mind. We are social workers."

Caught by surprise, Sami hesitated and thought of telling them not now, but he was not sure of the protocol.

"Just a minute." He closed the door and instructed his kids to stay in the bedroom and play with their toys while he talked with his visitors.

Chaaltu interrupted. "Dad, you promised to take us to the mall for ice cream."

Sami had no time for argument. "Yes, if you behave and play quietly." He put some toys and other items scattered around the room out of the way quickly to create room for his guests.

He opened the door. "You can come in."

After a brief introduction, one of the social workers, a lady, announced, "We received a report of child endangerment or negligence and stopped by to check the household and make sure that the children are safe. We react to concerns raised over the welfare of children within twenty-four hours, and we are here to investigate." Sami was utterly taken aback by this sudden intrusion.

"Do you have a warrant?" he asked.

The two social workers looked at each other, sullen and baffled at the unexpected request.

"We are not police officers, and you are not under arrest," one of them said.

Sami regained his composure. "I mean, who sent you?" Their silence prompted him to add, "What are you investigating? What did I do? Did the lady at the clinic lie about me?" His questions appeared confused and naïve.

One of the representatives responded, "We understand your position. We will try to make this visit short." Sami wasn't sure what the visitors intended to do. "We would like you to know that there was a concern raised regarding the child's welfare, and as part of the child protection team, our office will launch an investigation within twenty-four hours. Today, we are here to respond to these concerns, assess the situation, and decide on the appropriate action, which includes assessing the child's needs, the parents' capacity to meet these needs, living conditions, and the overall family and environmental situations."

He paused to reassure Sami that it was part of their routine to stop by homes when they got a call. Sami nodded. The social worker continued. "It is our responsibility to investigate if there's an allegation of abuse, assess the situation, and arrange for a conference to discuss the issue." He paused again as if he had forgotten something. "You will hear from us if further investigation is needed." He turned to face his colleague.

Sami remained mute, holding the door, thinking that they had to leave.

"Just before we leave, can we see the children?" the social worker said. "We have not seen them yet. Can you ask them to come? We would also like to see their rooms if you don't mind."

"Okay." Sami went into the inner room, brought out his children, and introduced them. The visitors greeted them and asked general questions about what they liked and if they knew what they would like to do when they grew up. Chaaltu was the only one answering for the rest of the kids. She told the woman about the roaches and rats in the house.

"Thanks for sharing," the lady said and then continued questioning further. "What happened to your little feet?"

"I stepped on broken glass," Musa answered. Chaaltu picked up from where Musa left off and narrated the whole incident.

Just before they departed, the lady took toys from her bag and asked Sami if it was okay to give them to the kids. "I only have two, but I am sure they can share, right?" She gave the toys to Sami.

"What do we say, kids?" asked Sami.

"Thank you!"

"You have lovely kids," the lady added.

"Thanks," Sami acknowledged.

The lady turned. "Where is the children's' mother?"

"Oh, she went to the store nearby."

The two visitors stepped outside to leave. As they walked back, they looked at each other.

"They seem to be happy," the lady commented.

"Let's try another time," her colleague replied.

* * *

Sami reflected on everything that had happened in the past week. He wrinkled the bridge of his nose and raised his cheeks, making a rugged face. He had a mistrust of human beings and of his ability to make things the way he wanted. It was inconceivable to think that he could be the one causing suffering to his fellow human beings, yet when the same infliction visited upon him, he didn't know how to react. Instead, he turned it against himself.

Sami got another call from Thoma on the issue of money. As he listened, the rage mounted as if the ground under him was about to swallow him. No words came out of his mouth.

"You know, brother, something comes up every time, but I believe this will be the final incident. The company has decided to use a formula to calculate the acre rate into rows worked. We also included the extra time taken by the seed company representatives into the calculation." He waited. "Sami, are you still on the line?"

A long silence engulfed the tense atmosphere. Sami stared at the phone receiver, holding back, trying to suppress the anger.

"First of all, don't ever call me brother. Consider me your enemy. What other lies do you want me to hear?" Sami still felt the pain in his knuckle. The exhaustion from detasseling seeping through his hands, legs, and all over his body. Most of all, he was touched by the physical drain of energy his wife had experienced during this time. She'd taken time off from work to help him when he'd told her that they would get over two thousand dollars, an assumption based on them doing twenty acres at the rate of at least $150, if not two hundred dollars, per acre. Sami wondered what he would tell her now.

"Today is payday, and if you are available around 9:00 a.m., I would like to go with you to the bank."

Another long silence.

"Did you hear what I said?" Thoma asked. "I will pick you up."

"You know my address. Send it by mail."

"I need your signature to release the amount."

Sami knew he had time. He thought of demanding that Thoma send his check by mail, but he was not sure about the signature. After a little hesitation, he agreed to go with him to the bank. He could not trust Thoma anymore.

Thoma was with his wife and another of his close henchmen. They drove to the credit union in silence, and just before they reached it, Thoma handed Sami a check for two thousand dollars in Sami's name, in an envelope addressed to Thoma, and went over the procedure again.

"As you can see, this check is in your name, but some of the money belongs to other crew members who worked in various fields. Per our calculations, your amount is four hundred dollars, but I have included a bonus of a hundred dollars for your good work. As I told you earlier, I had to distribute the money to other crew members. You will get some money through a tax refund as well."

Sami quickly shot back, "The crew members you are talking about did not work in my field. How can they get the share of my sweat?"

Thoma's friend jumped in. "The company calculated all the acres together and provided money based on the acres completed by a sub-contractor. They do not care how many people worked on those acres. They only issue one check based on a specific number of fields." He glanced at Thoma.

"He's right, and I think I have already mentioned this to you as well." Just as Sami was about to speak, Thoma raised his hand for attention. "Let me clarify. The fields you worked in and all the surrounding fields worked by other crew members were put under one subcontractor, and they issued a check under one name. I instructed them to do that because I can trust you. Again, the subcontractors, like you, get a bonus. The company considered that you were all working for me. They then divided the fields into blocks of fifty acres, and at forty dollars per acre, the amount under your name was about two thousand. You know very well that you did not work fifty acres, right?" Thoma looked at Sami.

"You can show him the list of other crew members' names, Thoma," his friend interjected.

"Sure. As you can see, here are the names of the subcontractors." Thoma showed Sami the list.

Thomas's friend moved his arm to reveal the hidden butt of a pistol.

Sami looked at the henchman, his eyes darting back and forth. He could not even see the man's face. He wore dark, glossy sunglasses; the only part that Sami could see was his thick, crooked rust-red teeth, with a missing gap in his lower protruding jaw. Sami could not stand the reeking, repulsive odor from his mouth. The man wore a hoody and appeared ruthless.

"Where is the signature you talked about?" Sami inquired.

"Cash out the money first and meet us here. We will be waiting in the car, and then I will distribute it later to the rest of the subcontractors like you," Thoma instructed.

The moment he cashed the check, Sami hesitated. Thoughts ran through his mind. As he walked away from the teller, he wondered whether he'd done the right thing. Something in him told him to keep all the money. Another part of him hesitated. He returned to the counter and deposited $850 into his account.

Sami entered the car. Thoma asked his wife to drive to an isolated park. She stopped the car in the parking lot and waited. "We will not get out of the car," Thoma commanded. Trapped in the center, between Thoma and his friend, Sami fidgeted.

"Let me get out of the car first."

"No," the henchman said with a grimace. Sami could sense the unfriendly tone.

"I don't want to hear from you. I work for Thoma, not you. I don't even know your name, and why are you here in the first place?"

"It's okay, Sami. He's my friend and a partner. His name is George. There will be no problem." Thoma looked at his friend. "Right, George?" The henchman nodded, flexing his bicep.

Thoma brought out his calculator and punched in some bogus numbers and formula until he came up with a number equivalent to the acres worked. "Give me the money."

Sami pulled out the envelope and handed it to him.

"It's $850 short," said Thoma. "I gave you a check for two thousand dollars."

"I deposited the rest. My share for ten acres, according to our agreement."

"Thoma and his friend looked at each other.

"What! Can I finish him off right now?" Thoma's friend said, revealing the full length of the revolver.

"Wait, George, put that thing back. Am I hearing what you're hearing? You mean you are keeping other people's money? I have explained to you the procedure, and you better come to your senses. I need the rest of the money by tomorrow, or else." Thoma did not complete the sentence.

George finished for him. "You don't want the papers to cover the sad accident of the foreign student in Ames with four orphaned children and a widowed wife. What a tragedy. You don't want your friends to read that." He kept his gaze on Sami.

Thoma continued. "Your amount is five hundred dollars, as I said earlier, for detasseling this season."

Sami now believed that Thoma's strategy was a bogus scheme to cheat and take advantage of international students. Why would a company issue a check in his name as a sub-contractor if they suspected that the money was not for him?

They would never conspire with Thoma about this back deal.

"You know what? I am not as greedy as you think. The check was in my name, and I should have kept everything. I was kind enough to accept the minimum you offered in the beginning and kept the amount according to our agreement of seventy-five dollars per acre. I have added the hundred-dollar bonus you promised, although I deserved more. Stop threatening me. I have called my wife from the bank's telephone booth and told her everything. I will also make a report to the police if you keep threatening me. Right now, my wife knows that I am with you, your wife, and this man. If anything happens to me, she will report this information to the police and all the other documentation that I made in the field. I am sure you and your wife have children to worry about in case the police come after you for these illegal activities."

Nobody spoke for a while. Thoma, his wife, and his friend talked in their African language, which Sami did not understand. His wife appeared agitated, and from the way she threw her hands up, Sami concluded that she did not want any trouble. They argued, and then Thoma spoke with a conciliatory tone.

"Sami, I have been very truthful with you about this money. There is no need for us to resort to violence over this, and you don't need to go to the police. We can resolve this through our African ways. Right now, the temperature is rising, George and I agreed that we could sort this out, and you will hear from me this evening or tomorrow." He looked at Sami." Going to the police will worsen things for you. Don't even think about it. They won't help you. There are so many ways that I can get back to you. Do you know this, man?"

The henchman showed the full revolver.

* * *

That evening, Sami's wife answered the phone, and somebody with hoarse voice warned, "Tell that husband of yours to act wisely. Otherwise, you and your children will be at risk. I am sure you don't want to lose your beautiful children." The caller paused and added, "Calling the police or anybody else will hurt you. Tell him to return the money, and we will forget everything. I repeat. Return the money."

When Sami returned from the grocery store, he found his wife frantic and in distress. "I knew this detasseling thing would come to no good. What happened?"

After he told her the whole story, he added, "I kept the money that I worked for, and I intend to keep it."

Sarah started crying. "No, you have to give back the amount he requested. You cannot take this risk and destroy us. I take the threat seriously. We can get money in the future, but our lives are precious. I will not allow it. Give me his number."

Sami arched his brows, twisting the side of his mouth. "Are you out of your mind? Why put yourself in a vulnerable situation? Leave this thug to me. Okay, I will return the amount, but you better keep out of this." Sami had no intention of returning the $350. He just wanted his wife to calm down. "Thoma has a lot to lose if he continues playing this game. We will report to the police if there is any more telephone harassment. By the way, we need to record the voice just in case. We can also change our phone number tomorrow."

Sami turned to his wife. "In the meantime, give me the number. I will call back. I suggest you take the kids to the playground. I don't want them to overhear our conversation when I call. I will arrange a plan," he lied.

Sami dialed the number and realized that it was to a payphone. He then called Thoma's home phone number and got him on the phone. "Thoma, I want you to leave my family and me alone. I will not return the money. I have told all my friends about your threat. We have also recorded the threatening phone messages you or somebody left. If you don't stop, I will share everything with the university police and the Ames police as well. I have documented everything and will indicate that you threatened my family and me. Then the police will have full information." He paused. "Stop threatening me. By the way, I can also hire somebody to target you, and I know who can do it."

Sami kept silent for two days pondering over the incident that happened. He still regretted why he did not keep all the money that landed in his hand, and then he remembered the subtle death threat from the henchman. He had not even seen his face.

* * *

Sami switched his mind to the discussions he'd had with Kumar about his wife's refusal to go along with his plan. "It's not against the law to marry after you divorce your wife, and on paper, everything will be within the legal parameters." Sami had argued with Kumar over this point several times, and his words still echoed.

"Forget the moral side of this issue until you get the card in your hand." Kumar had followed this with another reminder: "You can pretend to be somebody else."

Sami turned the words over in his head. Deep down in his heart, he knew the answer, but he was afraid to face it. Furthermore, he intended to get the green card, just like Kumar and others had, even if it was through illegal means, but it never occurred to him that what he planned to do was unlawful.

The word "illegal" was repulsive; some people even said "aliens." These words conjured in his mind a stream of thoughts. It was an impertinence, to say the least, for all those good people like Jose, officially unwelcome, whose only crime was to be in a place they were not allowed.

That's it. Sami took a deep breath. *I am going to tell Sarah the truth. The whole truth, without holding back anything. Yes.* He nodded to himself as if a great idea had landed on him that he could grasp and bring to the reality of his world. However, he had been in this mood for a long time and knew it was not as easy a task as his mind led him to believe. This matter was out of the ordinary, and even a twisted thought would have to have a real justification. The alternative option would be for Sami not to say anything to his wife in detail but give her only the information needed to raise her hopes.

Either way, the seed of discord had already taken root. He knew how she'd reacted earlier, and he would not just pop in and introduce the topic again, especially after the incident of the money mischief. At one time, he had planned to announce the plan once he'd earned the right amount of money from the detasseling. Now that the outcome of the detasseling had become evident, he had to bring himself to deliver lousy news about two things at the same time. It would be a heavy dose to swallow.

Chapter 26

"Father of Hawa, come and give me a hand," Sarah called from the inner room.

Sami had hoped for this moment. It was one of those rare occasions when his wife would sparkle. Her face glittered like a faraway star on a cloudless sky, exuding serene composure.

"Here." she handed him the curtain to hang. Sami felt unexpected satisfaction, hoping that he would get time to converse and share memories about the good old days. He often used such moments to talk about general things about living in an atmosphere of tranquility. He glanced at her, checking whether her mood was in the right spot, especially in the way she said his name, with a melodic tone using the traditional recognition, "father of Hawa," after his elder daughter.

Life, consumed by the daily struggle of maintaining the basic needs of survival, had revolved around school, work, and children. As Sami looked back, he realized how much he'd missed. A nostalgic feeling of euphoria of bygone days swept through his mind. It had been precisely twelve years ago when he'd gotten married, and he felt he did not know this woman, who, at one time, had appeared robust, calm, and full of energy, with a presence that would make all the problems dissolve.

The irony of life comes in many forms, and if Sami could identify when the mood changes reappeared, he would replicate and devise a strategy to harness the root source of this happy moment. Looking at his wife, he had mixed feelings. He did not want to spoil her mood by giving her news that she might not approve. He weighed his options and concluded that it would be better to deliver an unpleasant message to a person who was in a good mood.

Sami knew his wife would have the next day off. What perfect timing, he reasoned. She would stay up a little later than usual to watch David Letterman's late-night talk show if she had the next day off.

Sami sat close to his wife. She looked at him, knowing something was coming her way.

"It's about the green card. Do you remember some of the options I mentioned to you a while back?" He waited for her to respond.

"The crazy stuff you talked. What about it? There were all kinds of options you brought up. So what?" She shrugged slightly.

He glanced at her to make sure that her mood was still in perfect state. She nodded.

Sami allowed a moment of silence to slip in. Then he said, "I don't imagine doing it in the real sense, but if we need to get this card, I want you to consider it." His wife showed a strange reaction on her face. She appeared lost for a while.

"I don't understand what you mean. Do what?"

"Let me put it this way. I have to marry this lady to get a green card."

"You know my stance. What do you want me to do?"

He looked in her direction. "I need a document to prove that I can marry. We would have to pretend that we are no longer together and produce a document that says we are divorced. I know how strange and bizarre it sounds, but we are the only people who will know the truth."

Sarah turned and twisted her face in the manner of a person confronted with a repugnant odor, and she let out a sudden guffaw and mocking gesture. She stood up and went to the inner room. With one glance in her direction, Sami knew he had blown it again.

He tried the bolted door and sighed. *What a buffoon, and I knew it.* As he paced the tiny living room, he rebuked himself for causing such a blunder. He might as well make himself comfortable on the sofa tonight. He tried the door one more time, but without success.

"Mother of Hawa, let me finish." He tried the door again. "I have weighed this matter seriously and come to this awkward decision. As I told you, the woman is there for the money and is not in it for any close relationship." He waited. "Are you listening? Other people have used this approach, and the woman herself has done it three times before." Sami tried to make the situation appear simple. He had to beg her to come back and listen to what he had to say. It took a while for him to calm her. She unlocked the door and stood in the doorway.

"You're telling me to lie and drop everything that I have ever learned, and I can't stoop so low. It is very demeaning. You make me feel cheap and dirty. No, no, this corrupt choice is not for me. Do it without me." Her appearance suddenly changed.

"Calm down, please. I was telling you what is available. I heard many people had done the same thing, and it was perfectly okay."

"I can't believe that you said this is okay. No, no, it's not okay for a married person to engage in this. As I said, I will not be part of this."

"The transaction is strictly for business, with a fixed amount of $4,500."

Sarah raised her eyebrows. "Was that the deal you were offered?" Sami could see her instantaneous reaction, as her eyes opened wide and her mouth gaped. Sarah held both of her cheeks.

Sami continued. "After I finalize the legal document, I can then initiate the divorce process and get back to you and our normal life."

Sarah stood motionless. "Are you telling me that you were already in contact with this whore? How could you sink this low? What a disgrace! How could you even have considered this possibility in the first place?" She slammed the door to the inner room and then opened it suddenly and shouted, "If you get your green card through this filthy way, what about me? Marry somebody else, too!" She shut the door again and added, "Where will you get this kind of money anyway?"

Sami tried the bolted door again. He could hear her sniffling on the other side. He put his ears to the door; a soft sobbing sound reached him.

"Can you open the door, please? I will explain it. There is a serious misunderstanding." There was no sign of her reaction. He continued. "Please hear me out, and I can explain how it works. Remember, once I get the green card, everything will happen, as I stated. We will be together again. I guarantee this will not involve our physical separation, nor will I have any physical contact with her. The woman lives in this city. I don't have to go far in case I need something." Sami knew he was repeating the same words over and over. He paused, making sure that she was listening. "I have been struggling with this decision for a while. We are together as a team. Nobody else should know about this, and there's no way anybody else will know anyway."

"You have already decided, so why bother telling me about it now?" Sarah said, her voice inaudible. "How can your consciousness entertain this bizarre illegal idea?"

Sami did not offer any other explanation. He knew his wife had decided. Later, long after his wife had gone to bed, he lay down on the sofa and thought over all the options and considered how it would work. Having made this crucial decision, he decided to stick to it and make it work. That night, the sleep did not come on time. He tossed a load of guilt off his chest. He didn't know whether he'd eased his burden, but at least he had a feeling that the problem was not going to get worse. A sort of satisfaction came over his mind.

For the next few days, Sami and his wife did not talk to each other. There was nothing to talk about regarding the hasty decision he'd made. It had disrupted their inner thought processes. Sami could see the snapshot aimed at him from all directions. A slight drop of a spoon on the floor could be a cause for a quarrel. A minor issue with the children, one that would usually be insignificant, suddenly became a big one to deal with. Everything that went on inside the house had been laid bare and scrutinized. A reign of gloomy trepidation continued to linger and remained unchanged for several days. The children ceased to play. A sudden drastic rule became effective and enforced. Strict discipline became the norm, and instant punishment for misbehavior followed immediately. A terror in the form of silence descended over the family corner. The two adults in the house imposed a strict curfew on themselves. The kids looked from one to another and understood something was going on, but they didn't dare intervene. It was a situation that had to be left alone. Only time would sort it out.

***

At work, Sami and his evening crew went on with their regular cleaning job. "Hey, amigo, how did detasseling go?" asked Jose.

"Not good. I got ripped off." Sami was not in the mood to discuss his ordeal.

"I made some money and helped my friends from Texas as well. Better than last year." Jose twisted his face into a bitter expression. "The middleman did it again, and I swear next year things will be different."

'What will you do, knock him off?" Pablo laughed.

"He preyed on the vulnerability of those people without legal documents. This exploitation and cheating will continue. I understand it was our fault. We avoided publicity and exposure to escape deportation and accepted the lesser of the two evils." Jose nodded.

It was Sami's turn to vent his grievances about the detasseling. "I did ten acres and got seventy-five dollars per acre."

"You got a better deal, amigo, and should not have complained." Further probing revealed that Jose had hoodwinked his friends, too. After all, he was the middleman. "I am curious to know, Jose, how does the middleman work?" Sami asked.

"Okay, amigo. I tink it may be different for different groups, but it worked for me. I would bring a certain number of people to a contractor and tell him that I had a crew for detasseling. He would then agree to a rate of payment, probably lower than the prevailing market, because the contractor had to get a cut. I would negotiate the payment rate. You know, most of them don't have documents. Other people would give them a bare minimum amount per acre worked and then keep the difference. I gave them an extra dollar above the minimum, and they were fine."

Pablo was not amused. "You exploited them, too. I don't see any difference."

"No, I did not. Amigo, each of my crew, got about three hundred dollars for the two weeks they helped."

"How much per acre?" Pablo asked.

"They worked together, so I could not pay them per acres

worked."

"You paid them per hour worked? Let's see. They worked for fifteen days, and each day was eight hours. That adds up to 120 hours of work, and if you paid them three hundred dollars each, how much was their hourly wage? Not much. You should have paid them at least four dollars per hour."

Jose looked at Pablo as if he wanted to strangle him. "There were other expenses that I took upon myself, lodging, and food." To Pablo, he said, "You did not get a contract, and I am sure you feel jealous, right?" His face crinkled in sarcastic laughter.

"Jose," Sami said, bringing the attention of the group back to him again, "Did you also get some money from your tax return?"

"You pay taxes on all the money you earn. You know that already, and if you signed a contract for a significant amount of money, get ready for Uncle Sam's tax for the government to dip into your pocket."

Sami kept silent, but Pablo laughed loudly. "Criminals don't file a tax return. If they do, they cheat."

Jose turned to Sami. "Something wrong, amigo?" Sami realized he'd gotten lost in his thoughts. "No, I just remembered something else. I am fine. It's about the contractor I worked for."

"Amigo, with a little fee, I can arrange for someone to straighten out this guy."

"What do you mean, Jose?"

Jose smiled. "There are many people who can fix things for a small fee. I think Pablo can do it as well, although he appears secretive."

"Sure, Jose. I can do a better job than you. A clean slate," Pablo replied.

"No, Jose, I don't want to do any harm." Sami shook his head.

"No sympathy for a person like that, you know. He will keep exploiting other students. You will need to stop him. I consider you a friend, and in my world, we protect each other. Right, Pablo?"

Pablo agreed.

"Let me know if you change your mind. I can fix a smooth accident," Jose added.

"Thanks. You've scared me. I won't go that route," Sami acknowledged. "I am curious, though. How do you do it?"

"Pablo, how did you do it? Tell him." Jose nudged him.

"I won't tell that to a soul. You know that Jose." Pablo smiled.

"Or do you delegate to your weed-smoking buddies?" Jose laughed.

Sami joined the laughter. The break ended, and they all rushed to work.

Chapter 27

The next day, Sami came home and found his wife in a gloomy mood. His demeanor changed suddenly. "Did something happen at home again?"

Sarah did not respond. She pointed to the statement of a bill. The charges were from the clinic during the emergency visit when his son had cut his foot. A portion of the fees already paid through the state's children's insurance, but they had to pay the remaining balance of $450.

Sami put the statement on the little table. "You don't have to be sad. We can pay it off little by little."

"I guess we still have the money from the detasseling that you saved. We can use part of the money to pay off this debt," she suggested.

"We can pay slowly." Sami's voice quivered, fearing the surreptitious exposure of his plan for the money from the detasseling.

"A social worker stopped by our house today, supposedly to find out how we were doing."

"What do you mean? What did they ask you?"

"The usual things, always suspecting that we are not up to the job, asking me why I was not with the children. As if they care more for my children than I do."

"What else?"

"She gave me some coupons for some discount stores and contact information in case I needed to talk with some women support groups."

"Interesting." Sami got curious. "Did you call them?

"Not from the list she gave me. I also received some immigrant contact information.

"Tell me about it!" His appetite for this news began to rise.

"Some of those women used their cultural practices as justification to support their claim for not going back to their countries of origin. I cannot believe the things they said to stay in this country. One of them told me that she sought political asylum because she came from a troubled country."

"We all came from unstable and dysfunctional countries. What was the story about?"

"In her village back home, they practiced circumcision of young girls, and she feared for her daughter."

Sami laughed and stopped when his wife shot a disapproving look at him.

"Give me a break. As if she doesn't have any control over her six-year-old daughter? What a bunch of baloney. Nowadays, most governments are opposed to this practice."

Another frown from his wife. "What?" Sami asked.

"Aren't you doing the same thing?" Sarah shot him a disapproving glare.

Sami stopped halfway through the sentence. "I meant the reason was overused and seemed obvious. My case is different."

Sarah looked in the direction of the noise. The kids were fighting over a toy. She rushed to the scene to separate the two warring parties. "Give me that," she demanded. "Both of you will be in time out. Adam! Move to that corner over there and sit down. Chaaltu, go to the other end of the room and sit down."

Chaaltu obeyed the stern command. Adam, on the other

hand, was still crying. "One more warning." Sarah held her hand up. "I will ground you for one week." She stood her ground.

Adam was not entirely quiet. "She started it and snatched my toy first and refused to take turns," he said, his voice, between sobs, catching in a hiccup.

"I will deal with her later. Stop crying now."

Beyond that, Adam knew he could not win against his mother. She was a master of discipline and would not entertain any further discussions.

"What else did you learn from those women? I bet they were a bunch of feminists trying to influence innocent immigrant women. I heard some of them drive wedges between families in the name of progress and liberation for women."

"The women talked about their truth and the injustice that they confronted every day in their daily lives."

"Some of those women are notorious for destroying families and separating husbands and wives. I hope they don't confuse you into thinking that they can solve all your problems." Sami waited for her response.

He did not want to appear as if he were opposing his wife's views. Sami made some comments about gender issues in the past and got into trouble with his wife. Anytime he gave his opinion about women's issues, she became offended and protective. She condemned him as a macho and sexist or showered him with whatever label people use for gender sensitivity issues. Sarah would find quotes and prove the horror women undergo daily. Then she would add, "I am not saying this to seek any sympathy."

Sami stood up to stretch, waiting for the opportune moment to appear.

His wife pointed to a letter on the table. "The admission letter."

"I still have to figure out how to finance the program unless they provide a full assistantship."

"I thought that was the reason why you selected this department."

"Yes, but you're not guaranteed to get an assistantship. One has to apply and compete with the rest of the applicants. If only we had the document." He switched the topic. It was this single idea that their lives would improve when they got a proper document that kept driving him. It had become an obsession, a goal without which their American dream would never materialize. Sarah remained silent.

"I got the application paper," Sami reminded her. After she did not respond, he continued. "It just needs your signature. I hate to bring this up again, and as I said, it sickens me to bring the sanctity of marriage into this process, but the signature is just a formality that we arranged. It does not change the facts as we know them. It is a paper and not real. You will not be required at the court if the document is signed."

Still no response. Sami continued.

"Think about the result for both of us." Sami thought he had explained what this would mean. He had been explicit in his explanation about his role and made it clear to her so many times. "You can sign on the highlighted signature page, my dear. You will see a bold word with a 'sign here' arrow. I have it in this manila envelope. I will put it beside your bedside reading table. Read through it, and I will initiate the process next week." With that, he concluded his final appeal.

Sarah glanced at the envelope once and then looked away.

Sami realized that telling his wife that everything would be okay had not convinced her to implement an action that would nullify her marriage. Her understanding was different, and the signing of the paper was tantamount to ending what she believed in, even if, as he'd said, this was a fake process to free him to marry the other woman on paper. It was this fact of lying that she could not come to terms with. Sami, on the other hand, took the whole thing differently. He believed that if he still lived with his family and only limited his activities to the document and what he needed to do to facilitate it, things would go as planned. With Sami, it was easy. He thought his wife shouldn't make a big deal out of it since they would still be living together, and he would not be living with the other woman.

Sami found this situation acceptable, though a little odd, and he believed that this could be the simplest thing to do, except, of course, for the part about lying and cheating. He still had to figure out how he would live with the memory throughout his life. The only thing he needed to worry about was how to raise the money.

Chapter 28

For the next few days, life went on as usual. Sami reminded his wife about the document one more time and then decided to give her two more days to think. He turned his attention to the job search and applied for a recently advertised job. He sifted through the mail, picked up the job rejection letters he'd received, shuffled them, and threw them in the trash with a thrust. It was a display intended to show frustration.

Sarah watched. "I will be back in less than an hour. I am meeting with our neighbor Lucy and other women at her house. Take the kids to the playground. My friend's kids will be there, as well."

"Okay, no problem. Have fun." Sami looked on as his wife grabbed the homemade cookies she prepared. The women occasionally shared recipes and other amenities from their respective countries. Indefatigable, she looked forward to meeting with these women. Most of them were stay-at-home moms. A little time together must have provided them the sanity they needed to survive the turmoil of their daily lives.

"Does Lucy live alone with her children? Where are they from?"

"Guyana. She lives alone with her children. She wrote a good recommendation letter for my job. The others are from Brazil, Jamaica, Sudan, India, Ghana, Gabon, Congo, Nigeria, and Mali." Sarah stepped out.

Sami continued to fantasize about the opportunities that would become available to him when he got the card, including government loans to finance his education.

Days passed. The monotonous daily life of work continued unabated, a sharp reminder of the lives in America.

One Saturday morning, one of the rare moments when Sami and his wife were at home together. The nature of their jobs would not allow them the luxury of being at home together during the weekends. A day that one of them was not working left a financial gap in their meager income.

Sami no longer took things lightly. Whether he deserved this kind of life or not was a question that resided, dormant, at the back of his mind. It did not bother him as it used to. In the world he'd been brought up in, one would go through a sort of linear pattern, with the educated group having distinctive roles and getting the best positions.

"Let's face it," Sami said. "This is our reality now. I don't want to go on like this. We have already decided to go this route."

Sarah jerked her head. With some papers in his hands, Sami stood over her as she sat. She looked up, not sure what to make of this intrusion. "It is not perfect. It is not normal. It is even immoral and unethical, as you said. Call it whatever you want to," he continued. His voice raised to a peak. "In a normal circumstance, I would not have thought of this approach. Look at how we live. Think of what we would have accomplished if only..." He deliberately left the word hanging. He had recently acquired a manner of speech that questioned all that he did. He fished the two-page document from the manila envelope and thrust right in front of her face.

"You did not sign it." Sarah faced him. From the way he held the document, she had no choice but to pick it. Sami pointed to the page. "Sign here and here. You've had over three days to make up your mind." He guided her with his fingers. "That's all we need, and then we will wait for less than a year and then be back together."

Nobody else will know, he said to himself.

Sarah had thought about this for weeks and weeks and concluded that she would not go along with it. For her, it was an issue of right and wrong and would not be convinced. She'd also weighed the pros and cons. As always, she would rely on her intuition and say no. At first, she'd thought of consulting her friend, but her recent encounter with other women of similar backgrounds had given her something to ponder. She had to rely on her gut feelings and would not consult another person for something she knew was wrong. Sarah knew her instincts were right, although blurred by the chaos of their lives.

Deep inside her heart, a fear resided, fear of loss, and it had something to do with the nature of the work and the life they led. A soft voice whispered in her mind. *Are you afraid of losing this marriage?* She was not sure whether to protect the union or her integrity or even the truth. A feeling of guilt tainted with revenge acrimoniously swept over her thoughts. A silent consolation from her inner soul would bring a temporary relief with which she hoped to gain a little confidence that things would be better. When choices are limited, one will take whatever becomes available. Sarah had to face things and believe her intuition was right, although some strange ideas were creeping into her mind. After her full-term job as a social worker, she'd added nutrition, health, and wellness certifications, including mental health. All these had improved her chances of getting a job at a mental health clinic. She had some confidence that things would be better, and she did not need to break the rules to get the legal document.

Sarah looked at the document, making sure that it was the

same one Sami had given her and put back the papers without signing. She placed the envelope on the small table where they kept mail, took out another sheet of blank paper, and wrote, "I will not sign this demeaning and degrading document."

She stepped out of the room immediately. She didn't need anything from outside other than to get some fresh air. Sami, in the meantime, was watching her closely. He was not sure what she had done.

"Are you all right?" He opened the door halfway and noticed that she was sitting.

Sarah did not even look at him. She just sat as if nothing had happened, engrossed in a world of her own, contemplating and oblivious to her surroundings. Sami thought it would be nice not to disrupt her thought processes. He wondered whether she could be in the same thinking mood as he was. He had often fought the idea out of his mind, and whenever it popped up, he remembered his children and the struggle he'd undertaken. He'd often wondered whether it was worthy of going. Each time he sank to the lowest depths, a renewed resurgence of spirit revived him again. Determined to move on with challenges, he weighed his whole life and scrutinized it from the perspective of a person making a long journey, not a small series of trips filled with bumps.

Kumar might have some solutions, he thought.

Chapter 29

The next day, Sami called Kumar to arrange a meeting with him a little before he went to see Jasmine.

"My wife did not buy into this idea and won't sign the document. Do you think it is a dead-end?" Sami sighed.

"Not at all," Kumar replied. "Divorce in this country is not as complicated as you might think. Iowa is a no-fault divorce state, and you don't need the consent of the other partner. And you don't need an attorney to initiate the process. A simple citation of irreconcilable differences is enough to end the marriage."

Sami squinted, not sure he understood him.

"You want the document to look real? let me show you." Kumar leaned forward. "Do you have the application form that I told you to bring with you?"

"Oh, here. I have it." Sami gave him a folder. "She did not sign it."

Kumar took the form and browsed through the pages.

"What's her name?"

"Sarah."

"A beautiful name." He flipped through the pages. "I can see that you did everything else, just like in the sample. Don't sweat over little things." Kumar smiled and handed the form back to Sami.

"You can take it to the county clerk this week. I could come along with you if you want," Kumar suggested.

Sami nodded with a gaping mouth. Then he appeared calm and thoughtful.

"By the way, you have settled everything with Jasmine, right?" Kumar asked.

"Sure, I will be meeting with her soon. In about fifteen minutes before I get to work. I have to go now."

"Okay. If you ever need anything else, let me know," Kumar added.

The meeting with Jasmine was very brief. Sami gave her five hundred dollars in an envelope and left. He observed that she was not in a jovial mood like the other time he'd met her. She had something on her mind, and he was not sure whether to engage her in a conversation or not. Besides, he had very little time before work. He apologized and left.

"Wait." Jasmine took his hand. "When will I see you again?" She hesitated before continuing. "I mean, if you're ready for the process, I guess. Here is my number. A new number just in case."

"Is Antonio bothering you again?" Sami asked.

"I hope not. We had some discussions, and I am fine if he keeps away. He was working but did not want to tell me where."

Sami noticed a fearful expression on her face. "This Antonio guy has changed your mood. Are you hiding something from me?"

"I don't want to see him. He can be a stumbling block, jealous with rage, and can destroy our plans. If he shows up at my place, I will have to think a way of getting rid of him."

"What? Is he such a terrible person? What exactly are you afraid of?"

"He can blackmail me. I wish I'd never met him; Antonio has no remorse and would even sell out his mother." Jasmine shivered as she said this.

Sami processed the message and downplayed the tension by changing the topic. "After you change phones, the next step is to change your location. You can report him and get a restraining order."

Sami, you don't know what this guy is capable of. As I said, if he shows up, I will find ways to get rid of him, but I will not involve the cops."

"We will talk later, Jasmine. Thanks, and read my note enclosed in the envelope."

Sami was somewhat in a hurry to leave for the meatpacking factory. His mind constantly bogged down with all the other family and financial issues, yet he failed to understand her fears. However, he knew Jasmine had something on her mind and was choosing not to disclose it. He decided not to indulge in it either at that moment. Despite his aloof attitude, though, he had brought upon himself an extra burden. The saga of marriage for a green card looked good on paper, but Sami had not put the human faces to it. Physical appearance could be deceiving and misinterpreted. There were all those emotions and mental agony that one could go through, and one would never know just by looking at a person.

He noticed his wife's foggy appearance, devoid of vigor, and no matter how one looked at it, Sami had to admit that his wife was right about the purported document. It was a divorce whether he pretended and called it fake or not. She stopped talking to him and kept to herself, working overtime with disabled children to stay busy. Sami had less time to speak with her, and even his children had accepted the pattern of their daily lives. Sami believed that his wife was now a total stranger, and her thought processes were diametrically out of line with his point of view.

Sami met Kumar two days later in the parking lot of the

county courthouse. Kumar went through the document again and filled in some parts correctly, making sure that Sami followed the example. "I will wait for you in the parking lot. You can go now," Kumar suggested.

With his heart pounding, Sami presented his document to the county court clerk. The clerk looked over the papers and told him that the court would issue a final divorce decree within ninety days. Sami also learned that while there was no waiting period needed for him to initiate a remarriage, it would be a good idea to wait until he received the decision of the court.

"Congratulations, Sami," said Kumar. "That was the first step, and I am sure things will get smoother. By the way, have you heard from Jasmine lately?"

"No, why? Is there anything that I need to know? I met with her two days ago."

"She mentioned her family issues earlier. You also know about her former husband, Antonio. He's a criminal who will do anything. She's afraid of possible blackmail. She will let you know if there is any problem, I guess, but don't worry. She's solid."

"I hope so," Sami said. "Hey, I am going back to school just in case. Do you have any idea how long the whole process will take.?"

"Probably about a year or so. Why?"

"Just concerned about the expiration of my visa. I have to be in school to maintain my status."

"What area? No luck in your field of study? You better select one where there are job opportunities, like technology and health," Kumar advised.

"To be frank with you, the choice of my career in animal science was by accident. I got a scholarship opportunity and grabbed it, but I did not have a strong passion for the field. I am afraid the same thing will happen to me again with the future decision of going back to school."

"Another scholarship?"

"I have to keep my visa status. Unfortunately, I would take any assistantship they offered. The sad fact is, I don't have many options to consider."

"I think you have a choice, Sami. You must liberate your mind from your limiting attitude. You're in America, the land of vast opportunities, where you can envision, dream big, and create a future for yourself."

"Kumar, I am more worried about my current situation, which I cannot fix than the future."

"It's in your mind. I've listened to several motivational speakers, and all of them emphasize positive attitude, strong convictions, and a belief that you can achieve whatever you want if you vividly create a mental image in your mind."

"I don't know, Kumar. I have been looking for a job for the last two years. If you think it is about my mental attitude, my mind is already saturated."

"Anyway, good luck. Don't be too hard on yourself. People have failed and risen. Keep your mind on the target. Okay, I have to go."

After Kumar left, Sami thought over the discussions they'd had and shifted his attention to school, which he knew best.

Chapter 30

"I am here to see Professor Wheeler," Sami announced. The secretary lifted her head without saying a word and pointed to a chair to wait.

Professor Wheeler, the head of the department of plant physiology, was stout and bald. He didn't have the patience for those who took his time more than he could allow. He would set a timer and expected the students to get to the point. He had no time for any discussions outside of what the students came for. He would not entertain any "mumbo-jumbo" social preliminaries that people got involved in, and he was known for being direct and to the point. When the time was up, he would stand up to let students know it was time to go. Sami had heard from other students that the professor was not very friendly. However, that was also subject to individual interpretation.

Sami took the news with anticipation, creating in his mind a mental image of the horrible situation that he would face. He knew students could be biased and, if they didn't like a professor, they would always have something negative to say about him or her.

Equipped with a load of worries and confusion, Sami waited to see the department head of the newly created department. Professor Jonathan Wheeler was the favorite candidate for this job. After a brief internal selection to choose the best and most qualified candidate, he got the position, but the rumor was that he'd gotten it because his wife and the dean's wife were twin sisters.

Sami focused on what he wanted to ask. When it was his turn to go in, the professor got a telephone call, and Sami had to wait. After what seemed to be an extended waiting period, Sami was ushered into a big office and came face to face with the professor he admired and had heard about so much.

"What can I do for you?" Professor Wheeler asked.

Sami saw a timer on the desk. "My name is Sami, and I got the assistantship that you offered me. Thank you."

The professor looked up with a startled expression on his face, wondering why he needed to hear Sami's name since he already knew it from the appointment made. Sami continued.

"Sir, is it possible to get a half-term assistantship?" The professor appeared confused by the way Sami addressed him. An old habit does not fade away quickly. Sami was not yet fully adjusted to the nuances and practices of interacting with Americans, who didn't seem to care for titles.

"We have many applicants, and that was how much we could offer. With the quarter-assistantship, you can pay in-state tuition, and that will be helpful. Any other questions?"

The professor did not ask him about anything else, his interests, or what he could offer. He didn't even ask him whether he had a family or not or from where he came. In the society where Sami had grown up, people would inquire about each other's affairs and show concerns, and they were willing to give a helping hand. Sami still wasn't accustomed to this individualistic kind of behavior. The quarter-assistantship he would get was about five hundred dollars, and he would work ten hours a week. He had to buy books, pay tuition, and buy health insurance. They insisted that he buy the insurance for himself, but he could not afford the family package.

Sami had done his research and found out that the department had money and allocated some percentages for minority applicants. While he considered himself a minority, as an outsider and non-citizen, he had little chance for consideration. Sami learned that people of color were not the only minorities; others were Caucasian women and immigrants from Asia. This was not what Sami had envisioned. The color of one's skin was not the only determining factor, and the field was more crowded than Sami had previously imagined. This loophole allowed employers to do what they already had been doing. It was a matter of reinforcing and complying with the rules in the book.

What if the law were to suggest a ratio in each section of the department? With a specific percentage allocated for all qualifying races. This and other thoughts soon began to speed through his mind. The assistantship he'd received was for work with a professor who studied plant evolution, not one of his primary interests. What in the world would he do with a degree in plant physiology, a field where he would deal with the growth of plants?

The professor did not initiate any further discussions and ended the meeting. "Welcome to the department. We have high expectations for our students."

Sami had to readjust his life for the next few days. He could still work at the meatpacking factory from 4:00 p.m., at least for now.

***

"Hey, amigo, what's up!" Jose called from across the lunchroom as Sami entered. "I heard that you're going back to school. Good for you, man. You did the right thing. What are you studying?"

"Plant physiology."

"What is that?"

"It is about plants," Sami said to brush him off.

"What plant?" Jose was not satisfied.

Sami wanted him off this topic. He knew what Jose would ask next. How long would it take, how much it would cost, and what would his salary be if employed? Jose's mind reflected the reality of his own life. Having dropped out of high school, he had seen his classmates continue with education and take positions in government and various industries later. He attributed his status in life due to a lack of education.

Sami would not talk more about this any further. He did not want any questions asked. Sometimes he questioned the point of going back to school again if it meant facing the same struggle, with no job outlook.

"Do you know your class schedule for next semester?" asked Moses.

Sami turned. "Not right now. It may be possible that I go part-time if the schedule causes any conflict."

Moses shook his head. "Part-time will not work very well with this kind of job. Let me know as soon as you confirm your class schedule. Currently, we have no shortage of workers. We have people who are ready to work right now, but I will keep you on standby in case nobody shows up for work."

Moses had overcome the problem of absentee workers by providing them a ride to and from work himself. He had maintained a pool on a waiting list that he could utilize as needed. With the quick turnover of people, he had little options left. More than half of the people working there had been in jail or had some clashes with law somewhere in the state, some with serious crimes.

Sami would miss the company of this group. It was an experience he would never forget, although some of the behavior he saw was despicable. It was this tiny moment of joy that Sami would miss for sure. When the time for parting came, he would leave just the way he had come, and he would probably look for a job with flexible hours compatible with his class schedule. Life had become a permanent move from one misery to the next.

Moses had already spread the word that Sami would probably work only this semester and focus on school. Emilio took up the message and spread it further with a twist. "Sami is going to study weed, marijuana."

Pablo looked at Sami with a sense of euphoria. The mere mention of the word "marijuana" triggered in him a craving for his old habit, which was itching to come out. After he got out of jail, Pablo had tried to reduce this behavior and kept away from it.

"Amigo, I have an idea," Jose said to Sami. "We can make a deal in the backyard here."

Sami was not sure what was going on. He jerked his head. "What?"

"Can I have a word with you in private?"

Sami was not sure what Jose wanted. He hesitated and then stepped aside, closer to Jose.

"I have noticed that behind our parking area, dense trees, and high grass are growing all over. And nobody goes there, and it is very safe."

Sami squinted. "So, what are you getting at?"

Jose looked to see whether anybody else was watching.

"You said you knew how to grow plants, and I can see great financial potential from this backyard. We can grow weed here, and nobody will notice."

Sami froze and quickly looked around. "The place is already overgrown with dense, grassy weeds."

"No, Sami, not that kind, the smoking type. You know what I mean."

Sami realized what Jose meant. "No, Jose. I know nothing about this kind of weed, and I don't want to be part of it. No." Sami shook his head and stepped back. Jose noticed the fearful expression on Sami's face.

"Okay, Sami, I was joking. Remember, you did not hear or see anything." Sami nodded. "Let's join the crew." Jose went ahead and started talking louder. "So, you are studying plants?"

"Yes, I will study all plants and their functions, and the evolution of plant life."

"How many more years?"

Moses answered for Sami before he had a chance to talk. "Two years."

"I will be in Mexico by the time you graduate. Invite me to your graduation two years from now! Oh, man." Jose shook his head.

"It's a long time, yes, unless, of course, you are in jail," Emilio interjected, causing a roar of laughter from the rest of the team.

"What jail? No, unless you sell me out," Jose replied in jest.

"For less than fifty dollars, I would," Emilio added.

"Even your pajada money won't save you."

"I believe you, but you better not think about it." Emilio paused for a moment. "You may not live to enjoy your money." He laughed.

In the meantime, the clock was ticking. Sami turned to Jose and asked, "What is pajada?"

"It is the money for bribery in Honduras. They call it pajada, just like I told you about mordida."

Sami wondered whether this kind of talk was a threat or just jokes between friends. He'd learned during the previous conversation with Jose about people from his part of the world, where one even had to take jokes seriously. People had cliques, just like gangs, and they protected each other and their interests. Those from the same country had a connection based on the city from where they came. They could use the money they earned to protect properties they acquired there or even to ease their way with police using what Jose called *mordida*. A cornerstone of the whole triangle, it was bribe money, or what, in Sami's home country, they called *chai*, something for tea. In other words, the money offered to soften up the corrupt officials.

Jose had said, "Amigo, you better not make enemies with the people of your hometown. You never know what might hit you while you're here or even there. Your property, relatives, and everything you have ever owned could be a target. You do not want everything that you've achieved, all your hard work and the struggles you've gone through here, disintegrate. The worst could be to end up in jail somewhere, where you will remain forgotten for a good number of years in a dreadful, filthy cave of misery. I have seen people destroyed, their whole family wiped out, and nobody questioned them out of fear."

As he drove home from work, Sami reflected on his interactions with Jose and his colleagues. The philosophy of life he'd learned from people like Jose and others who did not have any document was simple. They moved from one state to another, hiding, working there and here and collecting pieces together from wherever of their wretched living conditions that they could. However, in working with Jose, Sami came to realize how knowing a person like him changed one's perceptions about illegal immigrants, and probably about human beings in general. He had seen how hardworking Jose and his friends were. They were amicable and kind people, a joy to work with, with laughter and happiness, taking things one day at a time. They all had families who depended on them for their basic needs, receiving remittance monthly.

All the cynical condemnation about illegals and unbearable situations depicted in the media about their struggle to get into the US and the border problems he'd read about only confirmed his convictions about Jose's resilience and Americans' failure to look at them as human beings. They had great survival instincts, risking jails, deportation, harsh weather conditions, and the perils of the wildness to acquire a decent livelihood. They seemed to be happy and did not dwell on petty things. To Sami, this survival approach to life was indicative of inner strength and flexibility. In his life, Sami had experienced the attitude that one had to wait for something to happen and then react. The inherent nature of human beings was to strive to achieve a better life; even back in the days of hunters and gatherers, the family unit moved in search of food to survive. In today's financial world, the same instinct and drive to better oneself had propelled Jose, Emilio, Sanchos, Petros, and Pablo to take this treacherous journey to the north in search of greener pastures. One should admire their audacity rather than condemn them.

For Sami, at home, things did not change. He and his wife were swamped and yet not making enough, and everything they owned was on credit, a vicious cycle of life, living from paycheck to paycheck, and with no savings. Under these conditions, Sami and his wife remained strangers to each other. They had little reason to interact beyond the regular symbolic connubial gesture of the daily routine with their children.

Chapter 31

Sami came home close to midnight and realized that he had to stay awake to get his homework done. As soon as he opened his school bag, he heard the snapping sound of a mousetrap in the kitchen. He'd used a glue mouse trap previously, and the rats had figured out how to bypass it and got away. He'd then bought a wooden snare. He started getting jittery.

Sami followed the sound and found a rat smashed in the wire trap. He was not ready to battle with this constant nuisance in the house. Roaches were another menace that he dealt with, and he was particularly careful when he opened his school bag. One time, a cockroach followed him to class in it. Sami still remembered when the ugly brown thing crawled out when he took out his book. He quickly covered it under his palm, and nobody saw it, but ever since then, he was overly cautious about his bag. The trouble with crawling things in the house had stressed out his wife as well. Cockroaches were everywhere in the room.

The following day, when Musa saw roaches in the cereal box, he decided never to eat that brand of cereal. He believed that they'd bred in the cereal box, and no pleading with him could convince him otherwise. The other children joined the silent boycott. Their favorite cereal became a haunted object, evoking terrible fear.

Sarah took all the open cereal boxes and disposed of them. She had to go shopping again for breakfast cereal. While helping put away the groceries, Chaaltu grabbed a cereal box, but then dropped it immediately as if she had a hot ember in hand. Sarah ran to her rescue, thinking that she had hurt herself. "What happened?" she asked.

"The roaches." Chaaltu pointed to the cereal.

"I just bought it. How did the roaches get in?"

"The cereal," Chaaltu insisted.

Sarah laughed. "We have not opened the box yet, and we will seal it afterward." It then struck her that the kids were associating the roaches with their favorite cereal. She tried to reassure her daughter that everything would be okay. "We are looking for another apartment until the new university apartment becomes available. We will move out soon. Chaaltu, there are no roaches in the cereal box now." Chaaltu hesitated, still not convinced that the roaches would not return.

Sarah then transferred the breakfast cereal into a plastic container and closed it with a lid.

"Dad!" Chaaltu shouted, eager to get more support.

"Your dad is busy. What do you want?"

"I wanted to see the rat he caught last night."

"Just keep away from the trap," Sarah advised.

***

Sami reviewed his to-do list, which included Jasmine, green card, and Kumar and his new neighbor.

Sami was about to dial the number Jasmine had left for him when the phone rang. He picked it up slowly and listened. He kept quiet as he entered the bedroom and locked the door. "Jasmine, are you okay? I can talk now. Wait, calm down. I can't hear what you're saying. What about Antonio?" Sami waited. He sat on the bed. "What happened?" His voice was no longer a whisper. "What did he do?" He could hear only her sniffling.

I will be there," he confirmed.

Jasmine hung up while still sobbing.

***

Sami knocked and waited. He could sense the long waiting period, indicative of the precautionary measures she was taking. Jasmine opened the door and quickly looked outside as if in anticipation of an intruder. She locked the door and turned the knob, making sure that it remained closed. She then faced Sami slowly and cuddled up against him with teary eyes. "Antonio won't leave me alone." She sighed. Sami could see the fear in her eyes.

"Did he do anything to you.?"

"He tried several times to get me to take him back, but I refused. He then threatened to destroy me."

"How could he do that?" Sami asked innocently.

"Sami, you don't know Antonio. I could have changed my address and telephone number again. Antonio had nothing to lose. He accused me of damaging his reputation and is ready for revenge. He's such a lowlife, and he wants to bring me down to his level." She sobbed.

"I guess he got what he wanted from you. What else was he demanding?"

"Everything. To bleed me dry. The wretched scamp doesn't deserve anything. I can't maintain his addiction, and the sucker wants to drain me of everything I ever owned."

"Did you file a report?"

"No, I won't. I fear worse things will happen if I do."

"I don't know how you can live in this condition. You must do something about it. You should report it. Send Antonio to jail. Otherwise, you will be in constant fear. I am sure that's not how you want to live your life."

"I will give him one more warning, and then he will never

bother me again. I have planned the strategy out already. It's a perfect plan, but I need help." She looked at him with a pleading gaze.

Sami was ready to help if she needed it. "How can I help you?"

Jasmine put an arm around him and hugged. Her eyes were sparkling with satisfaction. "Can you help me?" she asked again.

"Yes, let me know what kind of help you need."

"Okay, I will let you know when the time is ready."

When the time is ready, Sami repeated in his head, wondering what Jasmine meant.

"I feel much better in your presence," she added.

"How often does Antonio show up at your place?"

"The two times that he came were during the weekend. He worked in the evening somewhere, and I was surprised that he didn't want me to know where he worked." She paused as if trying to recollect. "In the past, he worked at the meatpacking factory, restaurants, and also at a nightclub."

"We don't have anybody by the name of Antonio at the meatpacking factory now. Do you have any of his photos?"

"No, I destroyed all of them, even the ones with me in them. I did not want any trace of him in my life."

"You said he worked at the meatpacking factory in the past? Moses might know him unless he worked the morning shift."

"Wait, I think he did work the morning shift," Jasmine confirmed.

"Oh, then he won't know him. In any case, I'll ask, although it is unlikely that he would know because so many people worked there off and on. Are you afraid that he will do something to you?"

"I will be fine. Antonio can do anything. You're right, though. I will have to do something about this."

"I can see you have advertised for a roommate." Sami pointed to a sheet of paper on the table.

"Yes. I have an applicant who is ready to move in anytime."

After an hour of chatting, Sami left.

Chapter 32

One of those occasions where Sami didn't have to hesitate was when he encountered people from East Africa. In most cases, he could tell by looking at them, even to the extent of identifying their specific tribes. The distinguishing features were not only physical marks or general outlooks, but you could make a good guess from appearances. Most of his neighbors were students from other parts of developing countries. They shared similar traditional practices and beliefs. He often met with them at the laundry or playground, where they could chat and share information about their countries and the lives they led. Sami could still remember the first time he'd met his neighbor who'd come from Africa and the conversations they'd had. "You look like an Ethiopian, a Sudanese, or a Somali." Sami heard these kinds of comments several times wherever he met people from those countries. Even a classmate of his from Nigeria wondered whether Sami was a Fulani from Northern Nigeria or Chad. The fact of the matter was that everyone he met thought he somewhat looked like one of the groups from those countries.

Sami had neighbors from Ethiopia, Ghana, Ecuador, Iran, Sudan, Nigeria, Pakistan, Zambia, India, Mali, and Uganda, and they all lived in a two-bedroom apartment in an old university apartment building. The apartment units had been built in the 1940s to accommodate World War II student veterans and their families. These housing units, all arranged in rows, were only separated by a road. All the houses were similar in shape and color. Sami's apartment was across from his neighbor from Ethiopia. The houses were so close that if a person from one house called his name, he could easily hear it.

It was January, the spring semester had just begun, and snow had almost entirely covered the ground. During one of those casual meetings on campus, Sami got introduced to one of the students who'd moved recently into the apartments where he lived.

The main campus was within walking distance from these housing units. The path from each unit would converge and pass through a tunnel along the railroad track leading to the animal science's department horse barn.

Sami and some students from Africa would discuss university life and African problems. They shared the memories of their beloved homelands. It seemed to Sami that most of the international students from Africa were experts on African issues, and they appeared to know what caused all those miserable conditions in African countries. As usual, the majority were quick to blame the leaders in Africa, who amassed abundant wealth while their people suffered. The only thing they heard more often about Africa was news of poverty, hunger, diseases, and civil wars. Even natural calamities did not spare Africa.

With all these problems from their mother countries, it was evident in their discourse that international students should have a mission to accomplish. All of them had the desire to build their countries and make them better than the way they'd left them. However, it had become a mere delusion for most of them, who would never go back to participate in the building of their nations. Many believed that their skills and talents would be worth more here in the West. If not for visa restrictions, most international students would remain and not return home to face all those problems. Many graduate students got scholarships from their respective governments. Still, some of them got engaged in political views about the ways their countries were governed and feared retaliation from their repressive governments.

Sami heard many stories about international students and how some of them spied on each other, reminiscence of the cold war era.

"Welcome. You moved into the unit across from mine. I saw you this morning. Let me show you around," Sami offered.

Kebede Wolde, a graduate student in the department of statistics, was thrilled. He'd come a month earlier with his wife and two children, a six-year-old son and three-year-old daughter. The first few weeks had gone very well, and the family had soon adjusted to Iowan's life.

Sami took it upon himself to introduce Kebede to campus life and his friends from other parts of Africa. During the first few weeks, Sami also went with his neighbor to classes every morning, and sometimes they met on the way to school, a ten-minute walk to campus on the same path. It was natural that when you are with a person on the road every day to strike up a conversation.

Kebede tried to educate Sami about his country and the main tribes who lived in Ethiopia. "It is a known fact in Africa that major tribes fight to dominate each other, but in my country, we don't have tribal issues like most of the other parts of Africa. We are mixed communities with cultural heritage because of intermarriages. We have a lot of people who were assimilated and didn't even speak any other language other than our national language. In that regard, I think we are the only country that can claim a unity of language and has managed to forge an identity as one nation," Kebede concluded, with a sense of pride.

"You are not serious, my friend. No country in Africa has reached the stage you are claiming about your country," Sami replied.

"Well, at least we should get credit." Kebede was furious that any other language could be allowed in his country other than the national language, which was also the language of his tribe. Sami disagreed. "We should develop all the tribal dialects to avoid any dominance of one tribal group, and African countries should adopt a neutral national language like Kiswahili."

Kebede then stopped and asked, "Do you belong to one of those rebellious groups?"

"What do you mean?" Sami asked.

"Well, they are people opposed to the unity of my country, and they are waging war against our government. They want to claim separate regions for themselves when we all should be working towards the unity of all African countries as one united Africa." Kebede faced Sami. "Are you from Ogaden or one of the border tribes?"

"Maybe I am. What do you think?"

"You have a strong resemblance to either a Somalian or Ethiopian."

Soon after, Sami's encounters with Kebede on the way to school always initiated a further inquiry into tribal affairs in Africa. Sami was sure to surprise Kebede with historical facts that made him uncomfortable, like the European scramble for Africa. Kebede then decided to avoid Sami altogether and no longer shared morning walks with him to school. He either went ahead quickly or remained behind and changed his regular schedule.

***

Days passed, and life moved on for Sami and his colleagues at work and school. Jasmine, on the other hand, also tried to settle down. She kept her vigil, worrying that Antonio could show up again.

Jasmine stopped by Cub Foods and bought some groceries. The dark of the night was closing in when she reached her house. She parked her car, grabbed the grocery bag from the passenger seat, and turned to the sound of footsteps. Startled by Antonio, she dropped the shopping bag and screamed.

"Shh, it's me. I'm not going to hurt you." He held his hand over her mouth.

Jasmine struggled to free herself. "No, don't touch me with your filthy hand." She snatched up her grocery bag and rushed to the door. She groped around in her handbag for the keys to open it, but then, instead, she grabbed her hidden Mace defense spray and shot it at him. The stream of spray missed him. Antonio knocked it from her hand.

"Why did you do that, crazy woman?" He opened the door, pushed her in, and locked the door behind him.

"No, please don't," She pleaded.

"You asked for it. I did not come to cause trouble. You have to do what I tell you. I need some money, and you better shut your mouth. What are you up to these days, eh?" He fixed his gaze on her stricken, tearful eyes. "I have seen your boyfriend. By the way, he's a married man with four children. Are you now a husband snatcher? What a pathetic life. What happened to your green card business?" Antonio twisted his face mockingly.

Jasmine stared vacantly, and with each despicable word he uttered, her tears flowed, and her stomach muscles tightened. She writhed with vengeful hatred, regretting the day that she'd brought him into her life.

Antonio could see the rage in her eyes. He seemed to enjoy the scene. He unwrapped a stick of chewing gum and slowly put it in his mouth, pretending to feel sensational pleasure. "Do you want one?"

"Were you stalking me? Don't do that to me, Antonio." She tried to assuage her anger. "I can give you money if I have it, but I want you to leave me alone. You have already caused me more misery."

"You have a roommate, too? Really?" He snorted.

Jasmine did not answer. She went into her bedroom, brought back some money, and threw the envelope at him. Antonio caught it and ripped it open. "Is that all you have?"

"Why do you do this, Antonio. You need to go to rehab; even the two years in jail did not help? Are you on hard drugs now? Resorting to this miserable life? I will make sure that you go to jail or deported." She twisted her face, so the corner of her lip was pulled back in aversion. "Don't you work?"

He ignored her question. "Don't play any nasty games. Somebody will get hurt."

"Don't touch him," Jasmine pleaded again.

"You love him? I can see that in your eyes. Is it for the card or love?" He did not need her answer. Antonio trod towards the exit and stopped. He looked at her revealing what looked like the letters M and S and the number 13 tattooed around the dragon on the right side of his neck, which he'd acquired when he was in jail.

Jasmine kept quiet. Her eyes were attracted to the tattoo. She looked again to make sure that it was not the dreaded MS-13, la Mara Salvatrucha, the dangerous street gang where members were known to resort to all kinds of barbaric acts like murder, rape, and also maiming and terrorizing their victims.

When he was gone, Jasmine shut the door and leaned against the doorknob. Then she walked to the window, determined to resolve this issue that Antonio had to go.

Chapter 33

In the meantime, Sami occupied himself with school life, while his neighbor, Kebede, took every opportunity not to cross his path. Wherever he spotted Sami from a distance, Kebede made sure to dodge him and turn around. Sami thought the incidents were too numerous to be a coincidence. One thing led to another, and at first, Sami did not connect the dots, as they say.

One Saturday morning, Sami saw Kebede's wife and her son in the playground. The kids had played together before, and Musa rushed to meet with Kebede's son to share his latest toy with him. As soon as she saw him, Kebede's wife hurried her son out of the playground enclosure and left. Musa ran after Kebede's son to tell him to stay a little so that they could play. Kebede's wife would not allow her son to talk with Musa. She did not want to talk with Sami, either.

Kebede's son was innocent. Unaware of what his mom was up to, he invited Musa to his birthday party on Sunday. Musa felt excited and nudged his father to go straight to Walmart to buy a toy. He had already figured out what kind of cool gift to give for the birthday party.

The next day, Sami left after lunch to study at the library while his wife stayed home with the children. When he came home in the evening, he found his son in an unhappy mood.

It was rare for a kid to have a sad-looking face when his dad returned. That day, things were different. His five-year-old American-born child had, for the first time, experienced discrimination of a different kind. "What happened to you, Musa?" Sami asked.

"They won't let me in."

"What do you mean? Who won't let you?"

"Yohane's mom told me that she did not invite me to the party. She did not accept my gift and did not allow me to join the other kids."

"Did his mom tell you why?" There was no point for Sami to ask this question, and he knew it would not help.

"Not her, but her son told me as she was pulling him away from me. He said that I was from a rebellious tribe. Daddy! What is a tribe? And how come you didn't tell me? Do I have a tribe, and is my tribe bad?" He started crying.

Sami had a whole lot to explain. He was not sure whether his five-year-old could comprehend. He calmed his son, and at the same time, he became angry with his neighbor for putting his son through this archaic way of thinking. Suddenly, he realized that the tribal issues that he was trying to get away from would not leave him alone. Now he had to face the fact that even though his son was an American, the reality for him might be different.

Sometimes Sami got irritated with how some of the international students resisted change and clung to the status quo. No matter how far away from home they were, whatever was happening in the parts of the globe they came from would still affect their daily lives and impact their ways of thinking. To bring kids into a different culture from one's own, by itself, was a daunting task; nevertheless, Sami felt that he was bound by duty to teach and explain to his kids his cultural values.

Later that evening, the issue of his neighbor came up as he

was talking with his wife.

"Our kids are the reflections of who we are as people. The sad incident that happened to Musa will serve as excellent experimental material for learning. Kids are good followers," Sami said. "I'm sure my neighbor did a good job on that. We don't have to do the same."

He added, "However, we should not wait until they learn from strangers. It is never too late to teach our children what our concerns are. We have to do a bit of explaining and make it clear that it is not their fault if something like this happens." Sami kept talking even though he realized that his wife had stepped out. "Don't we have enough problems already?" he said when his wife rejoined him. "I was upset about the incident with Musa, and if I had been here, I would have stormed into her party and demanded an explanation. She portrayed mean, uncouth behavior not befitting of a mother."

Sami turned around. "Anyway, we can use this incident as a learning tool. We have to teach our children about our culture and language."

Sarah looked at him with that kind of look that he knew very well. She might be thinking, *Not again. It's the same story and discussion that we've had in the past.*

"I thought you said that you would be different." She paused.

"Sure, I don't like my children's minds poisoned by these tribal sentiments. On the other hand, it's better if they learn from me than from outside sources."

He was about to continue further when she interjected. "There is only one solution, and I have already figured it out."

"What?" Sami asked animatedly.

"Don't teach kids who were born here anything about tribal culture. Keep them clean, and I don't see why we should pollute our kids' minds with these toxic notions of tribal affairs anyway." She stood up to leave.

"Wait a minute. You are putting two different things together," Sami lamented. "Learning a language and culture has nothing to do with this. They will have no identity if we don't teach them about where we came from and some cultural values and language." Sami knew this had been a thorny issue with his wife. She was opposed to teaching them any tribal language, and she believed that the children should only learn American culture and nothing else.

Discussions about these issues had always evoked sentimental feelings in Sami. His mother desperately wanted to see his children learn the mother language. "I think you misunderstood me; I do not encourage our children to hate other cultures or people who are different. I am proud to tell them where I came from and what they need to know. Their identity."

"What identity?" she shot back. They are African Americans, and that is enough."

"I would rather call myself Oromo American, not that I am against the term African American. When an Italian or a British person becomes American, do they call him or her European American? No, they say Italian America or British American. Europe and Africa are continents, and I don't agree with the term used for Africa as if Africa is one country."

"Too bad, you can't change it." She shrugged in her defiant style.

"What is wrong with telling them which part of Africa we came from? I have heard Americans calling themselves Irish American, Jewish American, etc., and there was nothing wrong with that, so why don't we do the same?" Sami was furious. He thought his wife was showing an inferiority complex.

"I have already told you that I will not be part of this."

"Okay, fine, but don't stand in the way. I will teach them myself."

"You should have taught them about religion rather than this backward cultural thing you're talking about all the time." She was about to step out of the room, but then suddenly she heard a sharp scream from the kids' bedroom.

"Mom! It went under the bed!" Adam and Chaaltu dashed to the door and knocked each other on the head, sending Adam writhing to the ground with sharp pain. Musa followed, not sure what was happening. Sarah turned around.

"What is it?" Chaaltu could not catch her breath, and Adam was in pain. Sarah consoled Adam and attended to his swollen forehead. "Musa, tell me why they were screaming."

"There was a huge fat rat. It came through the opening and under the bed. Mom, it's huge, bigger than a puppy, I think."

"Wait, Musa!" Sarah held him.

"I cannot sleep there anymore, Mom," Chaaltu said. "No way. Dad, did you see?" She started crying.

"It won't harm you. It's afraid of you and has probably gone out again. I will block the hole. You will be fine. Did you see how it escaped? It ran away, right, Musa?"

"I told you," Musa confirmed.

It was Sarah's turn to express her grievances, and how she got fed up with the rats and cockroaches in this old university apartment house. "We have to get out of this miserable place. The kids have been traumatized by these pests."

"We can move out, but the apartments we can afford are not better than this. I saw some advertisements, one for a place not far from here. If you want, we can rent it. It is available. Remember, we are on the waiting list for the university's new apartment, and when it becomes available, we should move back," Sami said. Then he added, "And you know if we break the lease agreement, we have to pay the total amount of the remaining months in the lease."

"We have to leave. I don't want to fight with these rats and roaches anymore. We can check the apartment you talked about tomorrow afternoon," Sarah insisted.

"I will be studying with friends in the afternoon, but we can check it in the morning."

Chapter 34

Sami grabbed his school bag and proceeded to the door, but before he stepped out, he turned and said, "The first test surprised me, and I didn't do very well."

"Maybe you can consider reducing your hours at work and focus on classwork. I can work extra hours. I am sure we will manage," Sarah replied.

"Dad, I am coming with you," Chaaltu announced.

"Not today. Your dad will be at the library, studying with his friends." Sarah took Chaaltu by the hand.

"How about if we go to the park?" The rest of the kids heard Chaaltu's plan and rushed to join.

Sami walked to the university buildings, engrossed in thought. He knew the decision to return to school would add extra financial burden to the family situation. The truth of the matter was that the courses he took were hard, and he had little prior knowledge of the subject. Besides, there was no time for him to study at home, and as time had passed, he'd found himself getting low grades. Other graduate students in his class had similar problems regarding this course, and some of them had a study circle that Sami had decided to join.

The short walk to the library gave Sami time to reflect on another crucial pending issue to resolve. He had not heard from Jasmine, and he wanted to know whether she'd had any other encounters with Antonio. He stopped at the telephone booth and called her number, but no one answered. He then called Kumar's number and got no response. *She's still in the game*, he reassured himself.

Sami reached the library before his friends arrived, and he went through the references. Some instructors kept old exams at the library for students to practice with. "I am looking for any reference or past exams for this subject." He showed the course title and the professor's name to a library assistant.

The lady looked at the paper in his hand and shook her head. "We don't have anything for this professor. Many students were asking about this course. Maybe you can check similar courses in the biology department," she suggested. "A lot of students are not happy with this subject. They complained that the professor expects all students to master the subject and regurgitate the material from his lessons."

Sami got interested. "Did you take the course?"

"No, my friend took it. He said that students learned the tricks of this course and managed to pass." She started to move on.

"Do you know what the trick was?" Sami asked as he walked with her.

"Find old papers from a student who took his course, even if it was ten years ago. He never changes the exam questions. I have to go now."

Sami thanked her for this valuable information and returned to the study room that they'd reserved to wait for his friends.

Abdou, a graduate student from Mali, a French-speaking country in Africa, was the first to join him. He'd gotten a scholarship to study botany. Abdou had difficulty understanding the English terminology used in the subject. He did not fail like Sami but had a C grade and was still not happy with the score. Sami, on the other hand, would have been glad to get even a C; though that was not a good grade to expect for a graduate student, it was better than total failure. In any case, he was not supposed to get less than a B in any subject.

When the rest of the team arrived, Philip from Malawi, Romeo from Chile, Henry from Rwanda, and Ahmed from Jordan, they quickly got settled. Each one had a specific set of questions to prepare for. Abdou was the first to start answering his questions, and he immediately took on his role as a teacher.

"It was the analysis of the essay that I did poorly. I don't know why the professor took away points for writing and grammar," Abdou complained as he tried to make his point clear about the topic he had been assigned to discuss. "Do you know what the professor told me when I complained about the grade and wanted extra time for the test? I will prove to him that I can pass this course. I was shocked when he told me point blank that I should drop the course or take a lower-level course first."

"He told me a similar thing," said Sami, "and did not want the reputation of the university tarnished. The professor refused to give me extra credit, time, or another chance to repeat the test. This professor believed that a student who got an F in his class should drop the course." Sami's friends nodded in agreement.

"It's for this reason that we have to succeed in this course. We have to support each other," Philip added.

After hearing all these complaints, Sami thought that he would have to accept his mediocre grade for this semester.

"Okay, let's not get distracted further," Ahmed continued.

Each week, the group reserved a room in the library and crammed for the tests and answered questions, hoping that they would pass the course. Sami realized the difficulty he faced with the course was a lack of foundation at the graduate level.

As the group gathered to study, they also discussed other things that had happened to them and their daily toils and struggles, which were evident from the way they complained. Towards the end, they usually shared news from their home countries or discussed and argued about the general problems they faced in their daily lives. Abdou seemed to have had issues with student housing rules; he either had not read the rules or had ignored them. In any case, the previous week had been very rough for him.

Philip initiated the discussion. "What happened, Abdou? I heard you were in the paper."

"We wanted to celebrate our country's Independence Day. There are only three students from my country, and I am the only one with a family here, so I thought of having a goat feast to commemorate the occasion. We went to this farm that sold goats and sheep and selected an eighty-pound goat. The farmer even knew the ritual of preparing the slaughter in the manner required by our faith. Abdou pulled out the newspaper article from his bag and placed it on the desk. The story read: "A fire broke out in a student's apartment during a bizarre African feast ritual in the student's apartment, almost gutting the apartment where international students from Africa live."

"The incident did not happen as reported here, and they twisted and exaggerated the story. Look at what the article says. I wonder what bizarre African ritual the writer had in mind. A fantasy to create a sensation. Students from many countries live there, but he singled out Africa."

"Maybe they thought you did some voodoo practices of animal sacrifice," Romeo said.

"Let him finish," Ahmed prodded. "What did you do then?"

Abdou still had anxiety in his voice. "I was impressed and would never have thought that I could slaughter a goat here in the way we did in Africa. The farmer knew everything that I needed. He tied and held the goat facing the right direction of the Qibla required by my faith. After I pronounced the invocation and sliced the neck, he skinned and cut the meat into smaller pieces for me. His only request was that I not leave the skin behind and all inner organs like the stomach and intestines on the farm. The farmer was amiable, and he even asked whether the annual Muslim Ramadan of fasting was earlier this year."

"Come on, get to the point, Abdou," Phillip said impatiently.

"Okay, within twenty minutes, I packed the meat in a plastic bag, but I forgot to throw the skin and hooves in the dumpster as I planned earlier."

Phillip kept pressing while the others listened. "Give him time to finish his story," Ahmed said with irritation.

"My wife and my two children, seven and three, we're all excited to see whole meat put in a garbage bag. I helped my wife wash the stomach bowels in the bathroom. The smell was too strong, and I had to wash it several times, and still, we could not remove the odor. Finally, I remembered to dispose of the skin. I don't know why this silly idea came into my mind. I decided to burn it on the kitchen stove. I should have slipped it in the dumpster across the road. Nobody would have noticed, and that would have been the end of the story."

"What a foolish thing to do!" Ahmed exclaimed.

"A mistake I would regret later," Abdou replied. "My wife, who was new to the country, even advised me against it, and yet I thought I could do it quickly within a few seconds on the kitchen stove. When the fire alarm sounded, we panicked, and I turned off the stove, hoping that the sound would stop.

I was also aware that the family who lived across from where I lived had already complained to the university police to check out the stench coming from my apartment. She thought we'd brought manure home. We heard the woman neighbor shouting some words of obscenity at me. The university police had just arrived to respond to the complaint of the neighbor when the fire alarm sounded."

"You should have fanned and blown the air to stop the alarm."

"When you are in a panic mode, you don't think straight. Anyway, a heavy knock on the door thwarted our attention. Faced with two mean-looking university police officers, I didn't have anything to say other than to invite them in. They held their faces in a disgusting pose, trying to avoid the smell. That day, our feast was ruined. They wanted to make sure that the meat was inspected and certified. They could have thrown the whole goat away and served me with a substantial penalty. The university police considered my case a safety threat that endangered the lives of people around me, and they warned me about my risky behavior."

"What was the verdict?" Philip asked.

"I had to plead that I did not mean any harm, and it was an accident. The security team then made me sign some papers." Abdou paused.

"That's all for the mess you caused?" Philip wondered.

Abdou looked at him in a mean way. "I got away with a citation and met with the university housing committee for further disciplinary action. My plea of ignorance did not help much. The violation cited was fire alarms and equipment abuse. They warned me that the violation of this policy could lead to immediate removal from the residence facilities and cancellation of the housing contract. The decision is pending, and if I'm found responsible, I will have to pay for repair and replacement."

"I didn't know that there is such a rule," Sami said.

"I hope to get leniency based on my lack of understanding of the university housing policy. For sure, I did not tamper with the fire alarm and equipment, and I don't know why they charged me under this policy."

"Did you check the housing handbook? There are all sorts of obscure policies that we have to deal with, and until you break one, you won't know," Ahmed added.

"As I said, I had to plead that I did not mean any harm, and it was an accident. The committee made me sign some papers. The ordeal we went through that week was reported in the student paper, and the city newspaper carried the story with a twist. You can see the headline yourself." He pushed the article towards Ahmed. "The Feast of African Ritual Revisited."

"That was what happened. The writer flavored the story and added some other bizarre things that did not happen." Abdou ended his story and waited.

The room remained quiet for a while.

Sami broke the silence by telling them about his experience with a student counselor. "I struggled with this course from the beginning and needed academic tips on how to study. Frankly, I didn't know how to study. I tried to absorb everything at the same time, without any strategy, memorizing words and cramming in as much material as I could. I did not remember anything I read in the end." The team nodded in agreement. "The counselor reacted like I needed psychiatric help."

"What happened then?" Phillip asked. He could not wait for the answer. Instead, he confessed that he'd had a similar problem with remembering what he read and tempted to take a drug that another student claimed boosted memory.

"Let Sami finish," Ahmed called out.

"The woman brought a textbook and told me to use the

SQ3R methods of studying: survey, question, recite, read, and review. It was a slow process, and it took a while, but in the end, I got better.

Abdou shook his head when he heard there was a way to study. "I usually do what naturally comes to me: memorize the bulk of the material when preparing for exams."

"Abdou, I heard you cheated on the exam. Did you cheat?" Sami asked.

"No, Sami, I did not." Abdou laughed. "Let me explain. The answers to the questions were exactly from the notes the teacher gave. I memorized them and reproduced them word for word, and that was why she thought I copied."

Sami thought his ordeal and the others he'd heard were bad, but then he heard Henry's story. Henry told them what he'd gone through back in his home country of Rwanda, a country doomed by senseless tragedy, torn between two rival tribes. Henry had a relationship with both the warring tribes through his mother and father. His brothers were all married to women from one or the other tribe. The curse of his mixed-marriage blood, a blessing in peaceful times, turned out to be an evil act of destruction of the bloodline. It took him a couple of minutes to even say a word about his past. Nothing in this world would expunge the torment and painful feelings he'd experienced, as he watched his whole family wiped out. The few survivors, including one of his brothers and sisters, escaped from the appalling carnage committed by their family members. People as close as friends killed each other without any feelings of mercy or remorse just because of the so-called enemy tribes. An accidental choice of birth, one would say, and yet none of us have the liberty of choosing where we would like to be born.

The intensity with which he told his story moved them all, and it took some time for them to resume their group work again. As a matter of fact, after that story, the group could not proceed further. They had no concentration anymore.

Sami stepped out of the library with renewed confidence, sure that he would pull up his grades. He remembered to call Jasmine.

Chapter 35

Sami dialed Jasmine's number and waited. When she answered, her voice sounded shaky. "Are you okay?" he inquired.

"Where are you? Can we meet?" she asked.

"Sure, I have just got done with my studies and will be heading home. I could free up an hour if you want to see me."

"It is urgent."

"I walked to the library, so I don't have a car with me right now. I will have to go home first."

"I don't think it's fair to bother you with my problems." She hesitated. "Antonio has escalated his mischievous activities to a different level. He has been stalking us, and he knows about you." Jasmine sighed.

"I will be there as soon as I can," Sami confirmed.

***

Sami carefully listened as Jasmine narrated her ordeal with Antonio.

"You have to report this incident, Jasmine. You cannot keep quiet about this and expect him to stay away. Do you know where he lives"?

"I don't know."

"You said that he knew me? How come?"

"He said he was hiding in the parking lot in his car when you came with me one day, and he saw your face."

Sami had less time to figure out the approach he would take now, and he wondered how he could meet with Antonio. "Maybe you could arrange to introduce me to him so that I can know his face as well."

"It's better if you don't know each other. You can't predict what Antonio will do, and I don't want anything to happen to you." Jasmine studied his face furtively.

"If you don't have his photo anywhere, how will I know how he looks like? It's like unseen enemy lurking in the dark."

"I don't have any, as I told you. I have destroyed all, even the ones that I took with him." She sighed with a glimpse of triumph in her eyes.

"Maybe I have to wait around until he shows up."

"I will plan something and let you know." She then raised her head. "Wait. He has a strange tattoo that he got while in prison. I am not sure about it, but it looks like a dragon, and there's an inscription, MS-13, tattooed on the left side of his neck. I am not sure why he has it. This symbol represents notorious gangsters, and he was never part of this gang." With her cheek tilted, resting on her hand, Jasmine remained pensive.

"You never know. A lot of things happen to people in jail," Sami said. "That won't help me. Probably a lot of people who were in jail got similar tattoos. If you can describe to me what he looks like, that would help."

Jasmine laughed and then said, "I laughed because the only thing I can remember is that he points with his lips at people, especially when talking about the other person, and that could also be the culture of that part of the world where he came from." She paused. "He's Catholic.

Sami laughed. "I think you need to use adjectives like

aggressive, anxious, etc."

"Okay, he's about five feet six inches, shorter than you and heavier, with typical Latin American features, and to be frank with you, I cannot give a good description. It's difficult for me to differentiate him. He looks like a typical Honduran." Jasmine threw her hands up.

"Jasmine, I understand. That won't help me either. I don't know what Hondurans look like. Let's focus on the tattoo. How visible is it?"

"The dragon is visible, but you have to look closely to identify the MS-13 inscribed around it. I am afraid Antonio might have joined the gang while in jail."

"Jasmine, all criminals have some tattoos, and probably for fun. He might keep adding. Most of the people I work with have tattoos, at least Pablo, Jose, Emilio, and Petros have some on their bodies. All have some around their necks."

Jasmine grew interested when Sami mentioned his coworkers with tattoos. "Maybe I will stop by one day during your break time."

"Are you out of your mind? Do you want to check tattoos? Some of them have them on strange parts of the body, including thighs and other private areas. I have seen a dragon tattoo on Petros, Emilio, and Pablo." Sami frowned.

Jasmine laughed. "No, Sami, I can't do that, but I will know if Antonio works there."

"I don't think Antonio works there. Otherwise, I would know," Sami concluded.

"How would you know? He could be going by any of those fake names they keep."

"Jasmine, you have to report this guy. Do it now and request a restraining order."

"I wish it were as easy as you think."

"Jasmine, this guy has a lot to lose, and I am puzzled by your attitude. You don't want to help yourself."

After a long silence, Jasmine broke into tears and said, "He threatened to wipe out my family if I report him. He said he would start with my kids, grandma, and then come for me last."

"I am sorry to hear about this. What do you think is the best solution, then?"

"I will figure out something. I have a plan, but first, I needed to find out where Antonio works or lives."

"Jasmine, in the meantime, can you take his picture and share it with me?"

"He might suspect that I am after something if I start taking his picture."

"Jasmine, okay, you said he started blackmailing you. Is there anything else?" Sami waited.

"I think he's using drugs again, either marijuana or other drugs. If I only knew where he works." She twitched her lips.

Sami raised his head as if he'd remembered something. "Do you think he knew my home phone number?"

"I don't know. Are you suspecting something?"

"At one time, my wife complained that somebody called and told her that I was seeing another woman. I did not put a lot of weight on it because she knew I had talked with you and Kumar. It happened twice, and both incidents happened during the times when we met." Sami straightened his arm. "I did not take it seriously, but now that you brought this up, it could be another dirty trick Antonio is playing or even another person I have a problem with." Sami nodded.

He stood up and looked through the window at the parking lot. "Do you park your car there as well? I can see there are enough parking spaces for all the neighborhood."

Jasmine joined him. "Yes, I sometimes park there. As you can see, my driveway is too small for two cars, and when my roommate is around, I park in the general parking lot. The parking space belongs to the apartment building. On my right side is another rental house, and on the left is a home where an older lady lives." Jasmine paused and added, "It's a good place to live, and the majority of residents are students."

Sami, apparently musing about by all the tasks ahead of him, wore a somber expression on his face. "I am thinking about what you said. Can Antonio be a threat to my family? Why? I am not sure. I want to find out and meet with him face to face."

"I don't recommend this." Jasmine turned to face him. She held her face with an appealing gesture. Her eyes still fixated on him. "If cornered, he can act viciously. I think we have to find where he works or lives first. I will arrange to follow him. I tried once when he left my house. He stayed in the car for a few minutes to disguise his tracks. He will plan something for my upcoming birthday, and I will see whether I can take his photo."

"Jasmine, I don't understand. How can you entertain the man who terrorized you? What the heck? Are you hiding something from me? Do you take drugs with him? I need to know," Sami fumed.

Jasmine lowered her gaze. "I have to be honest with you, Sami. Not in the way you think. I started smoking marijuana when I had serious depression and stress, and it helped me to relax. I didn't use it frequently, once or twice a month, to help with the stress. I stopped for some time, but when Antonio returned. I got stressed and tried it again." She looked up. "I am not addicted to it. I just use it as needed."

"Tell me what you told Antonio about me. I want to know."

"Nothing new, Sami. He was jealous, like most men."

"Okay, but what you told him will make a difference in how he reacts towards me. If he thinks that I am competing with him, he has a valid reason."

Jasmine jumped in before Sami could finish. "Wait a

minute, Sami. I don't know what he thinks. I told him to keep away from you."

"You didn't give him a reason why he should keep away. Besides, he wants to get back with you. What if you tell him the truth!"

"No, he would blackmail me further and get you in trouble.

"Either way, I am already a thorn in his path. He will see us together more often, so you may need to clarify my role. Either we are just friends, colleagues, or students in the same department, whatever, so he doesn't take me as his competitor. Jasmine, I don't want to put my family in a collateral damage situation."

Sami sipped water and checked the time. "I need any description of him you can think of. I am concerned that he even knew how many children I have. I strongly believe that he misunderstands my role and relationship with you, and I hope you will clarify that and give me an update soon." Sami stood up to leave and turned. "This is my graduate students' office number. I am there most of the time, when not in class."

Jasmine stood up and hugged him. "Okay, I will see what I can do." She walked with him to the parking lot.

Chapter 36

It had been three weeks since Sami had seen Jasmine . He checked the mail and satisfied himself that his wife had not found a letter from Jasmine or the county court.

Sami brooded over the prolonged absence of Jasmine's whereabouts. He combed through the piles of papers, trashed the junk mail, and was about to stop when a single soiled envelope addressed to him caught his attention. His name was spelled with an error: "Sama." He tore it open. A small handwritten note read, "Keep away from that woman or else," and it ended with a death skull drawing as a signature and dated two weeks ago.

With his hand almost trembling, Sami stared vacantly at it, piecing together the possible suspects. Antonio and Thoma came to mind. Sami placed the note back into the envelop and put it in his pocket. With his mind preoccupied with a green card and schoolwork, he was not prepared for this new distraction, and he did not want to disclose it to his wife, either. He recalled the last discussion he'd had with his wife regarding the saga of getting a document and how upset she had been. Sami was afraid that any further push from him could open the fractured wound that he had tried to cover. Sarah had recently changed her mood and tactics. Her job situation had improved with flexible working hours, and she seemed to be happy. She had internalized the accumulated frustration of life by working continuously, even some days when she was off duty. Sarah would volunteer or work extra time. She attended a women's group with her neighbor and brought home some literature on women's issues.

***

After several attempts to contact Jasmine, Sami browsed through the daily papers in case an accident involving her had been reported.

The next day, life unfolded as it usually did, with the new day bringing a multitude of problems. Sami trudged on, one step at a time. He flipped ideas in his head. *No matter what happens after today, I will stay on track.* He looked around, making sure that no one was within hearing range lest a question pops up regarding the stability of his mind.

Sami stretched, and his muscle twitched. He needed to recoup his strength after this self-induced failure, exacerbated by his perceived pain and suffering that kept him stagnant. Over the years, Sami had developed a self-satisfying mode of reassurance, and he could even entertain daydreaming of a world of great accomplishments, what he would have been and what he could be in the future. The slow progress towards this ideal goal made Sami impatient and doubted himself. Still, he found ways to boost his morale and spirit by reminding himself. *After all, you're the only one from your village who has ever gone to school this far and gone overseas for further studies, and probably the only one from the clan to have ever boarded an airplane.* Sami had no control over these events, and yet he took pride in extolling them to boost his dwindling ego as if that was enough to propel him to move forward.

Sami reminded himself of the deal with Jasmine. A woman who could technically act as his wife no matter how much he denied having anything to do with her. Regardless, his close encounter and an episode he'd got involved in had paved the way for the establishment of a relationship. While Sami knew and believed that nothing would happen to disrupt his marriage vows to his wife, this episode with Jasmine would make him vulnerable. As a married man, he knew his place and the commitment to his marriage vows. He'd taken out a loan to finance this project and couldn't imagine losing everything. He would never believe that the money he'd paid could go down the drain, money desperately needed for his other essential daily amenities.

Sami glanced at the telephone several times. He paced the length of the room. "Why would I even think of expecting any call from her?" he said, trying to talk himself out of this strange mood. People in the village where he came from believed in all sorts of things, including witchcraft. If he were to apply similar logic, he might think that the events were the result of a powerful spell cast upon him. However, he doubted whether these kinds of things could happen in Jasmine's world.

At least she should call and apologize, he thought. The financial reality and the staggering debt he'd gotten into for the green card deal would soon haunt him. The fear of the unknown slowly seeped in. Sami tried to track his movements and encounters with Jasmine in his mind to find out whether he'd made an unforgettable mistake or left any clues. The sudden disappearance of Jasmine and the silence surrounding the deal had caused his paranoia. Sami remembered that his fingerprints could be all over her place. He'd even received divorce paper from the court that he'd filed without the consent of his wife. How could he face her if this situation failed? On top of all that was the imminent threat that he had to figure how to resolve.

The telephone rang. Sami turned with a pounding heartbeat and rushed to pick it up.

It was his wife. "Yes, they are okay. They ate," he told her.

"Is everything okay with you?" she repeatedly asked.

"Yes, everything is fine. Why?" Sami responded with anxiety.

"You sounded different."

Sami would not admit the dilemma he was in and that the agitation in his voice was because he did not get the telephone he'd expected. And then a big realization descended upon him; something rushed through his mind. *Does she suspect that I'm hiding something? Did she find out about the papers I received from the county court?* He waited for her to ask questions, expecting that the next would be the one he would hate to answer.

He was sure she was asleep when he arrived home late last night, and it should not have surprised her because he often came back when she was sleeping. It had been this way for most nights. It was a life he had come to accept unwillingly. It didn't bother his wife because she had to work early the next day and had gone to sleep early.

Sami said to his wife, "If we were in the village where we came from, you could have been ostracized for neglecting your husband."

She replied sarcastically, "You have to wake up to the realities of the real world."

The truth of the matter was their strained relationship. The issue worsened due to the financial situation and family problems that kept popping up. Preoccupied with getting a call from Jasmine, Sami had forgotten to prepare an answer in his head if his wife decided to ask. He sighed with relief when she ended the call.

Late that day, he received another call from Kumar, who said that he was just checking when Sami asked.

"I am fine. What happened to you and Jasmine? I tried calling several times."

"I don't know about Jasmine, but I am here now. I went for

a short vacation to Florida."

"Do you mean you don't know what happened to Jasmine?" Sami exclaimed.

"No, why? She had some family issues and planned to visit them the last time I talked to her," Kumar answered.

"There is something else that she might have told you about Antonio. She got scared. Antonio was stalking both of us."

Kumar laughed. "You're not serious. Why would that lowlife stalk you?"

"I got a threatening note telling me not to associate with Jasmine."

"Don't pay too much attention to it. Antonio is enraged with jealousy. I understand he wants Jasmine back, and she's not budging."

Sami did not respond. The silence prompted Kumar to ask, "Sami, are you still there?"

Sami held the phone with a tight grip as if he could squeeze every bit of information out of it that he could get. "Yes, still here." He waited. "You knew all this and didn't tell me?"

"I thought you knew."

"I knew one incident a couple of weeks ago where he threatened her. I advised her to report the matter, but she believed he would go away."

"Sami, are you considering a different approach to Jasmine?"

Sami was not clear what Kumar meant. Jasmine had not shared her whereabouts with him, nor the last incident with Antonio, and that bothered him. The fact that she had not talked to him before she'd disappeared made him angry. He had a feeling of uneasiness. This woman had come from nowhere. Why in the world would he have this kind of attitude? Sami thought she should be closer to him now than ever. He would stick to the deal, the agreement where there would not be any binding between the parties. Each of them would pretend not to know each other, working towards their goal of getting something from the other. As for Sami, it was the green card. He had put so much faith and hope in it that at times, he thought that without it, there would be no life for him in the USA. As for Jasmine, the money to curb her practical needs should have overridden everything else, and it was easy money to come by. With a stroke of a pen, she could put a few thousand dollars in her pocket. Jasmine knew how to deal with this kind of game and accepted only cash, and she could quickly cover her tracks once done.

Sami thought he had leverage because of the relationship that had developed. Jasmine could either stick to her previous plan or change her mind altogether. She was no stranger to this kind of game, and as such, she might as well exploit the innocent nature of Sami's personality, making him believe that she was interested in him so she could siphon even more money from him. Sami was afraid of what he could do. The series of events that had triggered his final decision had happened haphazardly. An erratic life hinged on a slippery string, prone to rupture at the spur of the moment.

"Okay, I will wait, then." On the other end of the line, Kumar had long gone. Sami put down the phone. His kids were already on edge, eager to get out of the house.

The door swung open, and the kids dashed out, chasing each other to see who would be the first to reach the playground. "Wait, Adam." Sami tried to stop him from running, but it was too late. Sami had to step out and watch as they raced to the swings. It appeared the small playground was empty. Sami jerked his head to the commotion in the house. His daughter Chaaltu was overturning the basket and spreading the toys all over. She was looking for her special toy to take with her to the playground. Then the telephone rang again. His daughter picked the phone up and talked for a few seconds and then hung up.

"Who was it?" Sami asked, with hesitation in his voice. It was common for his kids to answer the telephone, although he had trained them not to, especially since they had a phone-answering machine installed to leave messages. Sami thought that it was one of those stubborn telemarketers who kept calling to promote their products. He glanced at his daughter, who seemed to act as if the call had come from a friend.

"Who was calling?" Sami asked.

"Just a woman who wanted to talk with you. Her name was Jasmine or something like that, and I told her that you're busy. She said she would call later.

"Why didn't you tell me?" Sami yelled at her. "Did she say her name was Jasmine?"

"I am not sure. It sounded like that, and the lady understood that you were busy," Chaaltu said with a frightened voice, wondering why Daddy was so mad at her for not letting him know about this call.

"I am not busy. How many times have I told you not to answer the phone while I am around?" Sami belted out anxiously; he was undeniably irritated, and it showed it in his voice. He didn't know why he wanted to hear from Jasmine other than to tell her the outcome of the divorce decision. He had no explanation for his behavior. An urgent need to talk with her seized him, probably to secure positive reassurance that the deal would go through and let her know he was ready to file for the next step of the process. He approached the phone but realized that he had to attend to his kids for now. His daughter cowered away, wondering why Daddy was so mad because of a phone call.

That night, no other calls came. Sami slept, wondering what had happened. The phone number displayed on the caller ID did not work. In the meantime, life continued with its usual pattern, a twist, and uncertainty that led him to make another decision with ponderous reservations. Like all the decisions that he'd made during his lifetime, it was circumstantial. Sami found himself trapped by a situation that was beyond his control. As an international student, bound by some visa regulations and requirements, he had to monitor his status to avoid any violations.

For the next few days, Sami put some documents in order. His student visa would not expire until he gets done with his graduate work. However, his wearisome experiences with the job search had made him doubt future job prospects with the plant physiology degree he was pursuing. The decision had been made willy-nilly in hopes of satisfying the visa requirement.

A week went by, and even after several attempts, Jasmine did not answer her phone. Sami kept leaving messages, and when it became clear that she would not respond, he decided to check her place out. Sami knew where she lived; he'd noted down the address the last time she'd invited him over. It would take him less than fifteen minutes to get there.

Chapter 37

Sami drove slowly to see Jasmine, debating in his mind why she'd stopped calling and wondering whether she'd called while he was not at home. He feared that if his wife answered the phone, she might threaten her not to call again.

As he came closer to where she lived, he shivered, and an anticipatory mood overtook him. It was not cold, and the thought of not seeing her flooded his mind. His imaginary fear of deception crept in. *I am doomed. She's a fraud, and probably working undercover.* There was no car parked anywhere, a possible sign that there might be nobody in the house. He stopped in her driveway. He could feel the rhythmic sound of his heartbeat racing.

Sami got out of the car and tried the doorbell button once, and then twice. He decided to take a quick look around the whole house and walked towards the window. To his amazement, he noticed the curtain lift slightly, and he saw somebody peeping at him. He stood still and looked at the curtain, which had now closed. He looked again to make sure that it was not his imagination playing tricks on him. A glimpse of a dark figure silhouetted against the drapery emerged and quickly disappeared. Sami was sure he had seen a person, and he expected somebody to open the door. He went back to the front door and knocked again. No response.

He then left a sticky note at the door with his name and address for Jasmine.

Who could be there in the house? Her roommate? He thought. Before he could come up with any weird answers, a neighbor opened her door, looked at him, and immediately closed the door as if she was frightened. She appeared elderly. He felt a sense of aloofness in a strange place and feared what the neighbor would think about him. The way he dressed could fit the description of a burglar because of the disguise he'd put on to avoid being noticed by anybody who might know him. As he retraced his steps, he looked back at the window.

Before reaching his car, Sami noticed a police car coming in his direction. The vehicle approached slowly. Sami fiddled with his car key, trying to insert it in the lock. Once in the car, with an unsteady and shaky hand, he failed to start the engine. He caught a glimpse of the window, and this time, the curtain moved slightly, and he saw a hand sticking the middle finger up.

"Son of a..." Sami held in the temptation to curse. He began to sense the urgency of getting out of there, but at the same time, he wondered whether he should let the police know about this rude demonstration. The idea did not appeal to him because the police would ask many questions, and he could not answer why he was there himself. Sami had heard that sometimes they could turn things against you. From past experiences he'd had with police in Kenya, he'd concluded that cops should not be trusted. It was unfortunate that he took a generalized approach to this incident without any evidence of any adverse publicity regarding the police in this town. However, he'd had enough past experiences not to trust any cop anywhere in the world.

He recorded the time of the encounter and reversed his car. Suddenly a police car swung around in front of him with its siren on and flashing its lights. He had no idea what the policeman wanted.

"Step out of the car with your hands up!" a voice over an intercom commanded.

Sami was dazzled; he thought it was a dream. It took two more orders before he stepped out as commanded.

"I did not do anything wrong. I was trying to visit a friend." He'd heard cases of police shooting people who looked like him, and with no time to think, he raised his hands above his head and waited for more commands to obey instantly. "What do you want me to do?"

The policeman ignored him and pushed him towards the car while his partner searched the vehicle. They took his student ID and driver's license and told him to wait. After what seemed to be a long delay, the policeman relayed to him that the neighbors had noticed him hovering around the houses and the neighborhood. He also reported an attempted burglary.

"Are you trying to break into the house?" the policeman asked.

"No, sir, I was here to visit a friend. Her name is Jasmine. She lives in house number 215, I was here about three weeks ago," Sami confessed.

The policemen looked at each other. It was evident that they did not like his answer. "You were planning to steal something, right. A neighbor saw you trying to enter the house through the window."

Sami tried to say something, but the words could not come out clearly. "I swear, I was just visiting a lady friend who invited me a couple of weeks ago. I was concerned when she did not answer my phone call."

"What was the phone number? Give it to me," the police officer demanded. He looked at the phone number and checked some numbers; what they were, Sami was not sure. "You can go now. If there is anything else, we will get in touch with you." The police officer gave him a business card.

Haunted by the guilt of not knowing who the person in the house was, Sami got upset. The police episode was worrisome. He was afraid that his association with Jasmine could get him into further trouble. People in the wrong neighborhood could get shot. Many unanswered questions went through his mind as he drove away. He kept looking in the rearview mirror to make sure that the police officers were not following him.

***

"Hello, Kumar, it's Sami,"

"Oh, you sound different."

"Just a little upset. It's about Jasmine. Can you tell me what happened to her?"

"We can meet if you want. I will be at Hy-Vee in about an hour, and we can meet at McDonald's just across on Lincoln Way."

"Okay," Sami agreed.

When Sami arrived, Kumar was already seated and sipping his coffee. Sami joined him and opened the discussion. "I haven't heard from Jasmine, and when I went to her house, I saw another person lives there. What do you know about her? Did she leave town?"

Caught by surprise, Kumar thought for a moment. "Well, sort of, and surely not what she does on a day-to-day basis."

"Let me get this straight. You don't know about Jasmine's married life?"

"Do you mean this kind of marriage?" Kumar asked.

"Yes."

It took a while for Kumar to respond. He kept sipping his coffee. "Do you want to know? Does it matter if you get what you want? You are getting too close, eh." He winked.

"No, not the way you think. You know, I have a wife. I wanted to clear my consciousness and get through with this document without any complications. For instance, you don't know very much about her green card marriages and whether it was successful or not."

Kumar looked at him in a way that suggested that he was hiding something. "Not in detail, but from what I gathered, they processed the document, and her last husband got into trouble with the law and went to jail. Antonio, you know about him."

"Did he get the card?"

"Sure, he got the card, alright. Jasmine complained that he was violent and physical with her. It took a while before she recovered. He may also have leaked information about how he got the card. Don't worry too much. She had already decided to step out of this activity. That's the only thing I knew. I don't communicate with her every day. However, the last time we talked, she was thinking about visiting her family in New York. It was like an emergency. She hasn't called me, either, for the last couple of weeks."

"I am concerned. What if she disappears?"

"I think she will honor the agreement you made. Give it time and wait."

"Let's hope so. By the way, how do you know her?"

Kumar looked at him with a smile. He was not expecting this line of questioning. "I happened to know her, and it's a long story. A different circumstance."

"If you don't want to talk about it, I understand."

"I don't right now. Maybe someday. For now, just relax."

"That's fine. If you happen to hear from Jasmine, let me know. I would like to get over this matter."

"Remember, the nature of this work requires total secrecy, and you need to learn and practice the role you desire carefully and with precision. You will certainly encounter immigration officers, and they will have a preconceived notion about your marriage. You are always a suspect. You should know that."

Sami frowned, wondering why Kumar had used such strong words. "What do you mean, a suspect? I have not committed any crime yet."

Kumar let out a smirking laugh. "You're right; no crime committed."

"Okay, I get your point." Sami smiled. "Anyway, I have to go. I will call you tomorrow if I have anything else to ask. One more thing."

"What?"

"Never mind. Tomorrow, then. I will think about it," Sami said. Then he asked, "Oh, did she say anything about her roommate?"

"Not much, really, other than the fact that he was antisocial and mean. Don't read more into this."

"Sure," Sami agreed.

"Okay, I have to get something from the grocery." Kumar headed towards the store.

Chapter 38

A week later, Sami dialed Kumar's telephone number and heard the following message : "We are sorry . You have reached a number that has been disconnected or is no longer in service."

"Disconnected!" Sami exclaimed. He realized that was the only number he had. Sami went to the restaurant to inquire about Kumar.

"Do you know how I can reach Kumar?" he asked the restaurant waitress he knew.

"Kumar resigned a week ago and went back to India," the lady replied, but then she hesitated. "Did you check where he lived? I can give you the address we have if you want."

"Yes, please, that would help."

She wrote down an address and gave it to him. "That was the address listed."

Sami looked at the address and shook his head. "The university demolished that old apartment building a year ago. This address no longer exists."

The waitress shrugged, not sure what else to do. Looking back, Sami realized how the nature of this deal had made him keep everything secret, to the point where he'd overlooked its most critical aspect. Sami had met Kumar at work and didn't know where he lived. Kumar had preferred to meet at the restaurant where they worked and to discuss things after work. Knowing what he knew now, Sami became suspicious that Kumar knew more than what he'd shared about Jasmine.

Sami had heard many stories about fraud and how crooks cheated innocent people. He recalled the incident in the streets of Nairobi in Kenya, where he'd become a victim once and lost money when the card-playing trickster had duped him into playing cards.

The trick was for him to identify the original card selected. They called the game "pata potea," or "win or lose." The player would be shown playing cards and expected to recognize them. Sami thought that it was easy to pick the card from the deck. He saw a seven of spades, the card he'd betted on. When the trickster flipped the cards over, there were no seven of spades, and he lost. There was nothing Sami could do. Of the four who'd played the cards like him, three of them won. Sami heard later that those players were fake; they were on the same team, trying to lure people into the trap, pretending to be customers.

Sami would never have thought that his plan would fail. He'd believed what Kumar had told him about Jasmine. The only person who had been skeptical from the beginning was his wife.

***

Sami tried Kumar's number again, and a different person answered. He pretended to change his voice and tried a second time. He got the same message. "Wrong number." Sami thought seriously about the drama that he'd gone through; it was evident that Kumar, or whoever he was, had changed his phone number as well. Sami recalled the exact word Kumar said. "My friend introduced me to Jasmine." He wondered whether anybody knew who the real Jasmine was and where she'd gone.

Sami had no picture of Kumar either. The incomplete

information he had about Kumar Mehta did not lead him to any discovery. It added more suspicions in his mind about the relationship between Kumar and Jasmine. Sami wondered why Kumar had been evasive about questions regarding Jasmine and where she might be. He paused to connect and retrieve the series of events that had crossed his path.

***

Another week went by, and Sami moved out of the university apartment to one with three bedrooms near campus. He was hoping that he would return when the three-bedroom university family apartment rooms become available. This apartment was also walking distance from the college, and there were many grocery stores nearby.

Sami walked to the grocery to get the newspaper. At the entrance, he saw some advertisements for jobs and rental vacancies. He read publications by various organizations and became curious. His attention was attracted to the topic advertised: "Wealth and Happiness and How to Attain Them." Sami looked at his watch and realized that the presentation would take place in a church around the corner adjacent to the grocery. He reread the topic, "Wealth and Happiness," and wondered why they were holding it in the church.

Sami had never been a consistent worshiper, and at one point, he'd drifted away from religion out of ignorance. Although his parents were Muslim, he had not learned about Islam growing up. His nomadic parents, like the rest of the people in the area, continued with their cultural lifestyle and lived the ways of their traditions. The last time Sami had performed any worship was when he got married, where they practiced a mixture of Islamic faith and traditional rites.

Sami entertained his curiosity and wanted to find out more about the presentation. He entered the church, and somebody told him to move forward and sit, but he decided to sit in the last row so that he could get out when needed. The people started filling the rows in the back. Sami looked around and realized that this was a prayer service.

He turned to the person sitting next to him and asked, "What is he doing?" He gestured to the speaker. "I thought there would be a presentation on the topics advertised." He was sure about the venue and the time specified.

The man chuckled. "They do that all the time to attract people and then conduct secret fundraising during Saturday service. Aren't you a Seventh Day Adventist?"

"No, what is that?" Sami attempted to stand up.

The man gave him a strange look. "It is a Protestant Christian denomination. We do our observance on the seventh day of the week. Sit down. You will hear something on the topic, too."

"Shh, silence," a person in the next row snapped at them. Sami realized the trap and sat down. In any case, he thought that if it was a house of God, he might find inner peace in the presence of divine enclosure.

Sami felt that all eyes were on him, and he was in the wrong spot. The people who worshiped there didn't look like him, and it was as if they expected him to find his kind elsewhere in the city.

The pastor began the service promptly, and sure enough, the topic of the sermon was on wealth. He started with the story in Genesis and showed how God owned everything, and human beings were only managers of God's property. He then moved on to elaborate some passages in the Bible, reading Deuteronomy 8:17–18. "And thou say in thine heart, My power and the might of mine hand hath gotten me this wealth. But thou shalt remember the Lord thy God: for it is he that giveth thee power to get wealth."

The pastor read in another section of the Bible and

mentioned how King Solomon, the wealthiest person during his time, acknowledged the wealth God had provided him. Sami fidgeted. The only thing on his mind was how much more time was left.

"Money is the cause of all evils in the world." The pastor vehemently emphasized his point. Sami was dozing off and on, and he woke up the moment the pastor mentioned the word "money." He didn't know the background context used for this phrase, but he knew the idiosyncrasy behind all preaching. He listened attentively as the pastor preached. The language he used in the sermon, was ominous, powerful, nefarious, and delightful, all at the same time, and it captivated Sami. No matter what the preacher's views were, no one would convince Sami that money was evil. The problem was with the people, not money. They hoarded and kept for themselves while other human beings suffered.

Sami observed the donation box as they passed down the long pews. He watched as people put some money and checks in it. The person who sat next to him looked at him with a firm gaze, expecting Sami to drop money into the box. Sami frowned, thinking that giving contributions was a voluntary act. The way the person held his gaze indicated what he expected Sami to do. He had to put money in the box. Sami smiled to dispel the image of a grumpy face and pretended to search in his pocket for cash. Unobtrusive thoughts crept into his mind with an imaginary temptation. What if the lights were off? He could sense fingers groping in the dark, enticed by the bait of the treasure of the donation box.

When the pastor condemned the money, Sami thought that the pastor knew what was in his mind and had selected a topic relevant to his ordeals. The pastor talked about debts, money, family, alcohol addiction, gambling, and all other social ills. He seemed to suggest with a conviction that the victims were at fault. He stressed that people caused all sorts of problems to occur and emphasized the accountability that each member should have for their sins and transgressions.

Sami waited until the end of the service. Some people followed him with their eyes as he left the church. One person caught up with him and, with a weird look on his face, said, "You're not a regular worshipper here. Not from around here, right? I hope you got what you needed." His voice trailed off. "I am a frequent worshiper at this church, and I haven't seen you here before."

With a puzzled look on his face, Sami waited.

"I know one temple down on Eleventh Street where you might feel comfortable," the man said.

"Why do you think I should feel comfortable there?" Sami asked.

"I thought that you wanted to be with people you have something in common with."

"You mean this?" Sami held his hand up to show the color of his skin.

The man felt embarrassed and could not answer him any further. "I am sorry; I didn't mean to evoke these feelings in you. I thought you would be more welcome there than here." The man stepped back and prepared to leave.

"Do you mean that the God you worship and mine are somewhat different?"

"No, don't get me wrong. I was just stating the reality of things around here, and I am sure you're aware of it yourself." He waited, not knowing how Sami would react. "Some of your people worship at this temple around Thirteenth and Ontario Street. I saw some students going there in the evenings."

"It's called a mosque," Sami corrected.

He apologized and left in a hurry.

Sami turned around to catch up with the man, but it was

too late. He had cut a corner around the store and disappeared. Sami regretted his actions towards the man, who had been trying to help. A sense of guilt overtook him.

Sami revisited the question of money and the pastor's argument in his mind as he walked back to his apartment.

He entered the apartment building entrance, stopped at the magazine stand, and browsed through all of the advertisements posted. Then he climbed the stairs to his second-floor room.

Chapter 39

Sami paused on the stairs and looked down before he reached his apartment . His neighbor popped her head through the door and shut it quickly . Sami stopped to see what she was up to. He never saw her leave the room. Every time he came down the stairs, she would open her door, look, and close it. She did not respond when Sami tried to greet her .

Sami couldn't wait to share his Sunday morning adventure with his wife. He ran up the stairs, eager to spread the news, which he could inflate to his taste. "Mother of Hawa, you can't believe what happened this morning." Sami steadied himself with his hands on the door frame, panting. Then he grabbed a bottle of water and took a few gulps.

"We were wondering what took you so long to return. Did you go to the university gym to exercise?"

"No, I attended a fascinating presentation in the church on how to acquire wealth." He smiled.

"Oh, I thought people prayed and rested on Sundays. What kind of financial presentation on a Sunday morning in a Church?" Her facial expression extended to ignominious disbelief. She held her hand over her mouth, wondering what his real motives were. Indeed, he had not turned spiritual. A grip of fear engulfed her. Sarah knew Sami never showed interest in religious activities and was more inclined towards traditional ways of life.

The church episode with Sami added more frightening thoughts in her mind. She was afraid that his frustration with life could tip him over to try a new religion. She couldn't imagine that her children would embrace a different faith from her own. Up to that moment, religion was not an issue because the children automatically followed the parents. Fearful thoughts raced through her mind. Her maternal instincts aroused by the fact that she did not teach her children about religion, and she did not want them to learn from others. She had been shocked earlier when they'd asked her why they didn't celebrate Christmas.

With the available space of the new apartment, Sarah felt at ease and created a learning environment for her children. The kids were pleased with the new location. Sami could still remember their excitement when they moved in. "We rented a three-bedroom apartment," Mom announced when she picked the kids up from the daycare. The children felt happy; for the first time, they each had a room they could call their own. They ran around, jumping, and showing each other what they could do in their rooms.

"At last, we have a place of our own," the bigger ones commented. The little ones joined in and danced. They all put on their favorite songs and sang together. Unfortunately, the apartment they rented was on the second floor, and Sami would soon find out the limiting rules of the apartment's living conditions.

Soon the neighbors noticed the little feet tapping on the floor above. It was a little louder for one neighbor, who did not understand children. This neighbor kept to herself, and right from the time Sami's family moved in, she seemed extremely uncomfortable. They must not disturb her peace. Silence should be the norm, and these little rugrats must be tamed to keep quiet. It was unacceptable for the neighbor on the first floor. Kids running around in the house on the second floor, jumping up and down, singing songs, and reciting their ABCs, were too loud for this neighbor. "What could a five-year-old do to satisfy this neighbor?" Sami questioned. Well, the parents were to blame for not disciplining their kids. You might wonder how? The kids stayed in the daycare for five to six hours and were asleep by eight in the evening. They needed three hours to have fun and play in their rooms, and yet the law of the apartment complex stated that they had no right to disturb the peaceful nights of the adults' world.

In the little space that they called their home, the kids put their toys, stacked them together, and pretended to make them jump up and down.

The second week after they moved into the new house, Sarah suddenly became angry with the kids for playing. She told them not to jump up and down. The five-year-old could not understand why Mommy was not happy when he played. Mommy spoke with a raised voice, telling them not to run in the house, not to jump, not to dance in their rooms, not to sing loudly, and not to play hide and go seek in the house. The children found the new rule challenging to adhere to, and the parents became sad. The bigger ones thought it was the silly adults' world, where they sometimes pretended to be happy and sometimes sad.

"The little noises that you made in your rooms bothered another tenant on the first floor, and this is a warning letter from the landlord." With teary eyes, Sarah held the note in her hand. "I've told you several times. We will lose this apartment." The sobbing mother could not control herself.

Chaaltu, as usual, had a question for her mother. "Mom, why can't we play in our rooms.? We have enough space to play together in our new apartment, and if we can't play the way we want at home, where else can we play?"

"We will be thrown out of this house if we cause problems for our neighbors." The mother could no longer control the tears pouring down. She wiped off her tears and continued. "They said that we disturbed them."

"Mom, it is not fair that we cannot play in our rooms. You promised that when we moved into a new house, we would have our rooms where we could have fun. We feared cockroaches and rats, and now you grounded us because of a stupid old lady? I hate this stinking life!" Chaaltu cried. The sobbing mother held her daughter.

"It is the evil woman downstairs, right? She does not like us. Every time we come down, she opens her door, looks at us, and then shuts her door. She will burn in hell." Chaaltu continued with her tumultuous stream of curses.

"Chaaltu, honey, don't talk like that." Sarah held her close. "Where did you learn this kind of language?" Chaaltu detached herself from her mom but kept quiet. "We will one day have our own house, but right now, we are renting, and we have to follow their rules."

Sami and his wife received a complaint from a neighbor who lived on the first floor directly below their rooms. They went to the landlord's office to express dissatisfaction with the harsh, unrealistic expectations of the neighbor's claim. They told the landlord that their children played just like other children would play in their rooms and had not done anything wrong to cause a disturbance. Their words fell on deaf ears, for the landlady seemed to ignore this simple fact about children. The lady who'd complained had no children, and she had been living in that apartment for the last fifteen years, so the landlady considered her a valuable tenant and did not want to lose her. She would rather have uncouth people out of her apartment as soon as possible. Sami recalled how the landlady reacted even on the day she'd shown them the apartment.

When the children, out of excitement, jumped around. She looked at them and asked, "When did you come to America?" She then realized her suggestive bias, so when Sarah shot her unfriendly glance, she added, "Don't get me wrong; I have children, too. Sometimes they can act wild."

Sami felt pain while listening to the barrage of questions directed at him regarding his children. While he thought it was a good idea to have silence in the rooms and quiet time for neighbors, some of the demands were unrealistic and cruel to the little kids, whose only excitement was to have fun and enjoy each moment they had.

That night, the family felt the presence of a cloud of darkness. The happy moments and joyful evenings were things of the past. The kids did their homework and watched cartoons on TV until they went to bed.

"This is not the way our children should spend their evenings," Sami fumed.

"They are fine."

"How can this be fine? They watched passively. Didn't you see the laughter and joy when they played together? Their innate tendency to follow the natural growth with creative and childish sagacity that we are robbing them of by making them prone to inactivity."

"We have already received an eviction notice. What do you suggest?" Sarah shot him a glance.

"This is cruel and unfair. What are we teaching our kids?"

"Respect for others' property."

"Give me a break. You're taking it too far."

Chapter 40

A week later, Sarah threw a letter on to his lap. "Did you see what happened?" With teary eyes, she commanded, "Read! This is what you get!"

Sami had known that this was coming and didn't need to read. He browsed through the letter and read only the relevant parts. "We continue to receive complaints concerning excessive noise from your apartment... It has never been our intent to restrict your enjoyment of your home. However, we must consider the rights and privileges of all tenants. This is the second notice that you received regarding this violation of your lease, and due to your continued violation, we have no other choice left but to terminate your contract by the end of this month..."

Sami held the letter in his hand and paced the room. He was not sure what option to take. They'd spent only two months in this rented apartment, and this was the only time he'd felt his kids had a bit of freedom to play in their rooms, and now, with this newfound curfew and restrictions, he wondered how he could exercise his rights.

Sami's wife took things a little differently. She was ready to discipline her kids. She thought their behavior was not acceptable. She rebuked them for acting wildly, and she put the blame directly on Sami for inadequate supervision.

"It's all your fault. Who was the adult at home when these disruptions happened? You let the kids run around and jump on the sofa. We were on the first floor in a university apartment room, and now look what you have done," She broke down in tears.

"As I told you all the time, the kids used indoor voices. It was only normal play, and they are kids. What do they expect?" He shouted. "I know for sure the person who complained about us; it was that devilish-looking woman directly under us. I have seen how she holds her face wherever our kids come into the building. She does not like us. It is not about the noise. It is about who we are as people. Don't you get it?"

"You don't know about that, and there is no reason to assume.".

"What a life! I can't believe that our children don't have the right to play in their rooms. The landlord has no right to kick us out of the apartment."

"What rights do you have here? Especially when you trampled on the very rights that you are claiming to have," Sarah snapped. "You abused your privileges as a tenant."

rooms?

"You blame me for this now? Don't put up this deceptive act of masquerade. I cannot believe that you are on her side and agreed to this censorship." He knew their anger could spill into a heated debate. It just required a little tip.

"In America, you have rights, but you may not be aware of them. A landlord cannot kick you out without justification, without a court order of eviction." Sami paced the room again. "What if we ignore the request to move out?" he said to himself. "This is not fair. When you discipline your child, they come for your child in the name of protecting their welfare, and they call it child abuse. What do we call this now? It's discrimination against kids. They are helpless without a voice, and I have to be their advocate." Sami turned around abruptly. The loud laughter from his wife caught his attention.

"You're not serious." She continued laughing. "The landlady has every right to kick us out. It's her house and property, and if we do not follow her set of rules, we will not be allowed to live here. The law is on her side. You can even go to court, and the judges will rule in her favor. You have to know your place on the social ladder. You don't have a voice. If you don't vote, you don't count much because most of these landlords have the power to influence decisions."

Sami looked at her directly. "This is not a third-world country. Judges here follow the rules." He paused. "If you are such an expert in this area, why can't you fight for your children's justice? Yes, I have a voice if I use it in the right way. It's just that I do not want to be in the limelight right now because of my legal status." Sami showed frustration on his face, and he tapped the table in a reflective mood." I guess I have to rethink my life in this country."

This provoked another look of disapproval from his wife. He knew what she would say.

"You can buy a house."

Sami returned the look and murmured to himself, "It is not fair. I can take this matter and understand it as an adult. How do you expect the children to understand this treatment?"

"Don't make it a big deal. Let it go. There is nothing you can do about it."

Sami looked at his wife again. "I can file for a complaint based on discrimination. I did some research and found out that the behavior of our children that the landlady quoted was expected and did not reach the level of disturbance. They made noises while playing, which was an acceptable thing for children, so she was discriminating against families with children. There is something else. The landlady has to show that we did not provide supervision for our children. I bet that will be hard to prove. She may also have discriminated because we are immigrants. Did you recall how she reacted the first time we checked out the house?" Sami nodded.

"Come on, get real. You let the children run around in the room and jump up and down. They turned the sofa cushion into a trampoline landing pad as if they were competing for gymnastics. You would have complained, too, if it were you. The poor old lady must have endured sleepless nights."

Sami moaned. "I cannot believe that came out of your mouth. I am afraid you can even send your children to jail."

"They should learn to take responsibility for their actions. Everything has a consequence. I am sure you have heard the phrase, 'Spare the rod, spoil the child.'"

"The phrase refers to discipline in the case of unruly children and has nothing to do with this incident. Here we are dealing with injustice. How can you apply such an illogical and unfair assessment by not advocating for your kids? I cannot believe a mother could think the way you do." Sami looked at his wife. "Do you mean it?"

"What do you think? Don't try to make me feel guilty. This tactic won't work with me. When it comes to responsibilities, I don't mince words and sugarcoat it. I don't feel guilty about it, either. It is the way it is."

"Yes, I believe you are capable of doing that," Sami acknowledged.

She looked at him in a way that confirmed his thoughts.

"Do you also believe that it was my fault that I did not get a job in my area of expertise, even though you knew that I tried everything and unfairly treated? It blew my mind when you found fault with your kids."

Sarah kept quiet.

"A problem-free world does not exist. We got out of one

problem, and now another one has opened. You wanted us to get away from cockroaches and rats in the old university apartment, and don't you see? We are facing a different kind of problem."

"In both cases, we had to do our part, and we didn't." Sarah was back in her defiant mood. "As for the job, you have to change your tactics and attitude. That's all I can say."

"Okay, here we go again. I believe the world is not black and white, and there are some gray areas as well. We see things differently. Don't you see that everybody is for himself or herself? Everybody wants you to align with their views. We don't have to agree with anybody. If something doesn't look right, whether the law is on their side or not, I will oppose it." Sami was heated up. He had a list of grievances and was ready to unleash.

"They should not kick us out of the apartment because of not following the silly owner's rule," he added.

Sarah frowned, jeering at him in a disapproving manner. "You have no ground to fight the case when everything is against you. You violated all the rules."

"Let's not argue over this. In both incidences, they violated our rights, and we have grounds to sue for failure to provide habitable housing. This is our basic right as tenants. Why do you assume your kids were at fault? The university should have eliminated those pests that caused us inconvenience, and the owner of this apartment should have respected the rights of children to play." Sami looked at his wife, who was still moody.

"I am sorry you feel that way. We are still on the waiting list for the university's new apartment building, and they will soon allow the tenants to move in. We will move out, and since the landlord has agreed to forfeit the lease agreement, we can move out anytime," Sami remarked as if confirming his statement. "Don't you see the landlady does not want us here? Otherwise, she would have demanded the full payment for the duration of the lease. That is discrimination in its highest form. She is telling us to move out now and forget about the lease agreement, which is financially good for us. Don't think she is doing any favor for us."

"If you destroy her property, it's obvious that she will look after her interests. She has to get us out free to minimize more damages."

Sami laughed. Sarah looked at him. "What?"

"Nothing is free, dear. The landlord has already profited. Didn't you read what was in the letter about the damages we caused? There were scratches on the refrigerator and floor. She said that she was going to replace the carpet with our deposit money, and we will not get a refund. We were here for only two months. It is a rip-off." Sami shook his head. "I have one regret. We did not take pictures when we moved in. Anyway, let's move on. There are greater things to worry about than this nuisance."

Sarah busied herself with kitchen chores. She turned on the radio as she worked. Sami, in the meantime, started playing with his kids. After dinner, the kids settled down and got ready for bed. He read them bedtime stories and told them some bits and pieces from his tribal folklore.

Once again, the contentious issue that muddled their thought processes lingered on. Neither Sami nor Sarah wanted to bring it up. For Sarah, the green card saga that had overtaken Sami's day-to-day life was never an issue. She dismissed it outright and kept herself out of it. No matter how carefully she avoided the path Sami was pursuing, she was disappointed that she'd failed to dissuade him from going forward with his wild idea. Sarah believed that he had not gone through with the process. Otherwise, she would have signed the document. In any case, she felt confident that her employer would waive her visa status. She could not wait to surprise Sami with one secret that she was not ready to disclose at this moment.

Sami, on the other hand, could not explain how all his efforts had evaporated. Kumar's and Jasmine's disappearances had left him on a path with a dead end. He could not face his wife to disclose what had happened, and he decided not to tell her. He pushed aside conflicting thoughts and focused on what to do next.

Chapter 41

It was one of those Friday evenings when students' frenzied lives sprang to new heights of unruliness . Sami looked forward to these delightful events . He had an appointment that Friday and was not working at the meatpacking factory.

The town adjacent to the university had always been the center of fun for students. Sami was about to walk home when he bumped into Abdou. "Hi Abdou, how are you doing? I forgot how to say that in French."

"It is comment allez vous?" Abdou hugged him. "I am in a hurry to catch a green bus. See you later. Oh, are you coming to the party this evening? I will be there later." He ran off to catch the bus to the students' housing complex.

Sami debated whether to go home first. Friday was the day he relieved his load of guilt and exhaustion after a week of physical exertion and the accumulation of all kinds of frustrations and miserable feelings. Rather than take the bus, he strolled along the sidewalk towards his house. He could use the time to reflect on things that had happened during the week.

As he was crossing the short stretch of a path towards the agronomy and horticulture buildings, he came to a halt. Jasmine saw him first and came to him with hands outstretched to hug him. She had a new look: An Afro hairstyle with a mixture of peacock's color styles that Sami had no idea from where it came. It looked like different hair colors incorporated into one strand, yet he didn't know what to call it. With a strutting display, Jasmine portrayed a charming and appealing theatrical persona.

"Nice to see you." She squeezed him, and it took a while for him to regain his composure. "I called you several times and left messages. I had to leave the city for a while, and besides, I wanted to start afresh." She paused.

Sami didn't know what she meant by starting afresh. Her casual approach puzzled him. "What are you up to?" he asked.

Jasmine exuded a vibrant, dazzling demeanor. She had disappeared for over three weeks without warning, and now she'd shown up as if nothing had happened. He refrained from making any comment and waited. He was a little surprised, though he'd somewhat expected this kind of reaction considering his strange fake marriage proposal. Something must have happened, he thought, and he feared that she'd changed her mind about the whole idea.

"I had to sort out some family matters," Jasmine announced.

"You kept me in suspense." Sami paused for a moment. "I was concerned. Anyway, we need to talk."

Jasmine suddenly turned around and stepped out of the path of an approaching student on a skateboard. "Watch out, asshole!" she cursed. The student swung by fast as Jasmine gasped, shooting out multiple words of profanity. Another student sped by and almost knocked down Sami.

"There is a party that I am planning to attend, and if you don't have other plans, maybe we could talk at that time. What do you think?" Sami asked.

It was one of those things you do when an awkward situation arises. Sami felt uncomfortable standing in the middle of a road with a woman. A sight, so palpable to the passers-by, and ripe for the spread of rumors. Sami was not ready for a scandal to emerge. He then switched his mind to the money matter and wondered how she could explain her long absence.

"I would love to. I have been invited and am heading that way." Jasmine nodded.

She glanced at him with a seductive wink, her eyes dancing with the joy of the moment. Jasmine could put up an act.

Sami smiled, hoping to hear what she had to say about the issue that she'd left hanging.

Jasmine stayed calm as she started walking.

"I guess you have a lot of explaining to do," Sami acquiesced halfheartedly.

"I do, and I had a strong reason. See you then," Jasmine affirmed.

Sami continued walking, hoping to get some answers to his questions. It became clear to him. It was not a question of right or wrong. He had to move past this stage regarding his decisions. Feelings of guilt crossed his mind off and on. With his mind fixated on the wrong side, and his senses numbed to sins for a long time, Sami felt the right decisions would vanish quickly without *a trace.*

The Friday nightlife had begun already when Sami arrived. At the door, there was a long line of students pushing to get in; some barred temporarily from entering due to their age, but somehow, when the line gets shorter, they would find themselves inside. They would pull every trick possible, like borrowing ID cards from each other. Those at the door merely glanced through the ID's and did not scrutinize them thoroughly, creating a set of loopholes for underage students to slip in.

Sami and Jasmine sat in a corner. "I am thirsty. What do

you want to drink?"

Jasmine had already ordered some drinks while waiting for him. After he ordered a soda, Sami had to find the right words to initiate the discussions. "Where do we begin?"

"I know. To be honest with you, I am struggling with it, too," Jasmine agreed.

"I appreciate the honesty. Let's get to the point." Sami could not wait to hear her explanation of why she'd disappeared for a while and why she now appeared to be a different person with a changed look.

"You have a right to be angry with me, and I don't blame you for that. I have acquired knowledge because of the experiences I got, and you can argue the pros and cons of this journey of my life that has shaped my attitude, political views, and the look you see today."

"Kumar also disappeared. I heard he returned to India. Do you know his whereabouts?"

Jasmine laughed. "Sorry, it was the way you said it. We did not disappear. You said the same thing about me. He went to see his mother, who was sick, and I think he will be back soon. Anyway…" Her eyes found Sami's. "What I was saying earlier was probably confusing. Let me make it clear. I have become an activist."

"What issue are you fighting for?" he inquired.

"Against drug overdose and misuse of drugs." She paused, assessing whether Sami was with her or not. He appeared at a loss, not expecting this side of the story from her. "Do you understand my argument?" she asked

Sami smiled. Jasmine thought that he was not able to understand the political jargon of the American system, but she was mistaken. Unlike American students, who were ignorant of the outside world, Sami, like most international students, was aware of political situations around the world and was fully engaged and interested in what was happening. Just a few days ago, he had been discussing with his international student friends about their experiences in their own countries.

"You have seen what happened during the election season in our country. The political bandits and some of the harsh critics of our government would turn to airwaves and scrutinize everything. I love our democracy, which, as you know, some of the countries where you came from can only dream about."

Sami kept silent. He did not like the pretentious way she was presenting the facts. He was sure she had little knowledge about developing countries.

"By the way," she continued, "I have seen many foreign students on campus; maybe you can share with me your experience about your own country someday."

Sami was a little taken aback by this request. In most of his experiences with other American students, whether they were black or white, none of them ever asked him about his country. He felt as if they all thought they knew his country better than him.

"Let me know when you are ready. I would love to share with you what I know."

"Okay, I am curious. You don't have to go into detail. All I know is what comes from the media," Jasmine added.

Sami acknowledged her observations. The media depicted Africa as a poverty-stricken continent. He was pleased that Jasmine was at least interested in finding out the truth.

"Let's get back to the issue at hand," he interjected.

"If you have any problem that needs a solution, nobody will do it for you. You have to learn to figure out how you will do it yourself first." Jasmine was intense in her discourse. Sami leaned forward, sipping cold soda as she gathered her momentum. "The world is ruled by a few idiots who, for various reasons, found out that most of the people are uninformed and don't care. So, they figured out how to shape their destiny. Do you see what is happening in politics? You heard people complain about issues when the campaign was over. What do you see now? You can take a hard look. You will find a whole segment of disfranchised community members in a perpetual race to meet their basic needs, yet unable to help themselves." Sami nodded as Jasmine continued. "You would think that if people were so passionate enough to care about their conditions, they would do something to improve them, right?"

Sami had not spoken much, but it was evident from his petulant toss of the head that frustration was gathering behind his troubled face. He allowed Jasmine to explain her situation.

Jasmine was adamant and viewed the world differently. What, exactly, had happened to change her stance?

As if reading his thoughts in his mind, Jasmine declared, "We should be part of the solution."

Sami looked up.

"You know, before my brother died…" It took her a while to compose herself again. "I didn't care or bother to know what a drug overdose was all about." She paused. Sami was not surprised by this reaction. People tended to shun those who were involved with drugs and did not learn about the issue.

"A drug overdose is considered a medical emergency and requires medical attention to help prevent death or lasting health consequences. Many states have passed 'Good Samaritan' laws that legally protect the victims of overdose. Even those who call 911 to report the emergency are also protected." She sighed. She did not wait for Sami to reply before adding, "You can help, you know."

Sami was not ready for this turn of events.

"I know what you're thinking. We cannot succeed without

your help and everybody around us. The drug overdose issue is bigger than you and me." He nodded, and she continued. "If we combine our efforts, it will become part of the greater society. You can help in any way you can."

"How can I help?" he asked.

"I am glad you asked because you are not alone."

"If you can help educate people, your close associates, friends, and neighbors, that would be great, and you have done your share. Just pass out these flyers and postcards. That will do."

"Here." She gave him some to take with him. "I know people think that they can't do anything. Their efforts add up. It may take many years, but someone somewhere will listen. In any case, it is better to do something than nothing."

Sami read the inscriptions on the postcards. "What you need to know about drug overdose and how to help." He flipped over and noticed a picture of a young adult.

Jasmine sipped a glass of water and continued. "We need this awareness, and I can count on you."

Chapter 42

"Jasmine. Give me your attention."

"Oh, I got carried away."

"Before you disappeared, we agreed to go forward with the preparation of the visa document. Let's address this."

Jasmine leaned forward with her elbows on the table, a surprised look on her face.

"Did you say I disappeared?" She smiled. "I took a break! Honey, I am here now."

The air in the room intensified with heated conversations in all the corners of the little space. Students jeered and howled across to each other. One might wonder how anybody could hear what someone else was saying when everybody was talking at the same time. Oblivious to the surroundings, Jasmine continued her crusade against what she perceived to be an ignored epidemic due to a lack of education. She was conscientious about carrying out her work, to the point where she had memorized all the steps of the actions needed.

"I stopped by your house and got a rude welcome. Do you know who lives there?" Sami asked, breaking her chain of thought.

"I no longer live there. Probably my roommate, and you know we didn't get along. I had to leave the house." Sami looked surprised, wondering how a female could have a male roommate. "Don't worry about him. I don't think he will do any harm to you."

"I am surprised that you had a male roommate."

"Sure, it was fine with me. We had separate rooms and lives. Nothing in common. We only shared the kitchen and living room."

"Did you hear from Antonio? Do you think he might know where you live now?"

"Not yet, but it may not be difficult for him to find out because I left a forwarding address."

Sami brought out the handwritten note that had warned him about Jasmine. "Do you think you can recognize this handwriting?"

She read the note, and her facial demeanor dropped flat, portraying a state of uncertainty. "It's Antonio. The wretched animal is still on the loose. He promised not to bother you." With rambling speech, she attempted to hide her vexation.

"Okay, we will get back to Antonio later. Let's talk about the main issue. Are you still in the game?"

Jasmine's expression became somber. "This will be my last project, you know. I committed to the deal and will go through with it."

"I have completed the application and done everything needed from my side," Sami said.

"Which application? Things have changed a lot since the last time we discussed this." It took a while for Jasmine to realize what he was getting at. "Oh." She darted sideways glances, murmuring in an excited tone of voice. Her facial expression removed from the reality of the moment.

Sami was perplexed and had to regroup his mental positioning and wait for another opportunity to strike. As he juggled the weird thoughts in his mind, it became apparent that he had to deal with the dark cloud over him. He needed to know whether her choice of public life would conflict with her previous clandestine activities.

"Are you waiting for an answer from me?" She asked after a long silence. She paused for a while and continued. "I could help you with the promise I made. You have to understand my current position. I have to do everything right and earn a clean record." She knew she had no problem marrying and later divorcing, and there was nothing illegal about that, but she'd also received some payments. Surely, she would erase this part of her history, and she swore never to do what she'd done earlier in her past. It was something she would not like to display in public. Divorced three times, and with three children who now lived with her grandmother, Jasmine desired a regular marriage. Her old habits crept in when she needed money. If this situation had happened today, she would have declined the opportunity.

"You know how difficult this will be considering that my situation has changed," she repeated.

"Jasmine, I want this document finalized and filed for the change of status at the same time. As I indicated to you earlier, I have the divorce paper from the court. We can now process the marriage document."

"I thought you said your wife was against it. She finally came on board, right?"

Sami ignored the question. "I do not want to delay the next stage further." He glanced at her.

"As I said, I will do it. If we file the marriage document right away for a green card, I think it might raise suspicion."

"I heard that it was okay to do it. People have married and separated several times, and nobody questioned it." Sami had his deadline to meet at the end of the semester, which was when his regular visa extension would end. He did not want to delay the process.

"Is there anything else you want me to do?"

"No!" Sami replied. "Nothing else. If we get done with what we have just discussed, we can then go to the county courthouse and finalize it this week and complete the immigration application at the same time. It might take some weeks, or even months before we can enact the process of applying for the green card." He looked up, making sure that Jasmine was following. "I researched the information, Form I-130, the relative petition, and I-485, the adjustment of status can be filled at the same time, and we can get this part out of the way, Jasmine."

"I get your point. There's more to it than what you would think. I would prefer a proper, official marriage, and through the church first before the court," she said.

"I would rather have it simple. I know it sounds artificial, and that was precisely why we went through all these steps. You knew all the formalities." Sami caught a glimpse of her reaction from the corner of his eye. Jasmine sensed the urgency and desperation with which Sami was pursuing the issue. Faced with the dilemma of her new change of look, she had to attune herself to this kind of living.

With unanswered questions in his mind, Sami tried to understand what the new Jasmine could offer. "Can we skip the church? I don't belong to the faith. We can do it at the county courthouse." Before Jasmine could speak, he said, "I have to go now. Can we meet to begin the application process?"

"We can meet at the library around 10:00 a.m.," Jasmine shifted her position.

"Wait..." Sami hesitated. "How about tomorrow at Memorial Union hall to finalize a couple of things. I will be available at 10:00 a.m.,"

Jasmine hesitated. "That would work for me."

The evening air turned crisp and chilly with Friday night's disco flavor. The party, still in its infancy stage, continued unabated and engulfed the atmosphere, dominated by a social life of its own. More students trickled in and out while Sami remained mesmerized by Jasmine's new look.

He glanced at her and envisioned his new role. He tried to rearrange the next step in his mind. Sometimes he would rehearse precisely how he would break the news to his wife, and he took pleasure in amusing himself with an opening line: "Honey, I have officially arranged for a fake marriage with a lady, and I'm ready to sign the papers. Everything will be all right." With his wife's relentless opposition, he had to take a cautionary approach. He kept the divorce papers securely hidden at the bottom of the drawer in the same envelope where he stored his certificates. He checked it regularly.

Chapter 43

Sami woke up a little earlier the following day to get ready to meet with Jasmine . He went to the bedroom and pulled open the drawer where he kept the recent document he'd received from the county office. He opened the envelope and held it up as if hesitating what to do.

"I will take the kids to the mall," Sarah announced. Sami dropped the envelope in his hand. He had not noticed his wife entering the bedroom.

"What's wrong? You appear shaken," Sarah commented.

"No, I am fine." Sarah looked at the envelope that he'd dropped with her penetrating gaze and turned away when his eyes met hers.

"I will go to the library," Sami chirped, concealing the surprised look on his face. *Does she know?* He asked himself.

Sami stopped by the Memorial Union Hall cafeteria. He got a cup of tea and waited. He kept to himself and watched the news on the TV screen as he tossed around the plans in his head.

He tried to deflect the true nature of this incident with Jasmine and its moral obligations.

"Hi, Sami," Jasmine said, surprising him from behind.

After a few seconds, Sami asked, "Can I get you

something? Juice, coffee, or donuts?"

"Thanks, I will get it." Jasmine joined the queue.

Sami turned around. They were some students at the table nearby within close hearing range. He moved to an empty table in the corner. Jasmine joined him.

"You know, I have been thinking."

"About what?" Sami paused.

"We can make it official. Well, sort of," Jasmine replied.

Sami was not sure what she meant. "Do you mean the document?"

"Yes, we are here to finalize the application and get ready."

"How long do you think it will take, and what else do we need?" Sami was trying to read her mind and get clues from her facial expression, which revealed nothing.

"Honey, it is up to you. You can do whatever you want; it is official. You finalized the divorce papers, paving the ways for a new beginning."

Sami kept silent, so Jasmine continued. "We can be good partners. I am now a bit hesitant to do it in a secretive way. I will consider this marriage proposal official. We will review everything tomorrow." She smiled.

"What?" Sami appeared off the track, not sure where the discussion was going. He had different thoughts, and his mood began to change. Jasmine realized the impact of her words. She stretched out her hand to pat him on the back. "Things are coming all at once for you, right?"

"Let me get this straight. What exactly do you want me to do now?" Sami asked

"Bring all the questions you have tomorrow when we will start the process," she said with a gleeful laugh of confidence. Sami got the opening he needed.

She unzipped her purse and took out a wrapped stick of chewing gum. She offered Sami a stick as well. "The timeline is critical, and we have to do it now." She unwrapped the second stick of gum. "I have quit smoking, and this helps me."

"This is a daunting task." Sami winked.

"I do understand. A big decision with risks involved." Jasmine nodded.

"The procedures are the same ones as with all the supporting documents." Jasmine opened a folder with sample applications. "Once you complete it, the United States Citizenship and Immigration Services will review the application, which can take months, and sometimes even years. They will then send a notice for us to appear for an interview."

Sami frowned. Jasmine continued. "Honey, they will scrutinize thoroughly and ask all kinds of questions to make sure that the marriage is legit and meant for real. After we pass this stage, there will be an adjustment of status, and then the rest will be history, and you will obtain your green card." She ended with a broad smile.

Sami reviewed the process in his head and realized how simple it could be if everything happened the way she'd said.

"You don't seem to be excited, Sami." She prodded him in the ribs, and he laughed. "I didn't know that you're ticklish." She prodded him again. "Now, I know." She then browsed through the form.

"Jasmine, I am okay. My only concern is about marriage in the church, and I also thought that we should get an attorney."

"We will get an attorney if we need one. I have some referrals. Don't worry about the church document; this will validate our marriage and can be a good supporting document to help during the interview." Jasmine looked at him. "Relax." She patted him on the back again.

Sami tried to move away, thinking that she would tickle him.

"Got you. I was not going to tickle you." She laughed.

"It won't take long, right?" Sami turned.

Jasmine gave him a sideways smile. "The process might take time."

"I heard that immigration procedures could be very slow in processing documents," Sami concluded.

"I have to go now," Jasmine announced. "This is my new address and phone number. Call, and we can talk." Jasmine picked up her purse and prepared to leave. "You know what? Do you have time now? I mean, this afternoon?"

"Sure, what is on your mind?" Sami leaned towards her.

"I was thinking of getting this over with, as you suggested. We could finalize the process this afternoon instead of tomorrow if you want to. I just remembered another appointment I made earlier for tomorrow. My pastor will always be available in the afternoon. I can call and have him ready for us this afternoon instead."

"Jasmine."

She turned.

"The church thing makes me uncomfortable."

"It adds credibility, honey. I have the form that we use in our church with me." She pulled out a form.

"I thought you said that you did not belong to any denomination?"

"No, Sami, I don't. It is a convenient tool. I volunteered there. We can give it a trial, and don't worry; it will not interfere with your faith if you have one. I do not belong to this faith, either. We can make it simple, what they recognize as a common-law marriage. I think we agreed on that, and you had no problem with it. Here, I have it copied. This clause suits us well." Jasmine removed a copy of a document and showed him the portion regarding the common-law marriage.

"I bet you did your homework on this," Sami hinted.

"A witness will add extra validity to the marriage," Jasmine added. "We can have this format and a pastor as a witness. I can include my niece as well; she's in town."

"No problem. Where do we meet?"

"At the library, where we agreed earlier. We can walk to the pastor's office."

"Okay."

Jasmine turned, and Sami stood as if he had something on his mind.

"Do you have something to share with me?"

Sami hesitated. "Yes, Antonio contacted my wife, warning her about you. Did you see him after you came back?"

"Nothing unusual happened, right?" she asked. Then she thought for a minute and asked with a surprised look on her face, "No, wait! Did you send any flowers to my house recently?"

"No, why?"

"I received a bouquet of roses with a note that read, 'From your secret new admirer,' and I thought you sent it."

"Not me. Maybe it was Antonio."

"I don't know, Sami. I will have to wait and see. Anyway, see you this afternoon at the pastor's office."

***

Sami met Jasmine and her niece in the parking lot, and just before they entered the church office, he stepped closer to Jasmine and whispered. "What did you tell the priest to do?"

"In the Methodist Church, we have a pastor. I think he will make us take a vow and then witness it. There will be a standard form we need to sign. It is common to all marriages, where you put your name and declare that we agree to the vow. I have a copy here. Look it over."

Sami read and confirmed that it was the same sample that he'd seen. "And then what?"

"This is the form that we will take to the county court to

278

get a marriage license."

"What did you tell the pastor to do?" Just then, the door opened, and Pastor James Brandon ushered them in. He started with a few minutes of general preliminary advice before he administered the oath.

"I understand you are ready for this important event in your lives, and this is the form you will need if you have to apply for your license later. I have prepared it, and you can put your full names in the blank space." He looked at Sami with a smile. "I understand that you are a little shy and wanted to do it in private. I respect that."

Sami was shaken and confused. He looked as if he did not want to be there. Jasmine, on the other hand, was relaxed and at ease. She even held his hand as they were sitting. She sensed the stiffness in his muscle and held him until they left. They completed the whole process in about thirty minutes, although it felt like more than an hour had gone by as Sami kept glancing at his watch.

"Thanks. Everything happened so fast," Sami said, trying to regain his composure. I will be free tomorrow and Friday. We can go to the county court and apply for the adjustment at the same time."

Jasmine looked at him with a smile. "Honey, slow down. We just got married. The honeymoon period is not yet over. I don't want to generate any suspicion. We can do that after three months."

Sami looked at her with a disheartened facial expression. "I thought we agreed to do it immediately after the marriage. I need to have it before I graduate."

"You have to make this situation look real and practice it. You were so tense and nervous, and when immigration invites you for the interview, with grueling questions, they can easily detect and interpret your actions and pin you down. These people study behavior psychology, and they are good at what they do. A small mistake can jeopardize the whole thing. We need to do it right, and I don't want any faulty steps to emerge."

Sami turned to her. "I will prepare for the interview. Jasmine, why do you think I will fail? Do they use a lie detector screening method?"

"Not yet, but they look at any tiny bit of information and piece it together to create a picture of the type of marriage with which they agree. If the marriage lasts less than a year, it does not sound real, and that could cause more scrutiny."

Sami felt there was no need for further questions.

"Honey, we can still meet and get to know each other more; it will help in the interview process just in case they ask difficult questions. You never know what they will ask. I have heard a series of strange episodes when people go for quick-fix stuff."

Sami understood the need to take precautions.

"All these preparations will come later. Now we need to do what we agreed upon in the first place. Are you suggesting that we wait three months after the church document to process the marriage license?" Sami raised his eyebrows.

"Three months will be a good time. If you insist, we can wait one month and then go to the county clerk and get the marriage license. After another two months, we can process the change-of-status document with immigration, and then everything will fall into place."

Her statement did not convince Sami. "Jasmine, look here. You know what I want, and the quicker we get done with this, the better for both of us. My visa will expire soon, and I have already delayed my graduation. I cannot afford to be out of status. That would be catastrophic. Time is not on my side."

"Can we meet tomorrow? I will tell you why it's not a good idea to rush to get the documents. I would like this to succeed, and we need to do it the right way. Trust me; it will work. Meet me at the library at 2:00 p.m., and we will discuss it more. The same place."

Sami agreed.

Chapter 44

Antonio sifted through the pile of envelopes that he'd picked from Jasmine's mailbox from her previous address. He focused on two letters, one from the credit card company and another from the post office. He wrinkled his face with a smirk of rancor. He flipped the envelopes over and clenched his teeth, seething with rage as he read the note from the credit company. "How can she do that to me?" He puckered up his forehead. "She will pay heavily for this," he murmured to himself and looked through the pile of papers once more. His eyes caught two more envelopes. Like a bird of prey hovering in the air in anticipation of an attack, he narrowed his target and fished out an envelope. He tore it open slowly and removed the pre-approved new Visa credit card.

Antonio smacked his lips with an air of relish as he surveyed the discovery. It was like manna from heaven when he plucked up the glittering plastic. He could now strike her with a savage vengeance for what she'd done to him. Antonio then picked up the enclosed mover's guide packet. He thought for a while, as his old habit was itching to delve in. The old method in the past had worked well, and he could try once more. He scrutinized the contents of the package with scrupulous care. He needed just one week to redirect her forwarding address to where he lived and finalize the credit card process.

He paused, never expecting that anybody could beat him at his own game. Jasmine had used the trade Antonio knew so well against him. It reminded him of those days when he'd snooped through the neighbors' mailboxes at night to steal piles of envelopes for bank statements, credit card bills, reordered paper checks, and even junk mail, accumulating a vast collection of coupons.

Antonio realized that the two years that he'd spent in jail had turned out to be a cash cow for Jasmine's indulgences.

***

The next day, Sami arrived at the library ahead of the time scheduled.

"You look better than yesterday," Jasmine commented.

"I did a lot of thinking. There were so many things I did not know."

"We are almost at the finish line. With a little patience, everything will work out." Sami's patience was running out, and he did not hide it.

"We lost three weeks when you went away, Jasmine. Further delays will get me out of status, and I do not have other courses left to take for my graduation."

"We can get done with all the requirements soon."

"At least the application process should have been done before the expiration of my visa."

"Okay, let me say something. I am sure you would like to know more about me and what I think about this situation now."

"Sure, why not."

"There should not be any suspicion about this marriage; once you clear the divorce papers, as you indicated, then we will initiate the process. There is no mandatory waiting period for divorce."

"I read about it, and after the court clears it, it is over. There is an urgency in this matter," Sami emphasized.

"Sure, I understand. We can process the application of the marriage license and the adjustment of the status. However, I want us to do it at one-month intervals. I do not want the same mistake to occur again."

"What mistake?" Sami turned to face her.

"In my previous marriage, we processed the document quickly and ended the marriage quickly as well, and that created some suspicions. There was an issue."

"What issue? Why was there a problem?"

"He boasted about how he got his green card, and word got out and created attention. On top of that, he got himself into trouble." Sami shook his head as Jasmine continued. "It was a foolish thing to do. I understand you don't drink," she added as an afterthought.

"No, I don't. Drinking has nothing to do with this situation."

Jasmine noticed the expression on his face and quickly resumed. "When people drink, they do and say stupid stuff that can get them into trouble. On my part, everything was alright except for this connection that tainted my name, although the investigation proved that I was innocent and nothing like what he said happened."

"What did he say?"

Jasmine was hesitant to answer that question. "Anyway, he was saying that I facilitated the documents for him to get his card."

Sami smiled. It was the way she'd said it. Jasmine was trying to filter her words and make it appear to be a legitimate marriage that had gone wrong.

"Were you under investigation?"

"Not really. Antonio denied boasting about the marriage for the card. He got into trouble for something else. Smoking weed and causing disorderly conduct." She looked around. "The marriage was not under any suspicion. I just wanted to straighten things out a little, and if we follow the steps I've suggested, there will be no issue."

"Can we then identify a day that we can focus on the application process?"

"This week, I will be tied up. How about next week on Wednesday if that is okay with you. I will be available. We can go to the county clerk's office and apply for a marriage license and then go from there. I think it will take about a week before we get the marriage license, and then we will process the remaining part."

Sami was about to give up hope, and he worried that she was delaying the operation.

"That would work for me as well," he finally agreed.

"One more thing. For the next couple of weeks, we may need to see each other more often. It would make a good impression if we were together and also arrange a wedding. I will rent a wedding gown, and we can take some photos together." She hesitated for a moment and then continued. "There are other documents that we may need as well."

"Are all these necessary?" Sami asked.

"Yes. You never know when we will need them. The immigration officers will even scrutinize the authenticity of such a sacred thing as marriage. Nothing will stop them, and as I said, we would rather be prepared."

"What preparations do we need?"

"You may need to readjust and show up with me for some events. You will need to change your postal address, and you will receive some of your correspondence through my address. You can write down my new address; I will soon be receiving all my correspondence through this new address. We will need to have joint accounts, joint lease agreements, and most of the things that regular couples have together.

Remember, there will be no room for any suspicion."

Sami appeared lost for a moment.

"You seem to be surprised. I thought Kumar told you about all the preparations that you needed to undergo."

"I did not know that we had to live together physically and own everything together. I had the impression that the whole thing was just a formality."

"Honey, reality dictates that we do it the right way and the best way to get you what you desire." She looked him over. "You can make the marriage work."

"I am not sure I understand what you mean."

Jasmine smiled.

"What?" Sami asked.

"I love your innocence." Jasmine shot a glance at him. "When all the legal documents indicate that we are married, we will get the marriage certificate, and I was thinking to make this marriage work for real."

Sami realized that he was still not sure what Jasmine meant by "real." He'd gotten into this marriage with a goal in mind and the end in sight. He had some questions, but he was not sure whether it was culturally appropriate to ask them. He resisted the approach he would have had if assessed from his cultural point of view.

Sami cleared his throat to get attention, the old habits of his culture catching up with him. "I do understand the precautions needed, and frankly, I have more to lose. At the same time, I did not expect to live with you while I have a wife and kids at home. My understanding was to visit you occasionally and sign any documents if needed and stick to our agreed plans."

"Yes, that was part of the deal. The authenticity of the marriage requires more, and we need to work on it. We will start the initial process and work through it. The divorce document proves that you are no longer together with your wife," she reminded him with a smile and affection. "You have a new wife." Her eyes glittered with the satisfaction of comfort. By all accounts, Jasmine had taken the marriage agreement to heart and was determined to make it work.

Chapter 45

That evening, Sami came home looking slightly weary.

"Is everything okay?" Sarah asked.

"A bit exhausted." Several conflicting ideas bounced around in his head. Sami was more worried about the expiration of his visa.

Sarah, on the other hand, was in an excellent mood. She seemed to have adjusted well to her job and even received excellence awards for work ethics and her commitment. She'd also joined the healthy living club with her friends and practiced yoga. She felt relaxed, especially after moving into a new university apartment with three bedrooms. With the kids' playground just in front of the house, Sarah had nothing to complain about.

Sami did not allow his conscious guilt to haunt him. He brushed it off, hoping that the result would be worth the risk that he'd taken without his wife's knowledge.

***

The next day, Sami and Jasmine went to the campus town to take wedding photos. Jasmine was in her best mood. She had arranged with a photographer to create unique wedding photos.

"I have taken care of everything we need for the photo album. You need to dress your best and smile. Do not be surprised. Act natural, and we will complete all this within a few minutes."

"Jasmine, this sounds a little extreme. Can we tone it down a bit? We can take the photos, and no need to make a big deal out of it."

"To prove authenticity, it has to be done this way. I have already told you."

When they arrived, Sami was stunned to see that Jasmine had arranged everything for the occasion. She had her wedding gown, Sami's black tuxedo with black bow tie, and five wedding helpers, including the bridesmaid and the best man, lined up to simulate an actual wedding. The young girls with a bouquet of brightly colored flowers had African braided hairstyles fit for the ceremony. It took about forty-five minutes to shoot the photos.

Jasmine took Sami aside and whispered, "I negotiated down the price, and since I know the photographer, he asked for only $850."

"What! I was not expecting this, Jasmine."

"I thought we'd agreed about the photoshoot; it is embarrassing to cause a scene. Give me your card, and we will get it done. I will pay for lunch, which I have also arranged." She nudged him.

Sami reluctantly handed her his credit card, deepening another hole in his financial debt.

As they were having lunch, Jasmine kept glancing at Sami. "My apartment is not far from here. The address I gave you." She wrote it down. "In any case, I will be on campus for most of the day, working at the student center bookstore and spending my free time in the afternoon at the library. I will be on the second floor on Wednesdays and Fridays. You will see me as you come up the stairs. You can't miss the desk in the right-hand corner."

"No more surprises, right?"

Jasmine smiled. "No more."

After lunch, Sami went to the library, and then he had an appointment with his advisor about the graduation plans. As he was stepping out of the office, he saw Jasmine waiting for him.

Sami was not expecting her. He had been to the department's picnic with his wife and children, and he didn't want the secretary to speculate.

"I know you did not expect me to be around your department."

"Yes." Sami looked on, hiding the discomfort he was experiencing.

"I do understand. It will take time to get adjusted."

After Jasmine invited Sami home, she sensed his unwillingness to accept the offer. She then changed her tactics. "To have coffee," she insisted. Sami felt pressured to go along. Her apartment was walking distance from the university.

Jasmine kept her two-bedroom apartment neat and well maintained. Unlike the other time when he'd visited her house, Sami did not find pictures hanging and got curious about what photos she'd kept from her previous marriages. He decided to remind her of the wedding photos that she'd taken with him the other day and thought that could be an opportunity to dig a little deeper into her marriages and find out what kind of photos she'd kept. She might have taken some pictures of her previous weddings as well.

"Did you get the photos?" he asked.

"Oh, I did not pick them up from the studio yet. I will share them with you when I get them. It will take a few days." Jasmine noticed how Sami's eyes were focusing on the photo album near the TV stand. "That album has my family photos. Here." Jasmine picked up the photo album and handed it over. She flipped through the photos of her family members, her brother, aunt, mother, and grandmother, and her three children. There were no photos of any of her previous husbands. Sami wanted to ask, but he held back. She was deliberately keeping them away, and he wondered why she'd hidden them, or maybe they were in a separate album?

As if answering the question in his mind, she commented, "I keep the photos of my family together in one album."

"What happened to your other photos?" Sami scanned the room.

" I keep them in a separate album. Yours will be different, you know," She added.

Sami did not say anything. He continued looking at the pictures. "You have beautiful kids."

"Thanks. They are the love of my life."

"I am sure you miss them a lot."

"Sure, I do. I talk to my children almost every other day. Bless my grandma. She loves them so much and won't let them out of her sight."

"What about their dad?"

Sami regretted asking that question. It took Jasmine a while to respond, and it was apparent she had not expected it. "I would rather not discuss their dads."

"I am sorry if that brought out some unpleasant memories."

"Not about that. It's just that some things need to be left alone and forgotten, and I want to forget that part of my life. At least for now." She then pulled out another smaller album with some wedding photos. Sami picked it up and started flipping through the pages. Then he suddenly stopped. It was the wedding photo of Jasmine, and he held it closer to the light.

"You know that person, right?"

"I was trying to see whether it was the person I knew or

not," Sami said.

"You know him. Who do you think it is?"

"Kumar! The photo looks like him. You can tell me. Is it Kumar?"

"Yes."

"Were you two married?"

Jasmine smiled, confirming Sami's suspicion. Sami did not need an answer. He held the photo to the light, "What kind of marriage?" He felt that it was not a proper question to ask. He reframed his question when Jasmine did not respond. "When were you married to him?"

"About three years ago, and we remain friends." Sami's suspicion about Kumar and Jasmine's partnership in the deal became evident. There was no need to ask further questions about this relationship or any other. He turned over a few more pages of the album, continuing to look at the photos, and then handed it back over to her.

"What about your other husbands?" he asked.

"I destroyed all their photos. I would rather forget them." She shrugged casually.

"More coffee?"

"No, thank you."

"I am curious, Jasmine. Are you together with Kumar in this business?"

Jasmine took a long pause and then replied, "He gets twenty-five percent for connections. As I said, this will be my last venture." She smiled and then added, "Whatever happens in this room stays in this room."

"No need to worry," Sami replied.

He walked home from campus, slowly piecing together the incidents he'd encountered. He did not doubt his position and the possible outcome of the deal in which he was involved. Time was the only thing not in his favor at this point, and he vowed to press Jasmine to make it work. She had a soft spot for him and had taken the marriage to heart. By any account, Sami needed to see the reality of his marriage. The marriage plan, according to Jasmine, was real. She took each step assiduously to simulate the actual wedding. Sami might as well embrace the new married life.

"A second wife?" This seemed a fantasy in the making, yet the document and the legality had proven him wrong. "No, it's not real," he tried to convince himself. "It's a fake marriage, and Sarah is still my wife," he murmured.

Chapter 46

Sami learned that in this part of the world, individual interests come first. Many of the people won't do anything for you unless they receive some benefit in return. He had, therefore, positioned himself to get what he wanted, even if it meant going along with Jasmine's suggestions for the long-term prospects.

Two weeks had gone by since the last time Sami had met with Jasmine. He browsed through his to-do list and circled the words "marriage license" and "visa adjustment."

Sami picked up the phone in the graduate students' office. Jasmine was on the line.

"Hi, honey. What time shall we meet tomorrow?"

"I have blocked off the time in the afternoon at two." Sami then realized how she'd addressed him and the tone of her voice.

"Okay, I'll be at the library, and then we can walk to my house and go from there," Jasmine said.

They arrived at the county courthouse office a little early and waited in the lobby. Only two clerks were working, and the place was almost empty. When it was their chance to see the clerk, Jasmine held Sami back. The man was beckoning with his hand.

"It's our turn," Sami said.

"We will go to the lady when she becomes available."

Sami obliged, not sure what to make of her decision.

Later, when they got out of the building, Jasmine commented, "I did not want the man to serve us because he will be biased."

"Why do you think he would be biased? Do you know him from the past?"

"It was the way he asked me a question the other time. I did not like it."

"He probably wouldn't recognize you." Sami did not think it was a big deal.

"He will. I know the type. He's one of those who find faults in everything. We didn't have to deal with his unnecessary questions."

"We filled out everything on the form as requested, so why would he ask any other questions?"

"He would pretend to be friendly and ask some questions that would make you uncomfortable to answer. He might ask you where you came from and how long you have been here in the USA, and why entertain such nonsense from him? It's none of his business."

"I am glad we got done with this part. And hopefully, next week, we can start the next step, right?"

"In about three to four days, we will receive the license in the mail, and then we can start the visa adjustment application immediately." They drove in silence, except for Jasmine's few remarks about her activist's role, which she had abandoned when she'd gotten busy with school.

"I thought you were doing a good job about the awareness of drug overdose issues. I saw posters in the students' center."

"We should have done more through advocacy, education, and to strengthen our activism's role better." She turned left on Lincoln Way onto Beach Avenue, towards the Maple

Residence Hall. Sami realized that they were heading towards her apartment.

"I can take the bus from here if you can drop me off just around the corner," Sami requested.

"Oh no, we are going to my apartment. You can have a cup of coffee, and then I can drop you off." Sami went along with the suggestion. He had told her earlier that he was not a coffee drinker, but she must have forgotten. Either way, she had already turned the corner, and the next stop was at her house.

Jasmine went to the kitchen right away. "I am hungry; can I fix you something, too?"

"No, thank you."

"Coffee?"

"Juice will be fine." He still felt uncomfortable being alone with Jasmine. Although in his mind, he considered this encounter a strict business deal. He was sure Jasmine did not take it as just business anymore. Her subtle reactions, the tone of her voice, and the way she engaged him in discussions all carried the mark of a determined, calculated person planning to lure him in. At this point, Jasmine had leverage and a winning card to play in the form of the marriage platform and the subsequent visa adjustment process that Sami desperately needed. The mutual agreement worked for both Sami and Jasmine, but it looked like Jasmine's part of the bargain was strengthened. Sami picked up the daily newspaper, browsed through it, and then stopped. Jasmine noticed.

"I sent them to the papers to celebrate the occasion, and it looks great. I am delighted; the pictures came out fabulous."

"I did not want that kind of publicity, Jasmine; neither did I expect it. Our deal must be secret. What if my wife and friends find out?"

"What's wrong, honey? You should be excited. They will

not question this authenticity. A picture says it all."

Sami kept a moody silence.

"You know what?" Jasmine broke the train of his thought. "I think we should attend church together this Sunday. Do you remember the pastor who officiated our marriage? We have not visited his church. He will be delighted to see us again."

Sami was not expecting this invitation. It took a while for him to get composed, and as if searching for the right words, he pondered.

"Sami, the pastor would be happy to see us again. I want to show him respect."

Sami sighed, not ready for a more monotonous activity that he did not plan for, and yet he had to go along with this absurd idea anyway.

"I have to go." He prepared to leave.

Jasmine came closer to him and stopped when he tried to move away. She was sensing how uncomfortable he felt when she invaded his space.

"Relax, we are no longer strangers." She looked at him as if waiting for a sign of invitation from his side. "Officially married," she added with a smile.

Sami remained mute. Finally, he said, "Yeah, I guess so, but I have to go now. See you on Sunday then. Remember, I will not worship or participate in any rituals that you do in the church. It is against my convictions."

"I thought you said that you were not sure about which religion to adopt."

"No, I said that I did not practice any ritual as I was growing up, and I did not learn about my religion and practiced it. When you get children, things could change drastically in your life, and I was ashamed that I was not able to teach them about my religion because I was ignorant about it myself. I hope to change that, and from what I gathered, it is a straightforward, sensible religion to follow."

"How did it make sense to you?

"I worship only one God, who created everything without going through any intermediaries."

"In our church, we don't go through intermediaries."

"Well, it is more about the doctrine that I do not subscribe to."

"There are still many complicated tenets in religion that I do not know," Jasmine added. "In any case," she continued. "I am fine with what I know for now. Besides, I am exploring other options and will adopt anything that suits me from other religions. I liked the involvement of the community aspect of religion. For instance, the doctrine of the ecumenical movement appeals to me. It is about universal Christian unity, and we should be working towards universal religious unity." Jasmine was in an excited mood. When she was passionate about something, she elevates her voice with intense conviction and energy. Sami knew he had to interrupt her.

"Good luck with that. I would rather pick one religion and understand it first. People tended to twist, choose, and ignore aspects of their religion and, by doing so, dilute the authenticity of religions. You claimed to follow Jesus, right?"

"Yeah."

"Are you exactly doing what he did in your rituals? People change things and pick and choose what they want to follow. I think we better understand the religion that we claim to follow thoroughly. We will then find more similarities and common values and benefits. You might even find a universal appeal in a particular religion." Jasmine nodded in agreement as Sami continued. "Otherwise, if you pick what you want from each, you will end up creating another religion. We don't need any new religion right now."

"Anyway, that was an excellent healthy discussion about

religion. When you come on Sunday, you will sit with me and watch what I do and follow as much as possible. Your presence is sufficient for the occasion. I have seen people who sit at the back throughout and sleep. They show up when there is a social gathering, which sometimes turns into cookout lunches with hamburgers. Oh, one more thing. You can bring copies of your documents as well so that we can complete the application and then post it on Monday."

"Okay, I have to get going now." Sami proceeded to leave.

"I will drop you off. Where?"

"I will be fine at the Pammel Court grocery store. I have to pick up something from there and then walk to my apartment."

Chapter 47

That Sunday , Sami did better than he expected . He took some more pictures with Jasmine , and from the looks of things, everything went well. Sami was more open this time, and he freely talked with a member of the congregation who commented on his accent. Jasmine took the role of an expert and explained to the church member how the English language was diverse in its dialects . The church member confessed that he got interested in Africa after he'd watched the movie *Roots*, and he had already staked a claim to the ancestral line of Kunta Kinte.

Sami excused himself. "I have to go now," he whispered to Jasmine.

It was clear from the way Jasmine acted that everybody thought Sami was her new man, and she was eager to introduce him to everyone she met. That was not what Sami had expected from this arrangement.

"Let's drive to a couple of scenic places to take more pictures, like Reiman Gardens and the Furman Aquatic Center."

"I thought we were anyway, don't we need an attorney for this application?" Sami asked.

"We don't need to pay an attorney for the application; I know how to fill out these forms if you have all the documents needed."

For the next thirty minutes, Sami and Jasmine filled out the form for visa adjustments and attached all the necessary documents required. Satisfied that everything was in order, Jasmine reached out and hugged him passionately.

"Congratulations, this will bring us closer, and after two or three months, we will hear from them." She glanced at him with a tantalizing gaze and affectionately touched him, leaning closer until her dress brushed against him.

Sami was not sure whether to rejoice or not. The mere application of the form did not guarantee that he would get his visa adjusted and receive the green card. In the meantime, he prepared for the mock immigration interview that Jasmine had arranged. She gave him a list of questions they would likely ask.

"How you respond to these questions will have to come from the heart. They will detect mechanical answers without emotion. You need to show emotion, and your body needs to react," Jasmine advised. She was taping the session for his future review.

"How would that work?" Sami asked.

"You need to show feelings, and right now, I don't see it in you."

"What do you mean? You don't know what is in my heart."

"No, it's not that." Jasmine laughed. "How do you see the feelings I put into this marriage and how I act towards you?" She smiled.

"Very friendly, borderline affectionate," Sami confirmed.

"It is more than that, and I even did not want to admit it myself." She cast a glance at him as her mouth slightly opened. She had a glittery look in her eyes. "You lightened up my life from the time we met, and I cannot stop thinking about you." Silence engulfed the atmosphere. Jasmine leaned toward him.

"Jasmine, I have to go."

She held onto his hand, and Sami released it slowly. He was not sure about the impact of the change of venue and the emotions that she'd displayed. He'd never thought the deal he made with her would extend beyond the intended. He'd entered this arrangement with one thing in mind: get a green card and get out.

"See you tomorrow." Jasmine held on to his hand. "This will work out fine. I want this relationship to be different."

"I will mail the document tomorrow, and then we will go from there." Sami avoided direct eye contact and headed towards his car. Jasmine walked with him.

"I will see you at the school library, then." She planted a soft kiss on his cheek. "Okay, I will let you go," She squeezed and then released his hand.

"I will be there, Jasmine. I have to go. My kids are waiting for me to take them to the mall. I promised them earlier."

***

Sami came home excited. His wife had noticed the excitement and knew that he was up to something. She glanced at him and waited for him to say something. The kids were already waiting and would not give him any time to talk.

"Let's go, Dad. What took you so long?" Chaaltu asked in her usual assertive tone.

"I am ready, honey." He nudged Adam, who was tugging Chaaltu from behind.

Sami looked askance at his wife, and from the way she returned the look, he knew she would make a jeering remark at his efforts. He remembered how she reacted the first time he'd brought up the visa plan, but for the last three months, he had not mentioned it.

Sarah did not expect to find anything new in his

excitement towards the idea. He had gotten busy with school and kept quiet about the issue. Sarah had kept herself out of this process and told him not to involve her in what she called a shoddy deal. However, she continued pursuing visa adjustments on her own through her work. That day, when Sami beamed and exuded joyful countenance, Sarah held herself back.

***

Antonio browsed through the items in the electronic section at Walmart. With his eyes on the cashier counter, he strolled through the aisles, scanning the environment. There were only a few customers still in the store, as it was soon closing for the night. The two teenagers in the electronic section frequently glanced at him. One of them was on guard while the other tampered with the electromagnetic strips to disable them. It was a known strategy, but today, Antonio wasn't considering any of those tricks. He picked up the items he wanted and slowly moved to the counter. The cashier, a young lady, probably a high school student, looked over and yawned.

"A long day?" Antonio commented.

"Yeah, I did a double today. A co-worker called in sick. Are you ready to check out?" she asked.

"Sure." Antonio had been waiting for this moment, and he initiated a quick exchange of words with her to distract her attention as she swiped his credit card, commenting about the Nintendo her brother had recently bought.

"I can't wait to play the game," he replied, waiting for the cashier to run through all the items: pedicure foot spa, infinity necklace jewelry box, and an assortment of perfumes. "She will love that. Is it her birthday?" the cashier asked.

"You guessed it," Antonio replied with satisfaction. He had rehearsed the moment and was ready for any question that might come up. He held his breath as she looked at the screen for the transaction to go through. He pretended to check the total of $1,760 and scribbled his initial for signature.

Antonio slowly gathered all the items and walked out of the store, only to look back casually, clutching the grocery bag with his right hand. He then drove to Target, which would close in less than an hour. He stopped by the music section of the store and grabbed the latest CD releases and portable speakers, and then headed to the counter to pay with his credit card.

"Your ID please," the cashier demanded.

"Why do you need my ID?" Antonio asked and fiddled with his pocket as if looking for his wallet.

"To verify, and it is part of our policy. The name on the card shows Jasmine."

"Oh, sorry about that. It is my wife's card. I forgot my ID. I can come back later." Antonio took the card and left.

Later that evening, he pulled out the change-of-address form and forwarded Jasmine's address back to her current address, as she'd initially planned. It must have been two weeks, and she was not receiving any mail. He needed to mail the form tomorrow.

Antonio sat back and relaxed. He picked up the *Ames Tribune* from the table and browsed through it, stopping when he recognized the picture. "What!" he brought the paper closer to the light.

He then stepped out to get milk from the grocery store across the street. He dialed Jasmine's number from a payphone. "Congratulations. I saw it in the paper. I thought you stopped the game," he blurted out mockingly.

Jasmine knew he didn't mean to wish her good. "I told you never to call me again. Keep away from me, or I will call the police."

"I know you won't call a cop. Go ahead. Make my day. You have more to lose."

"Antonio, why are you doing this to me?"

"Payback, baby! Did you forget? I can't get credit because of you and that debt you put me through."

"We were still together at that time," Jasmine confessed.

Insinuating his sarcasm with a snicker, Antonio replied, "Yeah, you're right. The two years that I spent in jail, you were enjoying life at my own expense and plunged me into debt. Do you think I could forget that easily? It's my turn now. Get ready."

Jasmine hung up the phone.

Antonio smiled. He looked at the photo with intent.

***

Jasmine was startled when she heard a knock at the door. She looked at the time, and it was late, and she wasn't expecting anybody. She approached the door, thinking it was Sami. She peeped through the peephole and saw a red rose. "Who is it?" she asked.

Antonio changed his voice and replied, "It's me, sweetheart. Open up."

Jasmine opened the door and then suddenly pushed it back, but it was too late. Antonio was already in the doorway.

"I told you not to come to my place, Antonio."

"I came to apologize but allow me." He offered her the flowers and a boxed gift. "Give me a final chance."

"Antonio, I can't accept this from you. I am married."

"What do you mean? Is this for real? The guy is married with four children. Are you practicing polygamy in America? That would be great historic news." He whistled.

"No, we are officially married, and it is in the record. So, please leave me alone. I am expecting Sami anytime now."

"Something looks fishy here. Why would a guy leave his beautiful wife and four great children? Are you in your old game.? It must be for the card." He looked her in the eyes, and she didn't blink, showing a sign of stubbornness.

Antonio had to try a different strategy. His old tactics would not work anymore. Jasmine had taken him back several times in the past when he'd pleaded and showered her with gifts, but now she was putting her foot down.

"You have to leave," Jasmine ordered in a calm voice. Antonio had underestimated her move and realized there was no point in fighting. He took several steps back without further confrontation.

"I have nothing else against you; I hope you respect my stand. I am no longer available for any negotiation. Our romantic relationship is over. You must understand that it ended two years ago. I wish you good luck. Take back your gifts, and don't send me anymore." Jasmine bade him farewell.

When the door closed behind him, Antonio snapped. He always got his way.

He threw the flowers at the door and left. He had the receipt to return the gift tomorrow, but now he plotted what to do next.

Chapter 48

At the mall, Sarah and Sami watched their kids in the indoor playground center.

"I may surprise you soon, dear." Sami winked. Sarah waited to hear another joke or bombshell news.

"I have to see it in my hands." Sami tapped his lips in a gesture, indicating closed lips. "Until I feel it in my own two hands."

"What do you mean?"

"The looming uncertainty that has clogged my daily life will soon evaporate. Soon I will lay my hands on this precious thing."

Sarah looked at him with a frown on her face.

"I mean the green card," he added.

"What makes you certain that you will get it? It's a tedious process."

"I know. I am pushing it hard so that we can arrange for the marriage."

"What marriage?" Sarah asked.

"Did you forget? I have to remarry you to make this work." Sami did not want to open up this topic again, but he was excited and optimistic about his green card endeavors. He knew how Sarah was opposed to the idea despite his efficient strategy to convince her that he was still married to her.

"It's too late, and I don't know how you can reverse it."

"What?"

"You will create more suspicion if you act hastily. Even if you get a visa through marriage, you won't divorce the other lady right away. You should have known that by now," Sarah quipped.

"I know we are doing all kinds of things to minimize suspicions. I wanted it quickly done so that we can formalize our marriage union and move on." Sami tried to make it sound simple.

"Don't worry about me. I will be fine, and I don't need to adjust to your status."

It was Sami's turn to raise his eyebrows. He snorted. "What is the matter? Don't you believe me? Wait until you see it."

Sarah stood up. "Anything is possible. I am just letting you know that, as I said earlier, I do not have positive feelings about this green card business. I am glad I was not part of it."

"You are already part of this. I don't know what you are talking about," Sami retorted.

"You cut me off. Did you forget? When I objected to your plans. We are divorced, and I don't see why we are even discussing this matter." Sarah kept up the argument. "I want you to leave."

"What do you mean, leave?"

He recognized the penetrating look that she had. He observed his surroundings as they walked, catching up with the kids in the mall. He looked around, thinking that they were not supposed to be talking about this in public. "How did you know?" Sami realized that the secret was out. "We will talk about it later at home. Not now."

A long silence engulfed the atmosphere as they left the

mall and went to a nearby park without uttering a single word between them. Sami stole glances, trying to decipher Sarah's facial reactions. He did not notice any unusual change, and there was no anger on her face, either. The smooth radiance illuminating from her face gave him false hope of reassurance, while her body language and reactions showed some lack of passion.

By any legal standards, the news Sami was afraid to share indicated that the marriage to Jasmine was real. The documents proved it, and now, with Jasmine's request for joint ownership of everything, Sami could stop pretending. *What does it mean to act real?* Sami asked himself, and then he answered his question. He wondered about the motives Jasmine had for turning the deal into marriage for real. The nature of Sami's agreement required that he do what couples were supposed to do, and Jasmine had the right to demand them. Sami reflected over this for a long time and finally succumbed to the pressure. He had nothing to lose at this point other than what he'd lost already. There was no obstacle left between him and the card. He then remembered what Jasmine had said when he'd hesitated about the joint bank account, taking photos together with her, and even taking joint loans together: "From now on, everything depends on you if you want to get this card. You have to take risks and go the extra mile."

As a reluctant customer, Sami wondered how all these would help. "The immigration officers will look at all those things. The documents will automatically prove the legitimacy of the marriage. Only genuinely married couples can have joint bank accounts and co-sign loans for each other." Jasmine's words had echoed in his mind, and in the end, she'd won the day. She included his name on the rental lease and made him a joint owner on the car that she bought without his knowledge. Sami had already accepted his fate, and when she brought him some papers to sign, he signed them all.

When they returned home that evening, Sami needed enough courage to tell his wife all that he'd done and how far he was with the green card pursuit. He realized how much progress he'd made and remembered the last time they'd talked; he'd insisted that she sign the document. Time had gone by, and Sarah had gotten busy with her nutritional health and wellness research project at work and even bragged to him that she didn't need to get a green card through his process. After all these months, Sami had not told her all the activities he'd done with Jasmine, although he'd been faithful to his marital vows and came home in the evenings.

It was Sarah who broke the long silence during the evening after the kids went to bed, and the discussions took an entirely different turn.

"I will be going to Omaha, Nebraska, on Wednesday with a friend to take care of some of the immigration issues and will be back in the evening if all goes well."

Sami was stunned and mesmerized by her statement, and with a worrisome look on his face, he turned his body fully in her direction. "What for, and who is the friend?" He fixated his eyes on her, a rather piercing stare. Sarah knew what was on his mind and was ready to tease him further. She waited for his next move, the exact question he was concocting.

"One of my friends in the women group and an attorney."

"An attorney? what for?" Amazed by the turn of events, Sami remained mute in his thinking process. "What is the purpose of your trip?"

"Immigration interview."

"What! What kind? Really? How come?"

"A change of visa status." After a moment, she added, "You don't believe me, do you?"

"I don't because your visa is tied to mine."

"Things have changed." She glanced at him casually.

"Come on, give me a break. Stop joking." Sami stared at her with wide eyes, his jaws dropped. "This will never happen." He looked at his wife again. A second look in her eyes confirmed what he anticipated: her eyes glowed with pride, and yet hidden beneath the spectacular joy was a speck of sorrow, a sense of betrayal.

The magnitude of this abrupt news paralyzed him. He took a deep breath.

"Are you going alone?" he asked as if waking up from a trance.

"What do you mean alone? I told you I wasn't." Sarah understood his question and knew what he wanted to know. He would have to figure this out by himself.

Sami waited, but there was no answer. Sarah stood up and started moving toward the inner room.

"I did not remember signing anything," Sami said, his voice barely audible.

"There was nothing for you to sign."

When their eyes met, Sami understood what had happened. Sarah brought the newspaper with Jasmine and Sami's wedding photos and a copy of the divorce document that he'd hidden. "Did you forget all this?" She continued moving, and then she stopped, looked back, and added, "I will ask you to leave, and I expect you to honor it. You cannot live with me anymore. Live with her. She's your official wife. There's nothing for you here. I am no longer your wife."

"Wait a minute. You are still my wife, and you knew my plans all along. You can't do this to me." Sami did not believe her words. "I love you. You're the mother of my children, and I have never been unfaithful to you. It's not what you think." Sami rambled on in a confused state of mind.

"It will be on Wednesday morning. I will be fine. We have

an attorney with us, and it will be a smooth transition, and the attorney told me that they would ask some questions and approve it. I will then receive a green card in the mail later."

Sami paused, dumbfounded, shocked to discover what had happened. He tried to find encouraging words to say. "I thought this process would be complicated, and your visa and mine were linked and depended on how we came to this country."

"Not at all. You cut me off. Did you forget the divorce document?" Sarah realized how Sami reacted to this statement. Deep down, he felt the impending loss and the dire consequences of his decision to pursue this route on his own. Sarah, for her part, sparkled with agitation and a slight elevation in spirit and mood that Sami had not experienced the whole time during the green card journey.

A long silence ensued. "I was only doing it for us, I never intended to divorce you, and you knew it. I was afraid of deportation. I might have been wrong and impatient in choosing the illegal route, but I had no intention of abandoning you." With a weary outlook, Sami tapped the table in despair.

"I had to do what was best for me, especially after you went ahead with the divorce against my decision. You left me out, and I have settled the matter now." With that, Sarah glanced at him once more. Deep down in her eyes, Sami could sense a loving gesture. He yearned to reach at least the tip of her heart and reignite the dormant spark of love. He knew it was still there; he felt it.

"As I said, you can't live here with me anymore."

"Can you give me at least two to three weeks until I graduate?" he pleaded.

Sami stayed long after, reassessing the series of events unfolding. The lonely path he had trudged on had never been more lonesome. That night, as he tossed in his sleep on the couch, many frightening pictures emerged. It took him a while to reconfigure his approach. Things had taken a different path. What would happen to him once his wife got her status changed on her own? How would he reclaim what he'd lost? What about the role of Jasmine and the pursuit of a green card? All these questions popped up in his head without definite answers.

***

The next day, in a somber mood, Sami walked to the library and put the final touches on his thesis. He would soon graduate as planned and on schedule. He looked back and realized how much time was left and how he got consumed with one little piece of paper on which his whole career and the world of jobs hung. Suddenly, he felt the urge to see Jasmine. Not that she had answers for his daunting questions, which he knew the possible solutions to already. Sami wanted to hear a different explanation for his crooked path so that he could feel better about the whole situation. The previous scene reverberated in his mind as he pondered his entire life situation. Familiar incidents kept recurring in his mind with vigor.

He checked his time and had about an hour left before he was supposed to meet with Jasmine. He reviewed his to-do list for the week and felt satisfied that he had done everything except submit a job application.

He went to the second floor of the library and browsed through a magazine. As he navigated through the available jobs advertised, he noticed one in a small section of the magazine. It was a research assistant position in Ontario, Canada. This job was re-advertised, and it matched his qualifications. The application deadline had been extended and would arrive in a week. Sami thought for a while about all the previous job applications he'd made and decided to give this one a try. He had all his information on the disk, including copies of transcripts and some recommendation letters in a folder. He just needed to write a cover letter, and he could use the printer at the library and send the application.

Chapter 49

"You called me?" said Sami

"Yes," replied Jasmine. "Our lawyer got back to me. Do you remember when I told you about the guy joking in prison about the green card?"

"Do you mean your former husband?"

From the way Jasmine turned her face, Sami could tell that she did not want to associate herself with this man. "I wouldn't call him a husband. Anyway, immigration wanted to talk to me first before the interview."

"What does this mean? Did she tell you about the possible outcomes?"

"It could just be a simple question to clarify things. They already talked with me about this, and I answered truthfully, and they seemed to be satisfied. I don't think they have anything else new."

"Is this before we sent the application?"

"Yes, but I don't think this has anything to do with you. However, we needed to check a few things to make sure that we did the right thing and abided by the law." Jasmine noticed the surprise on Sami's face. "Not that we committed any crime, honey. Everything that was needed was in place. It's just that some people are skeptical by nature and want to find faults."

"I don't know what else we could have done. It has taken too long, and obviously, the original intention and plans are fading away. What else is left to do now?" he asked.

"I have completed everything on my checklist. We have a joint account, and both our names are on the rental lease and car to prove that we live together, and that will take care of things." She turned around with a surprised look in her eyes. "By the way, you need to deposit some money into the account. I checked it earlier. If you can deposit the remaining balance, that would help with the expenses."

"We can use the credit card," Sami suggested. He kept his gaze on her. "Jasmine, are you holding something from me? Are you under investigation? The decision has taken too long, and I don't want to delay it further. I am graduating three weeks from now, and my visa will expire right after that. Without any legal document, what will I do?"

"I wish I could expedite this process for you. In the meantime, keep reviewing the checklist again because the immigration officers will probably ask me about you. Do you have any pictures of your parents?"

I left them in Africa. Why do we need them?"

"Just in case they want to know whether I know about you. I am sure immigration knows a lot about you already. There is nothing that they don't know about us, but when they ask, I needed to produce something. At least give me their names, and you should know mine, too."

For the next hour, Sami and Jasmine exchanged background information about themselves. Their interests, hobbies, and anything they have associated with in the past. "I will quiz you tomorrow, and you need to do the same before I leave for my interview."

"If they set the interview date for you one month from now, that will be one week after my graduation, and then what? Will they call me after another month?" Sami threw up his hands. "I have a bad feeling about this plan. I will be out of status by then. They should have interviewed both of us at the same time!" he roared.

"Honey, unfortunately, they get to decide the time. They have their schedule and probably will have one of us together as well. You never know how many times they will conduct their interviews. The marriage issue is getting complicated, and we need to be patient," Jasmine said, trying to calm him down.

They ate lunch in silence. "Come on," Jasmine said, trying to cheer him up when she noticed the change in his mood. "It is strange how things are shifting."

He remained silent. Finally, he said, "I never thought that I would be out of status and an illegal immigrant. They even call us 'aliens.'"

Jasmine patted him on the back. "This is a country of 'aliens.' People came here from all over the world and settled. Only, my ancestors were brought by force as slaves, and they, too, survived. You will survive this ordeal. This little delay is just a formality, and you'll be fine."

Sami did not respond, so Jasmine continued. "That son of a...tainted my reputation. I am sure it was the same old story." She took a deep breath.

"What if they found enough evidence against you?" It was Sami's turn to question her.

"Trust me; there's nothing there. The guy is desperate and will do anything to save himself from the dungeon."

The look on Sami's face told a different story. There was another long silence before anyone spoke.

"Sami, I told you about Antonio, and the worst I expected had happened. I got a call from the credit card company that he used under my name. I have changed my phone twice, and I don't know how he got my number." Jasmine's face turned darker with distasteful rage.

"Why are you keeping this to yourself? I told you already. You should get the police involved," Sami suggested.

"It's not the way you think. The police won't stop him."

"They can at least put him in jail for some time. Didn't you say that he already served two years in jail for marijuana possession?"

"Yes, but he will soon be out again, and then the whole cycle will repeat. He has to be there for a long time or gone for good." She turned to face him. "Please don't judge me harshly. If I do anything, it's out of desperation. I would rather have him gone for good, whether deported or silenced." Jasmine appeared restless.

Sami was silent for a moment. "I don't know, Jasmine. I won't help with anything illegal. My only advice is to seek the help of law enforcement. Or, as you said, if he still uses marijuana, you can tip off the police and have him arrested."

"There is one favor I would ask of you." Jasmine waited until she was sure of Sami's attention." I want you to introduce me to one of the people you work with at the meat factory. I would give him a task to find where Antonio lives. If only I knew where he works. I will take care of the rest."

"Jasmine, I won't advise you to do anything silly. I would not recommend it if your goal is to hire a hitman for the job."

"No, I won't hire someone for that task. I want Antonio caught and deported."

"Jasmine, you know very well that they will consider me an accomplice if anything happens to him. By default, I have a motive. They will look for all kinds of reasons, and you will be the first suspect. I will be the next whether I like it or not." Sami felt anxious.

"Trust me on this, Sami. I will be the first on the police's radar. I am not all that stupid. I know how things work. I will work something out and have him deported, but I need to know where he works."

"Jasmine, I don't want to associate myself with this."

"That's fine. Tell me who is likely to do any task given. I just want to find out where Antonio lives or works. You mentioned two workers who were likely to take an assignment. Did you say, Pablo and Jose?"

"I think Pablo is more suited to any task you can give him," Sami answered.

Is it okay if I ask you for a little favor?"

"Sure."

"It's said that criminals will always return to the scene of their crime. I wonder whether Antonio works at the place he knew very well, the meatpacking factory, where he could work under a different name. It is the most likely place for him to get work easily." She looked at Sami for confirmation.

"Come on, Jasmine, he's not working there, not in the evening. Otherwise, I would know. Jose has worked there longer, and he would know. If you had his photo, that would help. They would recognize him if they could see the photo. For the morning shift, I don't know."

"You know he won't use the name Antonio, either." Jasmine nodded. "By the way, I am still eager to check your coworkers out, especially those who have tattoos like him."

"Pablo added more tattoos around his neck and ears. You won't get anywhere with the tattoos. They all have a similar design, as if in a competition."

"I will stop by tomorrow or the day after and check the morning crew and then return in the evening the same day or the next to check it myself. I know the strategic location to park and observe when they come out of work. I will then make the final decision whether to meet with either Pablo or Jose. This is the least I could ask you." She sighed.

"Sure, no problem. I could lure Pablo outside during break time if you want. He normally goes outside to smoke, and I can follow him and stay close. Remember, I don't want him to get the impression that I am connecting you to him. I do not trust any of these people."

"That's all I want you to do, and I will be fine," Jasmine reassured him.

"Jasmine, I know you have a lot of things on your mind right now, but I will be out of status by the time you see immigration for the interview. I wonder why they don't interview both of us at the same time. I thought that would be the logical thing to do."

"There is nothing logical in what they do. Immigration officers have separated families through deportations, and they don't care. They are numerous cases where they called a person for an interview and then held them for deportation. Can you believe that? You leave your home in the morning and are gone the next day. Deported."

"I heard there is an appeal process," Sami said.

"Yes, that can buy you time, but in the end, it is a hassle that you have to go through." Jasmine talked about this issue like she was an expert.

"Were any of your friends deported?"

"No, but I have heard a lot of strange stories. Don't worry; your case is different."

"Thanks for the reassurance. I am afraid that in a few weeks, we will not be talking about this when the visa expires. It does not look good." He paused with a thoughtful expression on his face. "You didn't tell me how many times you were married. I wonder whether your marriages might have something to do with this delay."

"Don't worry; my prior marriages have nothing to do with the delay. The only possible question they might ask will probably be about the short intervals between them. Again, marriages and divorces happen every day, and some last week or even less."

"I meant visa-related marriages. If all your marriages

ended up with divorce after your husbands got their green card, then one can question."

"Not really. It could just be a case of bad luck or poor choice of husbands. I had three in the past, and yours is, by far, quite different. All those things we prepared will make it special, so once we have that evidence, they will not question it."

"Let's hope so."

"You will be fine, honey. By the way, block the date, and we will go together. It would look good, and Omaha is just about a three-hour drive away, so we should be back in the evening."

"I don't think it is a good idea. What if..." Sami hesitated as if trying to find the right word. "They can stop me."

"Come on, Sami, nobody will stop you and ask for your documents. They will only see individuals with appointments. If you want, you can stay in the car or the waiting room."

The idea did not appeal to Sami. "I would prefer not to go."

"It is okay, then, and I didn't mean to make you feel uncomfortable. I understand your concern, although I believe that it is highly unlikely that the immigration officer will ask for your documents when you go there. How could they possibly detain you unless you meet with them?" She smiled at him.

"You know the U.S. Immigration and Customs Enforcement agents round up and deport illegal immigrants all the time." Sami was still not at ease.

"You came to the country legally, and that puts you in a different category."

"What difference does it make if you are out of status? You're still considered illegal without a visa to remain in this country."

Chapter 50

Jasmine recalled all the points of discussion she'd had with Sami and was less concerned , even if she had to face the stigma resulting from her actions. She felt the urge to act now more than any other time and determined to visit Sami at work during break time.

Jasmine's attempt to track down Antonio did not work. Twice she followed him to find out where he lived, and in both cases, Antonio noticed and kept her off the track. Jasmine recalled that Antonio visited her either on Saturdays or Sundays. With that, she concluded that the place he worked must have a rigid schedule where they didn't work on weekends. She had a hunch that Antonio might be working at a meatpacking factory or a nightclub, and she decided to start with the meatpacking factory first.

She drove slowly and arrived at her destination with confidence. The place had not changed much since three years ago when she used to give Antonio a ride there. She stayed in the car, making sure that nobody saw her. It was unlikely that anybody would be outside at that time when everybody was working. All the workers' cars packed tightly together, and she found a spot between two cars and parked.

A conspicuous bumper sticker on a Buick Regal with distinctive maroon color parked next to hers caught her attention: "Make Art, Not War." Jasmine froze and took a step back. She stooped to get a closer look again, and her jaw dropped open. The number plate and the bumper sticker caused her to take a second look with absolute disdain. "Oh my God, the scum is here!" Jasmine's shocking certainty of the evidence prompted her to get into her car.

She sat in the car for a moment and got out when she regained her composure. She put on gloves and tried the passenger door of the Buick. It was unlocked. A sense of relief engulfed her. She did not loathe the Buick but the owner. Now her plan had changed, and she had twenty-five minutes left to get out before the break started.

**

The next day, Jasmine got ready to implement her plan. She put on a wig, black leggings with an oversized sweater, and low-heel shoes. She then carefully packed the package, three ounces of marijuana, making sure that she wore gloves. She looked at the mirror once more with a smile of satisfaction. She had to be at the meatpacking factory one hour before the break.

Before she left her apartment, she peeped through the window. She scanned the parking lot for any of her neighbors who liked to hang around there and smoke. The darkness of the night had already intensified and settled. Jasmine walked to her car, got in, and waited for a few minutes before leaving.

She arrived at the meatpacking factory and parked her car at the end of the parking space near the trees, facing the building, where she could see anybody coming from the back door of the building where the evening crew worked. She planned to get away without anybody seeing her when the evening crew members got out for a break. She had forty-five minutes left before the break.

She stepped out of the car and stretched, leaving her car

door open, allowing her mind to rehearse how she would explain later to Sami why she had not shown up. The Buick was parked in the same spot. A sense of urgency overtook her. She had an alternative plan if the doors were locked. She took a deep breath, entered her car, moved it next to the Buick, and parked. She remained in the car and lowered her window. She had to calm down her anger and hatred. She would not allow her emotions to take over. It was the moment she'd waited. A sense of rage and intense revenge overtook her. She put new gloves on and took the package. The passenger door of the Buick was unlocked. She placed the parcel in the glove box, pushing it to the back.

***

"You have the right to remain silent. Anything you say can and will be used against you in a court of law. You have the right to an attorney. If you cannot afford an attorney, one will be provided for you. Do you understand the rights I have just read to you? With these rights in mind, do you wish to speak to me?" The police officer held the drug-sniffing dog tightly as he carefully recited the Miranda rights.

Pablo's response was unequivocal: "I want an attorney. I will not talk until I have an attorney."

The next day, the evening crew members clustered together and exchanged glances. Nobody was willing to talk and share the usual jovial jokes. Even Jose kept to himself. When Moses brought the papers to show them the news about the arrests made the previous night, they all wondered how little they knew about each other. "Amigo," Jose said, unable to hold it in anymore, "I knew it. What a fool, keeping three ounces of marijuana in the car. He outsmarted all of us." He turned to Moses. "You didn't know his real name?"

"No, Jose, he has a valid ID and goes by the name Pablo," Moses said.

"I wonder who tipped off the cops." Jose looked at Sami.

Sami remained silent, still in total shock. "Why are you looking at me as if I had anything to do with this, Jose? Not me. I had nothing to do with this incident."

"Probably one of his customers. Who knows? I saw strange characters showing up during break time every night," Moses said. "In any case, we need to move on."

***

There was great jubilation at Sami's house the following week and a flurry of activities, including many guests from his wife's work that Sami did not know. Everybody was in a party mood; his wife's friends, the women's group, were all excited and happy. Sarah was the center of attention as she was celebrating the success of her visa adjustment. Some women were congratulating him and were delighted with this transition to a green card.

Sami returned the goodwill gesture with gratitude. Of course, he was happy about the success of his dear wife. At the same time, in his heart, he felt a little sadness, but not because of jealousy or resentment. Enticed into accepting the path he'd chosen, Sami feared to lose his wife. The only thing he could do was wait. The heavy burden on his head tightened like a yoke on a plowing ox ready to plunge into a barren field. His desire, paved by illusion and the glory of what he would become when he got the green card, appeared within reach. The questions that Sami had to answer were many, and thoughts ran through his mind again. What would happen if Jasmine got into trouble? How could he pull out and get back to his wife? Would she accept him?

Sami should never have underestimated her. He would never have thought in a million years that his wife could pursue this route on her own and succeed. It was not that she was not capable; it was the way she did it behind the scenes. Surely, she'd gotten help from her women friends, and the speed with which she received it surprised him. In any case,

Sami's long battle would remain for some time until he had the document in his hands. In the meantime, with the developing situation, he had to consider an attorney before things got worse. The attorney specialized in marriage and divorce issues. He needed to confirm what he'd researched about marriage laws in different parts of the country.

As he pondered these thoughts, Sami concocted an alternative plan. What if his marriage in Kenya was traditional? He wondered whether it was still binding or nullified. He needed a lawyer who could argue his case since his situation was not bigamy. He'd married Jasmine legally here in the USA, but his previous marriage, based on his traditional culture, allowed polygamy, where a second marriage could not dissolve it. The only problem was that he'd officially indicated on paper that he had divorced his traditional wife. How could he reverse this trend? Sami tossed the idea around, but whichever ways he looked at it, it was about visa issues, and they would question his motives for both marriages. He was not even sure whether his wife would take him back.

How would she accept him back after all that had happened? She had already asked him to leave. Sami finally tried to assess it from a religious point of view, and even with that, he needed enough justification for divorce. A marital quagmire of indebtedness, for Sami, did not observe the expected waiting period for reconciliation before he ended the marriage.

***

Sarah enjoyed the mirthful week of celebration and continued until Sami's graduation day. With the whole family in a celebratory mood, Sami had to surrender to the festivity of his graduation willy-nilly. Everyone was in jubilant spirits, toasting the occasions. Jasmine was also present that evening. She did not get any private time with Sami, but she tried to appear in some photos with his friends.

A photographer, unaware of her surreptitious glances and her eagerness to be in the picture, spotted and captured a moment when she congratulated Sami. It was a perfect photo that would go into her secret photo album, and with other paraphernalia, she'd assembled for her upcoming event.

Chapter 51

"I think they are looking for something or found something on you. Otherwise, why would immigration separate our interviews?" Sami asked.

"Honey, let's put all the documents together and follow the checklist." Jasmine put some documents in an envelope labeled "immigration." "We will make an appointment with an immigration attorney now."

She opened the black notebook she kept in the living room and checked the schedule of her immigration lawyer in Des Moines, Iowa. After several calls, she made an appointment and Sami went along with her suggestions. He had no experience with attorneys, and what he'd heard from his friends about the exorbitant fees lawyers charged was not very encouraging. One of his friends who'd come to the USA on a J-visa had to pay a retainer fee for a year. Every time they met for consultations at the coffee shop, his attorney charged him even for snacks she ate during their meetings.

Jasmine assured Sami that there were always one or two bad apples in any profession, and she had a lot of confidence in her choice. "I did my homework on this and got a fine lawyer."

Sami felt an elevated pride in his accomplishments after he graduated with a second degree in plant physiology despite the hurdles that he'd faced over the years. The job opportunities for him in the US didn't appear promising with this degree. Sami was occupied with getting a green card that he almost overlooked the job applications and job search.

Jasmine, on the other hand, was working meticulously, making sure that everything she needed to prove that her marriage to Sami was legitimate. After three previous marriages, she was determined to make this succeed. She had buried the past and hoped that it would not catch up with her. Now, with Antonio out of the way, she hoped to solidify her current marriage to Sami.

She went through her checklists, which included marriage ceremony, news clip, numerous photo clips of wedding scenes, a county record, date, and place of birth for both Sami and her. Other significant information that Jasmine gathered included the year of marriage, their full names, the name of the pastor who conducted the ceremony, names and birthplaces of both of their parents, names of the witnesses to the marriage, her niece, and cousin, and her address. She listed that Sami lived with her at the same address after they were married. Jasmine was very particular about some African traditions of polygamy since Sami came from a polygamist family. She was more concerned about bigamy, which could be legal in some states if the marriage took place outside Iowa. Jasmine checked and confirmed that in Iowa, it was illegal and a misdemeanor with a maximum penalty of one year in jail. She would prove the legality of her marriage, and whatever weird thoughts Sami concocted about the traditional wedding with his previous wife would have no place in the USA. The records also showed that he had divorced, and that was enough for her to fight.

Jasmine stopped abruptly.

"Do you remember the exact date of your divorce?"

"No, why? Does it matter?"

"Yes, I need to see it." Jasmine was determined to make sure that the previous marriage had ended before she'd gotten into the agreement. She frantically checked her documents. "I don't have a copy in my file."

"Why? I think I finalized the divorce paper with my wife before we initiated this. Remember, it was around the time you disappeared."

"Thank God. If the other divorce did not happen, it would have been considered bigamy. It is a misdemeanor."

Jasmine made the appointment with a lawyer in Des Moines for the next day. Sami had a second phone interview in the morning for the research assistant position in Canada he'd applied for earlier. He felt confident about the interactions he'd had, and they'd invited him for an onsite interview.

***

The lawyer, Mrs. Jones, reviewed the documents and found that Jasmine had not fully complied with the request, and that could jeopardize her petition. The records indicated that she had three previous marriages that she'd filed petitions for, but in her document, she'd claimed there were only two. The discrepancies in the application could pose a serious issue if they discovered, and the United States Citizenship and Immigration Services (USCIS) could categorize the petition as marriage fraud.

"I have looked at your documents and everything that you presented to me," Mrs. Jones began. "The day of your appointment with immigration will not work for me. I have a court case on that day, but I think it will be a formality." Jasmine looked worried.

"It was about the marriage petitions that you filled for your previous husband. You did not state them correctly. You left one out, and that does not go well with immigration," Mrs. Jones confirmed.

Sami jumped in. "What will be the consequence of this error? Can it be corrected."

"Yes, it can be corrected. We can reapply and notify the immigration office of the mistakes made, but I don't know how much time we have left to rectify this before the interview in two days. You are also concerned about your visa expiration. Time is not on our side. As for your second question, the consequences can be detrimental." Mrs. Jones paused to make sure that her clients got the message without getting scared. "The USCIS will review the petition and conduct investigations on whether this marital relationship rises to the level of fraud."

"How can they consider this a fraud. On what basis?" Sami asked.

"They will look at her application, and her omission of one of her husband's petitions would reach the level of fraud."

"Is this a crime?"

"Yes. If found guilty, the penalty can be a maximum of ten years of imprisonment and a $250,000 fine."

"If mistakes happen, why won't they correct them? I guess they have her record."

"Yes, but her omission could have an impact on their decision for this case."

"What do you want me to do now?" Jasmine asked.

"As I said, we can do a new application if you desire, but the mistake can also be corrected at the interview before you take an oath."

"That option is out. It is too late. Sami's visa will expire soon."

"We can go ahead with the plan, but with the time left, there is very little we can do right now."

"Sami, do you have any questions for Mrs. Jones?"

"I was just wondering what the worst scenario for me would be. I know immigration can deny this case, but is there anything else that I should know?"

Mrs. Jones thought for a while before she answered. "I don't know. An immigration officer can look at everything and decide what to do. Even a mere submission of an adjustment of status application can be used as grounds to place you in removal proceedings."

"Do you mean deportation?"

"Yes, kind of." Mrs. Jones tried to calm the situation. "Don't worry. We would appeal if the situation reached that level." She hesitated and added, "This case can be complicated, and my strong suggestion is to withdraw the application and do it after Jasmine meets with them."

Sami and Jasmine left the office and walked to a café across the street. Sami was quiet for most of the time, and Jasmine kept on talking. She felt confident that everything would go smoothly.

"Jasmine, I feel like withdrawing from this deal."

"No, you can't do that now. It is better to apply before your visa expires. Otherwise, you will jeopardize everything you have done so far. You have to have legal status before you apply for adjustment, and if you withdraw, you will lose that privilege and expose yourself to deportation." Jasmine looked him over. "Is something bothering you? Come on. Things will work out. Don't stress yourself too much." She poked him in the rib. Sami smiled. "I know you're ticklish," Jasmine said to cheer him up. "By the way, I would also like you to come with me on that day of the interview."

"Jasmine, I just remembered a crucial appointment. I have a job interview scheduled on the same day, and it is in Canada. I would not like to miss it."

"Oh, you didn't share that with our attorney and me."

"I completely forgot. I got the news this morning after my phone interview. I have to fly out to Ontario, Canada."

She abruptly stopped. "Do you mean that you would

travel outside the country? Our lawyer should have known this new development. Can you postpone it? You should wait for the outcome of the interview with immigration. You cannot travel outside the country."

"I do understand the danger. Immigration did not even set an interview for me and kept me in the dark. Maybe if I get this job, I can improve my chances of getting the document. I want to get a job, and I need a legal document."

"Sami, I don't know whether you understand the gravity of this case. Right now, you are pursuing a document in the USA. You can be detained at the airport upon return or even denied re-entry into the country. Did you consider all these options? That's why we need to check with our lawyer. We must hurry back to her again. It is urgent. Let's go, please?"

"What are you up to?"

"We are going back to the lawyer. This information is critical, and she has to know it."

"It is not a big deal. I will be back the next day."

"I am not sure about that. Let the lawyer decide."

Back inside, they waited for Mrs. Jones to appear.

"What brings you back?"

"I forgot to let you know that I have an interview scheduled in Canada that I have to attend on the day of Jasmine's appointment. I have made arrangements already."

"What? You must be here. It can impact your case severely."

"Can we do something? Or prepare special travel documents for him?" Jasmine asked in desperation.

"We could request and file travel authorization with U.S.Citizenship and Immigration Services before travel and get approval. Otherwise, they will consider this as an abandonment at the time of your departure. You have to maintain continuous residence in the US between the date of filing and the date of the interview."

Jasmine looked at Sami with a worried look on her face. "I think this is not worth the risk, Sami. You can get a job in the USA if you have a proper document."

Sami shook his head. He knew the hassle of the job search he faced and had lost confidence in the biased system. "Jasmine," I have been there. There has been nothing for me for over two years. I lived through it, and I went back to college again, and if the opportunity comes along, I will grab it."

"Your head shake confuses me, Sami. You nod your head up and down and side to side, and I don't know what you mean."

"In my culture, when you shake your head from side to side, it means no."

"How do I know about your culture? It could probably also mean yes in some cultures. I would rather have no cultural mix-ups, please."

"Okay, Jasmine. No need to be upset. Those things come to me naturally."

It was Mrs. Jones's turn to intervene. "You should not go. It will nullify your case, and you will have no chance if you leave the country at this time."

Sami and Jasmine did not talk much during the forty-minute drive from Des Moines to Ames.

That evening, Sami made copies of all his documents, including those of his children. He put them in a separate binder.

"I've decided against following the advice of my lawyer. She did not want me to leave for Canada."

"What's the point of having a lawyer if you don't follow suggestions."

"I have decided to take this risk, and I strongly feel that I will get this job."

"Is there anything I can do to help?"

"I may need to borrow a little cash just in case. If I get the job, I will initiate the visa process from there."

"I thought you finalized your so-called marriage adjustment. Were you not called for an interview?"

Sami kept silent. Finally, seemingly as an afterthought, he replied, "Not yet."

"I am sorry to hear that. It does not look good if your visa expires before you get any feedback."

Another long silence.

"Jasmine has an appointment on the same day that I leave for Canada."

"Your presence is needed, right?"

"Not really. The immigration officer wanted to question Jasmine first, and I don't know whether there is any connection with this case or not. It could be about anything that is not related to our situation."

"What could that be? I am curious."

"Look, I don't know. I will leave my options open. Jasmine believed her previous husband lied about her on immigration. I don't know what to believe anymore."

Sarah helped him pack, and the kids had already sensed and settled on the notion that dad was going on a long journey. The older kids had figured out a long time ago that he was looking for a job. They held on to him, clinging tenaciously to every little bit of attention he could provide. It suddenly occurred to them that their dad would be leaving soon.

"You will be back, right, Dad?" Adam asked, not sure about where his father was going.

Chaaltu answered for him. "He will be back soon. He's going to Canada, not Africa."

"I will be back in just a day or two at most if all goes well." With that, Sami reassured them that he was making a short trip, but as a father advising his children, he added, "Help your mom in the house and each other."

"You can still cancel this trip. You know that immigration will not allow you back."

"I don't know the outcome of Jasmine's interview and my adjustment application. The mistake that we discovered very late could impact the outcome. Either way, my chances are limited."

"Your attorney can initiate a motion for a stay of removal, if that is what you are concerned about, and postpone deportation."

"I see this situation a little differently now. If I leave now, I am still legal since my visa has not expired, and I may have a chance to get back. On the other hand, if deported, the doors are closed. It is also a disgrace for me to bear the burden. I can't imagine being shipped like a cargo."

A moment of silence engulfed them. Sami looked at his wife. She looked back. He wanted to say something but could not think of a better word to express it.

***

Before he boarded the plane to Canada, Sami turned to his wife and said, "You know I still love you. As far as I know, you're still my wife. I don't know what kind of fate awaits me in Canada. If I get this job, everything will turn out okay, and I will have a chance to get back. Otherwise, I am willing to start things over again."

With teary eyes, he added, "I am sorry I have disappointed you, but I am determined to make it up."

He hugged and squeezed her tight. "Give me another chance."

***

As Jasmine drove to Omaha with her cousin on an early morning in June, she had every reason to be a little concerned. Her cousin kept propping her up to the enlightenment of music, constantly playing the recently released single by the Bahamian group Baha Men, "Who let the Dogs Out." Jasmine focused her attention on driving and tried to reassess what kinds of questions they would ask. There was one thing she was sure of, and even her lawyer had hinted about it already: it was unusual for immigration to interview her alone without her husband. She'd expected them to summon Sami and her together for the interview. She had rehearsed all the possible answers to the prepared questions that they usually came up with, and she was ready. Her lawyer thought this was unusual but had reassured her that it might be something that she needed to clarify about her previous marriage.

***

A week later, Sami read the news clip that his wife had sent, "A Case of Visa-Related Marriage Fraud":

Jasmine Thompson, a 30-year-old US citizen, was arrested on charges of fraudulent visa marriage. Jasmine married Antonio Rodriguez, who also uses the alias "Pablo," a Honduran illegal immigrant with multiple fake green cards. She divorced him within three months after he received his green card. Antonio is currently held in the county jail, awaiting deportation process.

As Sami read the article, he sipped his tea and sighed under his breath. "I wouldn't want to have it any other way." Sami had officially wrapped up his American rollercoaster saga. He folded the paper, stepped out of the café, and joined the stream of pedestrians on King Street West. He paused as he walked the lonely path amid strangers in downtown Ontario, Canada. A new dawn of realization came upon him.

About the Author

Dido G. Kotile is a native of Isiolo, Kenya. He holds a B.S from the University of Russia and a Ph.D. from Iowa State University. Dr. Kotile has been involved with private & charter schools since 2003 and worked as a school administrator, associate lecturer, educational consultant, and board chair of non-profit organizations from East Africa. He is currently a Director of a charter school, and lives in Woodbury, Minnesota, with a wife, and three young adult children.

This is his first novel.

didokotile.com

CPSIA information can be obtained
at www.ICGtesting.com
Printed in the USA
LVHW051740021120
670484LV00006B/1506